# Voices of World

## Antiquity to Pre-Modern Times

### Fifth Edition

Prepared and Compiled by:
Professor B. Carmon Hardy
Sharon K. Evanshine & Mary Marki

CENGAGE
Learning™

Australia • Brazil • Japan • Korea • Mexico • Singapore • Spain • United Kingdom • United States

**TVoices of World History: Antiquity to Pre-Modern Times, Fifth Edition**

Prepared and Compiled by:
Professor B. Carmon Hardy
Sharon K. Evanshine & Mary Marki

Executive Editor:
Maureen Staudt
Michael Stranz

Senior Project Development Manager:
Linda de Stefano

Marketing Specialist:
Sara Mercurio

Senior Production/Manufacturing Manager:
Donna M. Brown

PreMedia Supervisor:
Joel Brennecke

Rights & Permissions Specialist:
Kalina Hintz
Todd Osborne

Cover Designer: Ryan Duda
Cover Art: PhotoDisc Inc.



ISBN-13: 978-0-618-46329-9
ISBN-10: 0-618-46329-1

**Cengage Learning**
5191 Natorp Boulevard
Mason, Ohio 45040
USA

Cengage Learning is a leading provider of customized learning solutions with office locations around the globe, including Singapore, the United Kingdom, Australia, Mexico, Brazil, and Japan. Locate your local office at:
**international.cengage.com/region**

Cengage Learning products are represented in Canada by Nelson Education, Ltd.

For your lifelong learning solutions, visit **www.cengage.com/custom**

Visit our corporate website at **www.cengage.com**

Printed in the United States of America

# ACKNOWLEDGMENTS

St. Jerome's Epistolae, as found in James Hanscom, Leon Hellerman, and Ronald Posner, editors, Voices of the Past: Readings in Ancient History, (New York: The Macmillian Company, 1967, pages 172-173.)

Poem titled "Ozymandias" is translated by Ellsworth Barnard, editor of *Shelley: Selected Poems, Essays, and Letters,* pp. 61–62. Published in 1944 by Odyssey Press.

"On the Nature of Poetry," "On the Joys of Book Collecting," "On Quoting and Referencing Others," "Problem With Astrology," and "In Praise of Old Age" are all from *Letters from Petrarch* by Morris Bishop. © 1966 by Indiana University Press. Reprinted by permission.

Selections from *The Complete Writings of Thucydides: The Peloponnesian War* by R. Crawley (trans.)., pp. 109–114. © 1934 by Modem Library.

"Gregory of Tours on the Conversion and Baptism of Clovis" are reprinted from O.M. Dalton (trans.), *The History of the Franks,* Volume II. 1927 by Clarendon Press. Reprinted by permission of Oxford University Press.

"The Buddhist Doctrine of Emptiness," "Buddhist Urgings of Peacefulness," "Hindu Approval for Domestic and Civilized Pleasures," and "Islamic Thought in India," are reprinted from Sources of Indian Tradition, by Wm. Theodore de Bary © 1958, Columbia University Press. Reprinted with the permission of the publisher.

"Why is Buddhism Not Found in Traditional Chinese Texts" and "Memorial to the Sung Emperor, Jen Tsung" is reprinted from Sources of Chinese Tradition. by Wm. Theodore de Bary © 1960, Columbia University Press. Reprinted with the permission of the publisher.

"Eihard's Life—The Emperor Charles" is reprinted from *Early Lives of Charlemagn* by Einhard & The Mood of St. Gal by A.J. Grant (trans.), pp. 32–44. 1966 by Cooper Square Publishers, Inc.

Several poems are reprinted from *The Oxford Book of Greek Verse in Translation* edited by T.F. Higham and e.M. Browra, pp. 184–186, 201–202, 205–206, 210. © 1938 by The Claredon Press. Reprinted by permission of Oxford University Press.

Selections appear from *The Travels of Marco Polo,* revised from Marsden's translation and edited by Manuel Komroff. © 1953 by Modem Library.

Excerpt from" A Kung Woman's Memories of Childhood" is reprinted by permission of the publisher from KALAHARI HUNTER-GATHERERS: STUDIES OF THE KUNG SAN AND THEIR NEIGHBORS edited by Ricard B. Lee and Irven DeVore, Cambridge, Mass: Harvard University Press, Copyright © 1976 by the President and Fellows of Harvard College.

Excerpt "The Autobiography of Weni" is reprinted from *Ancient Egyptian Literature: A Book of Readings, Three Volumes,* by Miriam Lichtheim, pp. 18–22. © 19731980 by the Regents of the University of California. Reprinted with permission from the University of California Press.

Untitled poem is reprinted from *Ancient Egyptian Literature: A Book of Readings, Three Volumes,* by Miriam Lichtheim, pp18–22. © 1973–1980 by the Regents of the University of California. Reprinted with permission from the University of California Press.

"Oration on the Dignity of Man" by Giovanni Pico della Mirandola from *"The Renaissance Philosophy of Man* by Ernst Cassirer, Paul Kristeller, and John Herman Randall, Jr. © 1948 by the University of Chicago Press. Reprinted with permission from University of Chicago Press.

"Heroes and Immortality in Ancient Mesopotamia" is reprinted from Prichard, James, ANCIENT NEAR EASTERN TEXTS RELATING TO THE OLD TESTAMENT, Revised Edition. Copyright © 1975 by Princeton University Press. Reprinted by permission of Princeton University Press.

"Gaius Julius Caeser (100–44 B.C.) and His Commentaries on the Gallic Wars" and "Ammianus Marcellinus (Fl. 4th Cent. A.D.) on the Huns" is reprinted by permission of the publishers and the Loeb Classical Library from AMMIANUS MARCELLINUS, VOL III translated by J.C. Rolfe, Cambridge, Mass: Harvard University Press, 1939.

"fun Khaldun" is reprinted from Rosenthal, Franz; THE MUGADDIMAH: AN INTRODUCTION TO HISTORY, Volume II. Copyright © 1967 by Princeton University Press. Reprinted by permission of Princeton University Press.

From *The Life of Benvenuto Cellini Written by Himself* from the John Addington Symonds Translation, pp. 50–54. ©1949 by Phaidon Publisher, Inc.

Excerpt from *The Way and Its Power* by Arthur Waley. Copyright ©1934 by George Allen and Unwin Ltd. Reprinted by kind permission of The Arthur Waley Estate.

Excerpt from Records of the Grand Historian of China. vol. I, by Bunton Watson © 1961, Columbia University Press. Reprinted with the permission of the publisher.

"The Presocratic Philosophers" from pp. 44-45, 60, 69-71, 230-231 fromThe Presocratics by Philip Wheelwright, editor. Copyright ©1966 by Odyssey Press. Adapted by permission of Pearson Education, Inc., Upper Saddle River, NJ.

"Fragments from Protagoras" from pp. 239-240 fromThe Presocratics by Philip Wheelwright, editor. Copyright ©1966 by Odyssey Press. Adapted by permission of Pearson Education, Inc., Upper Saddle River, NJ.

"Fragments from Democritus" from pp. 182-186 fromThe Presocratics by Philip Wheelwright, editor. Copyright ©1966 by Odyssey Press. Adapted by permission of Pearson Education, Inc., Upper Saddle River, NJ.

Excerpts fromThe Epic of Gilgamesh: A New Translation, translated by Andrew George (Allen Lane: The Penguin Press, 1999). Translation copyright ©1999 by Andrew George. Reprinted by permission of Penguin Books Ltd.

From The Iliad of Homer and the Odyssey Rendered into English Prose by Samuel Butler. New York: E.P. Dutton & Company, 1923; reprinted in Volume 4: Great Books of the Western World, Chicago: Encyclopedia Britannica, 1952, pp. 156-159.

From The Iliad of Homer and the Odyssey Rendered into English Prose by Samuel Butler. London & New York: Longmans, Green, and Co., 1900; reprinted in Volume 4: Great Books of the Western World, Chicago: Encyclopedia Britannica, 1952, pp. 251-252.

Reprinted by permission of the publishers and the Trustees of the Loeb Classical Library from LIVY: VOLUME IX, Loeb Classical Library Volume 295, translated by Evan T. Sage, pages 413-419, Cambridge, Mass.: Harvard University Press, 1935. The Loeb Classical Library® is a registered trademark of the President and Fellows of Harvard College.

From The Kama Sutra of Vatsyayana, translated by Sir Richard Burton, Random House, Inc.

Excerpt from Leon Battista Alberti, The Family in Renaissance Florence, translated by Renee New Watkins, pp. 115-120. Copyright © 1969. Reprinted by permission of University of South Carolina Press.

# CONTENTS

# INTRODUCTION

This edition revises an earlier compilation of World History sources and reflects the efforts of my former graduate assistants and present colleagues, Sharon K. Evanshine, and Mary Marki. A fresh title, some new excerpts and discussion questions are among the changes, which constitute improvements. We have also shortened many documents and deleted others. For his generous assistance to our combined efforts, we wish to gratefully acknowledge Robert S. Evanshine, an expert computer consultant, without whose time, energy, and abilities, the book may never have reached completion.

Like the previous edition, the volume is divided into topical sections, each commencing with a lecture outline addressing some historical subject or period. The lecture topics begin with prehistoric man and conclude with the European Renaissance around 1500 A.D. Depending upon the length of the class, one or two topics will usually be addressed and completed each time the class meets. Sometimes, however, two periods may be required to cover the material in the unit. The outlines are taken directly from our lecture notes, thus students will be able to follow every lecture closely and easily. Because the outlines contain names, dates and other specifics referred to in the lectures, students should find note taking both more convenient and more accurate. Attending class regularly, using the outlines and taking complete notes will greatly advantage students in the examinations.

Your professor may assign a required or optional textbook and list the related pages in a class syllabus. Often, material provided by the textbook will overlap with what is discussed in the class lecture. At the same time, students should be aware that the lectures may include information not treated in the textbook.

A section of additional readings follows each lecture outline. These materials are usually copies of original documents dating from or bearing upon the subject matter treated in class. We have selected these primary source documents for the purpose of enriching your understanding of historical periods and events. They are also distinctive for their high interest and readability. Generally, students will find them to be interesting passages in their own right, apart from their relevance for the lecture topic. We urge students to read these important documents carefully as they will serve as a basis for class discussion and for questions on the examinations.

We believe that it is a vital part of the historical experience to assimilate the outlooks and world views of those we study. To accomplish this, we must spend time with them. Through exposure to primary source materials, we acquire the larger meaning of a passage, an understanding of the author's personality and something of the flavor of the time in which the work was written. In the process of compiling the additional readings, the documents have been edited. Consequently footnote references and other markings appearing in the body of the material have usually been deleted. However, a full acknowledgment of the sources from which the excerpts were taken is always provided in the headnote at the beginning of each section, permitting any student who wishes to do so to go to the original source and read further.

Students are invited to look upon the lectures and reading assignments as more than merely "requirements" for passing the course. They constitute an inquiry into the most fascinating subject we can consider: ourselves. They recapitulate our species' astonishing odyssey from prehistoric wanderings to encirclement and scientific mapping of the earth; they chronicle our rhapsodies on the miracle of self-conscious existence. If our collective history recalls things discouraging and melancholy, it is also rich with accounts that thrill and swell our optimism.

Although it is common to label such concerns as didactic, surely the educational enterprise may be justified on the grounds that it does more than prepare students to earn a livelihood. We all need to acquire an understanding of what our vocation *means* in its larger sense; where mankind's technical and commercial employments are taking us; and what our place and meaning as individuals is in our relationship with society as a whole.

The premise of this course is that these issues are best addressed in the context of the conversation humankind has had about them over centuries of time. Only by exploring the texture and boundaries of human experience can we assay our own potentials. By seeing life through the eyes of others, we enlarge our perspective and increase the likelihood for tolerance. In other words, this course first seeks to stimulate an interrogative mood, to cultivate our native inclination to question and compare. Above all, it is an adventure in our greatest gift, the capacity to wonder—taking as the chief stimulus for this activity mankind's long record of comment and self-reflection. We have prepared the readings in this book, as well as our lectures, with these objectives in mind. As educators, we look forward to seeing you in class and sharing the journey with you.

B. Carmon Hardy
Sharon K. Evanshine
Mary Marki

And now with art and skill I'll summarize
Another tale, which you should take to heart,
Of how both the gods and men began the same.
The gods, who live on Mount Olympus, first
Fashioned a golden race of mortal men; . . .

Hesiod (8th Cent. B.C.)
*Work and Days,* Lines 107–111

# LECTURE TOPIC 1

# *Early Humankind*

I. How Did Early Humans Evolve and Live?
   A. The Idea and the Discovery
      1. Charles Darwin
      2. The *Origin of Species* (1859)
   B. Neanderthal: 100,000 B.P.
   C. Eugen Dubois and Homo Erectus: 500,000 B.P.
   D. Raymond Dart, L.S.B. Leakey, Don Johanson *et al.*
      1. *Pithecanthropus Erectus*: 1,500,000–3,000,000 B.R.
   E. More Recent Forbearers: Cro-Magnon: 50,000 B.P.
II. Life in the Old Stone Age
   A. Paleolithic Society
      1. Nomadic
      2. Hunter-gatherers
   B. Record of the Caves
      1. Lascaux
      2. Les Ezyiers
      3. Altimira
III. The New Stone Age: Humankind's Longest Step?
   A. The Neolithic Revolution: 10,000–3,000 B.C.
      1. Angiosperms
      2. Agriculture
   B. Village Life and the Beginnings of Urbanism
      1. Walls
      2. Canals
      3. Government
   C. Divine Kingship: Government and Religion
   D. Family Life
   E. Property and Women
   F. Material Culture and the Division of Labor
      1. Trade Marks
      2. Communication and Writing
IV. What Is The Legacy of Our Prehistoric Heritage?
   A. Our Physical Stature
   B. The Impulse to Communicate and Wonder
   C. Village Life as the Basis of Civilization

# READING 1

## The Surprising Achievement of Paleolithic Humans

*Some of the most dramatic evidence we possess concerning the level of human intelligence and artistic capacity during the later period of the last Ice Age comes from the cave paintings of Western Europe. More than only symbolic or religious gestures, these depictions are important because they are aesthetic achievements of the first order. With these paintings, Cra-Magnon man announced the full arrival, both physically and mentally, of Homa-sapien's as self-conscious, reflecting human beings. The description of the great cave at Lascaux in France and other sites, provided below, is taken from Roger Lewin,* In the Age of Mankind: A Smithsonian Book of Human Evolution *(Washington, D.C: Smithsonian Books, 1988), pp. 134–154.*

---

### Discussion Questions

1. Were the cave paintings of Paleolithic humans works of art or religion?
2. Aristotle said art and religion are largely the same thing. Do you agree?

## ARTISTS OF THE ICE AGE

The reinforced metal door slams shut, and you stand in a dimly lit antechamber, the acrid smell of Formalin in your nostrils. Left behind is the dappled sunlight of a French hillside glade, and your eyes begin to adjust to a subterranean, crepuscular world.

Your guide, Jacques Marsal, whispers simple but vital instructions: You must dip your boots into the Formalin bath before going further. The sound of water dripping against stone can be heard. Another door opens—this one plastic—and you step from twilight into near-total blackness. Marsal snaps on a flashlight to guide your way down a flight of 19 concrete steps. You follow carefully, breathing the smell of damp clay, aware that the sound of dripping water has grown louder.

A second plastic door opens, and 24 steps take you yet deeper into this black, still world. Guided by a small handrail and the thin beam of Marsal's flashlight, you slowly edge some dozen yards along a crude pathway. Marsal tells you to stop and then moves away. His moment of drama has come. No one speaks. You wait nervously, your eyes straining to penetrate the cavernous darkness of the cave. Suddenly, the deep chamber floods with light, and you find yourself in the midst of chaotic visual activity.

To your left, a small herd of horses gallops away from you, their manes flowing, apparently fleeing from a strange horned creature at their rear. A massive bull arurochs—forerunner of modern domestic cattle—runs with them. Two small stags confront them head-on, then three more bulls surge around the curved end of the chamber at a terrifying clip. The last bull measures 20 feet from horned head to muscular rump. Smaller bulls, horses, bison, and deer dodge and leap among the racing herds. The more you look, the more you see. Animals materialize everywhere.

This is Lascaux, the most spectacular of all painted caves of Ice Age Europe. Here, encapsulated in sweeping lines and polychromatic images are clues to a way of life of people who lived some 17,000 years ago. The power and depth of the images speak directly to us, and we instantly recognize something germane to ourselves—here indeed is a cogent expression of the Age of Mankind.

Jacques Marsal's trick of taking visitors to the center of this first chamber of Lascaux—the Hall of Bulls—under cover of darkness, and then throwing the light switch, never fails to stir the emotions. How could it not? Here you stand, deep underground, surrounded by a scene so imbued with life that you can almost hear the thunder of hooves, smell the earthiness of the hides. Even the shadows cast by the billowing limestone roof add to the sense of surging energy. The myriad images are sharpened by the thin layer of white crystalline calcite that clings to much of the cave's rock face, a sparkling canvas for its ancient artists.

In 1940, when Marsal was only 15, he and three other boys were the first to enter Lascaux. The four young boys discovered a treasure far more incredible then they could have imagined. Located near the small town of Les Eyzies in the Perigord region of Southwest France, Lascaux is by far the most spectacular, prompting some to call it the Sistine Chapel of Ice Age art. In 1963, the cave was closed to public view forever, because of the tens of thousands of annual visitors had so changed the physical condition of the cave that the images had begun to deteriorate.

Now, just five visitors a day are allowed into the cave, whose atmosphere is carefully controlled by sensitive instrumentation. Potential disaster is averted by the air-lock entry system and the Formalin dip, which prevents corrosive algae and pollen from being carried into the cave on visitor's shoes. Marsal, who is immensely proud to be the Lascaux guide, is the steward of a fragile treasure, an irreplaceable link with our past.

While still marveling at the Hall of the Bulls, Marsal summons you into the Axial Gallery. . . As you enter the narrow gallery, a large red cow with a black neck and head appears on the north wall to your left. Called the Cow with the Collar, its rib cage bulges outward with the natural curve of the rock. Opposite the cow, a stag lifts back its head in a magnificent roar. Beneath the stag a mysterious line of 17 dots has been painted, finishing in a rectangle, one of the many enigmatic geometrical signs in the cave. Farther along the south wall two ibex face each other, locked in challenge. You begin to sense that this place was more than just a Paleolithic art gallery; Ice Age people must have come here not just to see the paintings, but somehow to be involved with them. . . .

Back at the entrance to the Hall of Bulls, Marsal now leads you left along a 55-foot-long passageway. . . Strikingly naturalistic color images seem almost to jump off these walls. . . . two male bison surge aggressively past each other. Here, perhaps more than in any other Ice Age image, the artist has captured spatial perspective, so you can feel the beasts readying themselves to swing around and charge once again. And . . . on the opposite wall, five stags with antlers are swimming across a river. Their bodies are invisible under an imaginary waterline, and their antlered heads are held high.

Other painted images decorate the walls in this section, but many have been lost to erosion. The most striking element of all, however, is the profusion of engravings, both large and small, etched with sharp flint tools. Unlike the calcite-covered walls of the Hall of the Bulls ant the Axial Gallery, the rock's surface here is soft. Several hundred simple images, including those of horses, bison, aurochs, and deer, as well as grids and abstract designs, adorn the walls. . . .

The most arresting engraving, however, lies in the deepest reaches of the gallery, a journey few people make. The trip is worth the discomfort and claustrophobia you fed, because here, 180 feet from the Hall of Bulls, is the Chamber of the Felines. Among a jumble of engraved signs, . . . are the arresting images of at least six cave lions. In one section a male is about to mount a female, who is flattening her ears and roaring in a characteristic response. Nearby, two males are apparently engaged in a territorial dispute. One threatens with outstretched claws and another growls and marks its territory by sending out a jet of urine.

Perhaps more than most images at Lascaux, those in the Chamber of the Felines capture elements of animal interaction with considerable acuity. These Ice Age artisans knew their subjects. These images, however, are not just naturalistic representations; several of the beasts have hooked lines impaled in their flanks. Spears? Perhaps. But there are crosses and other lines scattered among the animals, which suggest an activity *with* the image, not just an image *of* activity.

Finally, Marsal leads you to the shaft, site of Lascaux's most enigmatic and disturbing composition. Located just off the Apse, the shaft is reached through a trap door, which Marsal lifts with care and anticipation. A metal ladder takes you to the bottom of this 26-foot-deep retreat. The flashlight beam sparkles on the white and yellow calcite crystals. And then the beam of light falls on an incredible scene.

A great black bison stands poised for attack, its forelegs taut as a spring, tail lashing. The animal has been desperately wounded, a barbed spear crosses its body, its entrails spill to the ground. A man has fallen in front of the bison, and is about to be gored. But, unlike the careful naturalistic representations that characterize most of Lascaux's images, this image appears crude and infantile, a stickman with no life, wearing what might be a bird mask. Nearby is a bird on the end of a long staff, perhaps a spear thrower. And between the bird image and the man is a second barbed staff, too short for a spear, with a cross at the end. It is not clear what this scene represents. Depictions of humans are uncommon in Paleolithic art and, like this one, most are highly schematic rather than naturalistic.

Climbing out of the shaft, you have a sense of another's world of mythology, ritual, and tradition. Suddenly, you look at everything through new eyes. No longer do you ask merely what a certain image is, but what it *means.* One explanation . . . is called the era of "hunting magic." Abbe Henri Breuil, a magisterial figure in French archaeology for many decades, viewed the painted caves as essentially unstructured, as collections of images painted to increase the chances of a successful hunt—to ensure "that the game should be plentiful, that it should increase, and that sufficient should be killed."

Indeed, there are parallels for the hunting—magic idea among modern hunter—gatherers. Rituals are performed to ensure both a kill and safety for the hunters, often involving song, dance, and image making. As mentioned earlier, such rituals are not driven solely by self-interest; they are often meant in some way to propitiate the hunt's intended prey, which then becomes a participant, not just a victim, in the venture. In a manner that is almost impossible for the urban mind to grasp, hunter-gatherers view themselves as very much a part of nature. . .

Think back to Lascaux, to the Hall of Bulls, to the first image seen when entering the cave and the last to be seen when leaving. Here stands a curious creature. Animals ahead of it appear to be fleeing into the depths of the cave. Traditionally called the unicorn, although it has two horns, the creature defies ready identification. Upon its large body and swollen belly are drawn a series of circles and what appears to be the partial outline of a horse. A large, round eye is set into a head, with a long muzzle. Or is it? You squint, and suddenly you experience a perceptual flip, and you no longer see an animal with a long muzzle, but rather a man's face with a full beard, perhaps wearing some kind of mask It is a shock, one that deeply affects the way you think about the images of Lascaux, and of the world of Upper Paleolithic art as a whole.

As Margaret Conkey cautions, perhaps by the simple act of labeling what we see as "art," we limit the way we think about it and thereby fail to see far enough.

# READING 2

## Life Among Paleolithic Peoples

*This selection provides portions of an interview between Marjorie Shostak, an anthropologist, and a [Kung female from the Kalahari region of Africa. Paleolithic life yet exists in parts of the world. The interview is taken from Marjorie Shostak, "A !Kung Woman's Memories of Childhood," in Richard B. Lee and Irven DeVore, eds.,* Kalahari Hunter-Gatherers: Studies of the !Kung San and Their Neighbors *(Cambridge, Mass. and London: Harvard University Press, 1976), pp. 251–252, 258–259, 268–275.*

---

### Discussion Questions

1. Is the concept of "childhood" relative, varying from culture to culture?
2. Was !Kung society, as presented in this interview, patriarchal or matriarchal?

## "A !Kung Woman's Memories of Childhood"

(1) Long ago my mother gave birth to my younger brother Kumsa. I wanted the milk she had in her breasts and when she nursed him, my eyes watched as the milk spilled out. I cried all night, cried and cried, and then dawn broke.

Some mornings I just stayed around and my tears fell and I cried and refused food. That was because I saw him nursing, I saw with my eyes the milk spilling out. I thought it was mine.

Once, when my mother was with him and they were lying down asleep, I took him away from her and put him down on the other side of the hut. Then I lay down beside her. While she slept, I squeezed some milk and started to nurse and nursed and nursed and nursed. Maybe she thought it was him. When she woke and saw me, she said, "Where. . . tell me . . . tell me where did you put Kumsa? Where is he?"

I told her he was lying down inside the hut. She grabbed me and shoved me. I landed far away from her; I lay there and cried. She took Kumsa, put him down beside her, and insulted me by cursing my genitals.

"Are you crazy? By your large genitals, what's the matter with you? Are you crazy that you took a baby and dropped him somewhere else and then lay down beside me and nursed? I thought it was Kumsa."

I stayed there crying and crying, and then I was quiet. I got up and just sat, and when my father came home, she told him:

"Do you see what kind of mind your daughter has? Hit her! Hit her, don't just look at her. She almost killed Kumsa. This little baby, this little thing here, she took from my side and dropped him somewhere else. I was lying here holding him and was sleeping. She came and took him away, then left him, and lay down where he had been, and nursed me. Now, hit her!"

I said, "You're lying! Me. . . daddy, I didn't nurse. I refuse her milk and didn't take him away from her."

He said, "If I hear of this again, I'll hit you. Now, don't ever do that again!"

I said: "Yes, he's my little brother, is he not? My brother, my little brother, and I love him. I won't do that again. He can nurse all by himself Daddy, even if you're not here, I won't try to steal mother's breasts. That's my brother's milk. But when you go to the bush, I'm going to follow along with you. The two of us will go and kill springhare, and you will trap a guinea fowl and then give it to me."

We slept. When dawn broke my father and my older brother went and I ran behind. I knew that if I stayed in the village, mother would stinge her milk and wouldn't let me nurse. But when my older brother saw me, he pushed me away and told me to go back to the village, because the sun was too hot, and he said it would kill me. . . . (middle child - didn't belong?)

(9) One day we were walking, gathering food, and the sun was burning. It was the hot, dry season, and there was no water anywhere. The sun hurt! As we walked along, my older brother saw some honey. He and my father took it from the tree, and we ate it. I was so thirsty I practically drank it! I carried some with me and we continued to walk. Thirst was killing mother, and I was crying for water. I cried and cried. We rested somewhere in the shade and there was still no water. My father said to my older brother: " ≠Dau, your mother and I will remain in the shade of this baobab tree. Take the water containers, go and fill them with water. There is a big well way over at the Homa village."

≠Dau got up, took the ostrich eggshell containers, took a day pot, and went. I was lying down, thirst killing me. As I lay there, I thought, "If I just stay here with mother and father, I will die of thirst. Why don't I go with ≠Dau, go and drink some water?"

As soon as I thought that, I got up and ran. I cried after him and ran and cried and ran and followed his tracks. He still didn't hear me. I kept on running and cried after him. When he finally heard me, he turned around and saw me behind him and said, "N≠isa's here? What am I going to do with her now?"

When I finally caught up with him, he picked me up and carried me on his shoulder. My brother liked me. The two of us went together and walked and walked until we finally reached the water well. When we got there, we drank. I drank water and my heart was happy. Then we filled the containers. ≠Dau got them together, picked them up, picked me up, and carried me on his shoulders.

We started walking back and walked and walked, and then he put me down. I ran along with him and soon I started to cry. He told me: "N≠isa, I'm going to hit you. I am carrying these containers and they're very heavy. Now, keep running along, and let's get back to mother and father and give them some water. Thirst will kill them. What are you crying about? Are you without any sense?"

I said, "No! Pick me up. ≠Dau , pick me up and carry me on your shoulders."

He refused, and I cried. I ran along with him and cried and ran and cried.

After a while he said he would carry me again. He picked me up and put me on his shoulders and carried me a long way. It was far! Then he set me down again, and I ran until I was tired, and he picked me up and carried me. We finally brought the water back to our parents. Then we drank it and they said, "Yes our children brought water back and did well—we are alive once again."

After we rested, we left, and all of us went to live in Homa village, where the well was. We walked and rested and walked and rested until we got there. I didn't cry along the way and carried my honey with me. When we arrived, we drank plenty of water and settled there for a while. There was a lot of water and we had all that honey and my heart was happy. . . .

(18) When adults talk to me, I listen. Once they told me that when a young woman grows up, she takes a husband. When they first talked to me about it, I said: "What? What kind of thing am I that I should take a husband? Me, when I grow up, I won't marry. I will just lie by myself. A man, if I married him, what would I think I would be doing it for?"

My father said: "N≠isa if you agree, you will marry a man and get food and give some to him, and he will eat it. I, I am old. I am your father and am old; your mother's old, too. You will get married. Gather food and give it to your husband to eat. He also will do things for you—give you things you can wear. But if you refuse to take a husband, who will get food and

simple thinking of being a child (innocence/ignorance)
women considered property (have to marry)

give it to you to eat? Who will give you things that you shall have? Who will give you things that you will be able to wear?"

I said to my father and mother: "No. There's no question in my mind—I refuse a husband. I won't take one. What is it? Why should I take a husband? As I am now, I am still a child and won't marry. Why don't you marry the man you want for me and sit him down beside father? Then you'll have two husbands."

Mother said: "You're talking nonsense. I'm not going to marry him, you'll marry him. A husband, I want to give you. You say I should marry this other man? Why are you playing with me with this talk?"

I said: "Yes, that's what I am saying. Because you can see I am only a child, and yet you say I should get married. When I grow up and you tell me I should marry, then I will agree. But today I won't! I haven't passed through my childhood and I won't take a husband."

We continued to live and lived on and on and returned to just living. Then she talked about it again. "N≠isa, I should give you a husband. Which man shall give you?"

I knew which man she wanted me to marry. I said, "I refuse that man."

She said, "Marry him. Won't you marry him?"

I said, "You marry him. Marry him and set him beside father."

I stopped talking. I felt ashamed and was silent. I said to myself, "What am I doing? Later I will still go back to mother. When I speak like that, am I not shitting on her?"

I thought that. Then we all went to sleep. We continued to live and just kept on living and more time passed.

(19) Long ago my parents and I went to the village where old Kan/ / a and his son /"Tashay were living. My friend N!huka and I had gone to the water well to get water and he and his family were there, having just come back from the bush. When /"Tashay saw me, he decided he wanted to marry me. He called N!huka over and said, "N!huka, that young woman, that beautiful young woman. . . what is her name?"

N!huka told him my name was N≠isa, and he said, "That young woman. . . I'm going to tell mother and father about her. I'm going to ask them if I can marry her."

N!huka came back. We continued filling the water containers, then left and walked the long way back. When N!huka saw my mother she said, "N≠isa and I were getting water and while we were there, some people came to the well and filled their water containers, and a young man saw N≠isa and talked about marriage. He said his parents would ask you for N≠isa in marriage.

I was silent, just quiet. Because when you are a child and someone wants to marry you, you don't talk. At first my heart didn't agree to it. When they first talked about marriage, I didn't agree.

The next night there was a dance and we were singing and dancing, and he and his parents came from their camp and stayed with us at the dance. We danced and sang and danced and sang, and we didn't stop. N!huka and I sat together. /"Tashay came over to me and took my hand. I said "What . . . what is it? What kind of person is this? What is he doing? This person . . . this person. . . how come I'm sitting here and he came and took hold of me?"

N!huka said, "That's your husband. . . your husband has taken hold of you, is that not so?"

I said, "Won't he take you? You're older, and he'll marry you."

She said, "What! Isn't he my uncle? I won't marry my uncle. Anyway, he is asking you to marry him."

His parents went to my mother and father. His father said: "We have come here, and now that the dancing is finished, I want to speak to you, to /Gau and Chu!ko, N≠isa's father and mother. I will speak with you. Give me your child, the child you gave birth to. Give her to me, and I will give her to my son. Yesterday, while we were at the well, he saw your child. When he returned he told me that in the name of what he felt, that I should today come and ask for her. Then I can give her to him. He said I should come for her."

· women married young
· men chose women
· family "gave away" women

My mother said: "Yes. . . but I didn't give birth to a woman, I bore a child. She doesn't think about marriage, she just doesn't think about the inside of her marriage hut."

Then my father said: "Yes, I conceived that child as well, and she is a person who doesn't think about marriage. When she marries a man, she leaves him and marries another man and leaves him and gets up and marries another man and leaves him. She refuses men completely. There were two men whom she already refused. So, when I look at N≠isa today, I say she is not a woman. There is even another man, Oem, his hut is over there, who is asking to marry her. Oem's first wife is giving her things. When Oem goes gathering and comes back he gives things to his wife so she can give them to N≠isa. He asks N≠isa to sit with them. He wants her to stay and be a second wife. He wants her to take the food from his wife, so they can all eat together. But when his wife undoes the kaross and gives N≠isa food, she throws it down, ruins it in the sand, and kicks the kaross. It is because of that I say she is not a woman."

My father told that to /"Tashay's father. Then his father said: "Yes, I have listened to what you have said. That, of course, is the way of a child; it is a child's custom to do that. She gets married many times until one day she likes one man. Then they stay together. That is a child's way."

They talked about the marriage and agreed to it. All this time I was in my aunt's hut and couldn't see them, I could just hear their voices. Soon, I got up and went to my father's hut where they were talking. When I got there, /"Tashay was looking at me. I sat down. Then /"Tashay's mother said, "Ohhhh! How beautiful this person is! You are a young woman already. Why do they say that you don't want to get married?"

/"Tashay said, "Yes, she has just come in. I want you to take her and give her to me."

(20) There were a lot of people there, everyone came. All of /"Tashay's friends were there, and when they saw me, they told him he was too old for me. Each one said he wanted to marry me himself. His younger brother and his nephew were sitting around talking that way.

I went into my mother's hut and sat there. I was wearing many beads and hair was covered with ornaments. I went and sat beside mother. Another one of /"Tashay's friends came over and started talking as the others had, and I felt confused and couldn't understand why this was happening to me.

That night there was another dance and we danced and other people fell asleep and others kept dancing. In the morning they went back to their camp and we, to ours, and then we went to sleep. When the morning was late in the sky, his relatives came back. They stayed around and his parents told my aunt and my mother that they should all start building the marriage hut because they wanted to leave for another village. They began building the hut together, and everyone was talking and talking. There were a lot of people there. Then all the young men went and brought /"Tashay to the marriage hut. They stayed around the hut together near the fire. I was at mother's hut. They told two of my friends to go get me and bring me to the hut. I said to myself, "Oooooh . . . I'll run away to the bush."

When they came for me they couldn't find me. I wasn't by the fire.

"Where did N≠isa go? It's dark now, isn't it? Doesn't she know that things may bite and kill her when it is dark like this? Has she left?"

My father said, "Go tell N≠isa that if she behaves like that, I will hit her, and she won't run away again. What's the matter with her that she ran away into the bush?"

I had already gone. I stayed away a long time. I heard them calling.

"N≠isa-a! N≠isa-a!"

They were looking for me. I just sat, sat by the base of a tree. I heard my friend, N!huka, call out. "N≠isa-e . . . N≠isa-e my friend. . . there are things there which will bite and kill you. Now leave there and come back here."

They looked for me and looked and looked, and then N!huka came and saw me. I ran from her, and she ran after me and chased me and then caught me. She called out to the others. "People! N≠isa's here! Everyone come over here, come, take her. N≠isa's here!"

They came and brought me back. Then they lay me down inside the hut. I cried and cried, and people told me: "A man is not something that kills you; he is someone who marries you and he becomes like your father or your older brother. He kills animals and gives you things to eat. Even tomorrow; but because you are crying, when he kills an animal he will eat it himself and won't give you any. Beads, too. He will get some beads, but he won't give them to you. Why are you afraid of your husband and why are you crying?"

I listened and was quiet. Then he and I went and slept inside the hut. He slept by the mouth of the hut, near the fire. He came inside after he thought I was asleep. Then he lay down and slept.

I woke while it was still dark and said to myself, "How am I going to jump over him? How can I get out and go to mother's hut?"

That's what I was thinking in the middle of the night. Then I thought, "This person has married me. . . yes. . . " I lay there. I lay there and thought some more. "Why did people give me this man in marriage? The older people say he is a good person and. . . "

I lay there and didn't move. The rain came and beat down. It fell and kept on falling and falling and then dawn broke. In the morning, he got up first and went and sat by the fire. I was frightened! I was afraid of him and lay there and didn't get up. I waited for him to go away from the hut and when he went to urinate, I left and went to mother's hut. I went there and sat down inside her hut.

That day all his relatives came to our new hut—his mother, his father, his brothers. . . everyone! They all came. They said, "Go tell N≠isa that she should come and her in-laws will put the marriage oil on her. Can you see her over there? Why isn't she coming out so we can put the oil on her in her new hut?"

I refused to go there. Then my older brother said, "No, no. N≠isa, if you continue like this, I'll hit you. Now get out there and go sit down. Go over there and they will put the oil on you."

I still refused and just sat there. My older brother took a switch and came over to me. I got up because I was afraid of the switch. I followed him and walked to where the people were. My aunt put oil on /"Tashay, and his relatives put oil on me. Then they left and it was just /"Tashay and me.

(21) We lived together and after a while /"Tashay lay with me. Afterward, my insides hurt. I took some leaves and tied them with a string around my stomach, but it continued to hurt. The next morning I went gathering and collected some mongongo nuts and put them in my kaross. Meanwhile, I was thinking to myself, "Oooohhh . . . that man made my insides hurt. He made me feel pain today."

The next evening we lay down again. This time I took a leather strap, tied it around a piece of wood and then secured it to my genitals; I wanted to withhold my genitals. The two of us lay down and after a while he was looking for my genitals, and he felt the leather strap there. He said, "What . . . did another woman tell you to do this? Yesterday you lay with me so nicely when I came to you. Why are you today tying a piece of wood to your genitals? What are you holding back?"

I didn't answer. Then he said, "N≠isa . . . N≠isa . . . "

I said, "What is it?"

He said, "What are you doing?"

I didn't answer him. I was quiet.

"What are you so afraid of that you tied your genitals with a piece of leather and with a branch?"

I said, "I'm not afraid of anything."

He said: "No, no. Tell me what you are afraid of. Why did you tie a branch to your genitals? In the name of what you did, I am asking you.

"What are you doing when you do something like that? You are lying with me as though you were lying with a Bantu, a stranger. Why did you tie a branch to your genitals?"

I said: "I refuse to lie down because if I do, you will take me. I refuse! I refuse your touching my genitals because when you lay with me yesterday, my insides hurt me. That's why I am refusing you today, and you won't have me."

He said: "You're not telling the truth, now untie the leather strap. Untie the strap from around your genitals. Do you see me as someone who kills other people? Am I going to eat you? Am I going to kill you? I'm not going to kill you. Instead, as I am now, I have married you and want to make love to you. Don't think I would marry you and not sleep with you. Would I have married you just to *live* with you? Have you seen any man who has married a woman and who just lives with her and doesn't have sex with her?"

I said, "No, I still refuse it! I refuse sex. Yesterday my insides hurt, that's why." He said, "Mm. Today you will just lie there by yourself. But tomorrow I will take you."

I continued to refuse him and we just lay down. Before we went to sleep, he untied the strap and said, "I'm going to destroy it. If this is what use you put it to, I am going to untie it and destroy it in the fire."

Then we went to sleep and slept. He didn't take me, but he untied the strap because he was big and I was afraid of him. We went to sleep and got up the next morning. The men went out that day and then returned. That night /"Tashay and I entered the hut again and lay down together. I just lay there and after a while he touched my leg. I didn't move. I thought to myself, "Oh, what I did last night won't help me at all, because this man will hurt me. Then I'm going to give it to him, and he will have it. Some day it will no longer hurt me."

I said to him: "Today I'm going to lie here, and if you take me by force, you will have me. You will have me because today I'm just going to lie here. You are obviously looking for some 'food,' but I don't know if the 'food' I have is 'food' at all, because even if you have some, you won't be full."

Then I just lay down and he did his 'work.' Afterward he lay down.

(22) We lived together after that, but I ran away again and again. Once I ran away and slept in the bush and they found me in the morning. When my older brother said he was taking me back, I threatened to stick myself with a poison arrow. He got very angry and said: "If you try to stick yourself with an arrow, then I'll beat you and you'll understand what you were doing. As you stand here, talking very badly about what you are going to do to yourself. You are a person, a woman, and when you are alive you don't say those things. When you are alive, you should be playing.

"All your friends have gotten married and N!huka, too, she is going to marry your uncle and sit beside him. Don't say you won't come back to the village, because you and N!huka will have your own huts. Will your friend have a hut, and you won't? That's all. As I am ≠"Dau, your older brother, that's what I have to say."

I said: "Yes. This friend of mine has taken a husband, but surely she is older than I am. She is a grown woman. Me, I'm a child and don't think I should be married. Why have you come to ask me these things again?"

He said: "Put the *sha* roots you collected in your kaross and let's go. The person who sits here is your *husband!* He isn't anyone else's husband. He is the man we gave you. You will grow up with him, lay down with him, and give birth to children with him."

(23) When we returned to the village, I didn't go to my hut, but went and stayed at mother's hut. I went inside and rested. /"Tashay went to our hut and stayed there. He called to me. "N≠isa . . . N≠isa . . . "

I asked him what he wanted and left my mother's hut and went over to him. He gave me some *sha* roots he had dug. I took them, gave some to mother and went back to her hut and stayed there. Late afternoon, when dusk was standing, I went back to our hut and roasted some food. I took the food out of the coals and gave him some and set mine aside to cool. When it was ready, I ate it.

I ran away a few more times. I used to cry when he lay with me and kept saying no. People talked to me about it. Let me tell you what they said.

My mother said, "A man. . . when you marry a man, he doesn't marry your body, he marries your genitals so he can have sex with you."

And my aunt told me, "A man marries you and has sex with you. Why are you holding back? Your genitals are right over there!"

I answered, "I am only a child. This person is an adult. When he enters and takes me, he tears my genitals apart."

We lived and lived, and soon I started to like him. After that I was a grown person and said to myself, "Yes, without doubt, a man sleeps with you. I thought maybe he didn't."

We lived on, and then I loved him and he loved me, and I kept on loving him. When he wanted me, I didn't refuse and he slept with me. I thought, "Why have I been so concerned about my genitals? They are, after all, not so important. So why was I refusing them?"

I thought that and gave myself to him and gave and gave. I no longer refused. We lay with one another, and my breasts had grown very large. I had become a woman.

marriage of young female to older men
is seen as proper, but in turn takes
away the importance of sex (to be loved).

present western culture considers marriage
to be proper to adults who agree to it.
. sex has more meaning

# LECTURE TOPIC 2

## Mesopotamian Civilizations

I. What Was The First Writing Society Known To Man?
   A. Mesopotamia: "The Land Between the Rivers"
      1. The Tigris and the Euphrates
      2. The Area of Modern Iraq
   B. Cities of the Plain: Sumeria ca. 3200 B.C.
   C. Why Were the Sumerians Such A Remarkable People?
      1. Technological Invention
         a) Irrigation
         b) Wheel
      2. Cuneiform Writing
   D. What Were the Characteristics of Sumerian Social Structure?
      1. Government
         a) City-State
         b) The Ensi
         c) Divine Kingship
      2. Canals and Ziggurats
      3. Law
         a) *Lex Talionis*
         b) Tradition of the Blood Feud
         c) Inequality before the Law
      4. Religion
         a) Polytheistic
            (1) Enlil (Marduk)
            (2) Inanna (Ishtar)
         b) Mythopoeic
         c) Afterlife– Sheol
      5. Literature
         a) *Enuma Elish*
         b) Gilgamesh Epic
   E. What Was The Fate of Sumeria?
II. What Mesopotamian Societies Existed after Sumer?
   A. Akkadians: 2331 B.C.
      1. King Sargon
   B. Guti :2200 B.C.
      1. "Wild Beasts of the Mountains"
      2. King Gudea
   C. Sumerian Revival: 2150–1800 B.C.
      1. An Indian Summer
      2. Ur I, II, and III
   D. Amorites: 1800–1650 B.C.
      1. Also Called Babylonians

2. King Hammurabi and His Law Code (ca. 1750 B.C.)

E. Kassites:1650–1300 B.C.

F. Assyrians:1300–612 B.C.
   1. Capital at Ninevah
   2. Sargon II (fl. 722–705 B.C.)

G. Chaldeans: 612–549 B.C.

H. Persians

III. What Do We Know About Neighboring Mesopotamian Peoples?

A. Hittites:1500–1200 B.C.
   1. Capital at Hattusas
   2. Smelted Iron

B. *Voelkerwanderung* and Decline of the Hittites

C. Phoenicians: 1300–774 B.C.
   1. Maritime Economy
   2. Spread of Alphabet

IV. What Was The Mesopotamian Heritage?

A. Writing, Language, Literature

B. Mathematics: Sexagesimal Computation
   1. Water Clocks
   2. Lunar Calendars

C. Astrology and Medicine

D. Art and Architecture
   1. Potter's Wheel
   2. Arch, Vault, and Dome

E. Divine Kingship

F. The Urban Pattern Continued

# READING 1

## Gods, Heros and Immortality In Ancient Mesopotamia

*The Epic of Gilgamesh is one of the oldest and most famous of all Mesopotamian stories and is considered one of the great masterpieces of world literature. Based on older oral stories, it may be the first known piece of written literature in the world. The epic, which is founded on a real-life king who lived about 2600 B.C., was written over and over again on clay tablets in cuneiform script and is today a collation pieced together from various cuneiform tablets. The poem describes the adventures of its hero, King Gilgamesh, part-human, part-divine and a ruler of Uruk, one of the most important Mesopotamian city-states. More than an appealing story, it is a discourse on the human condition, which captures the imagination of readers thousands of years later. Certain themes and elements undoubtedly date from Sumerian times and many motifs find counterparts in literature the world over. Specifically, although part divine, Gilgamesh confronts his own mortality and must face the inevitability of his own death. After trying desperately to escape his fate, Gilgamesh finally realizes that his only means of gaining immortality is through the lasting achievements of his life. The following excerpt is taken from Andrew George, ed. and trans.,* The Epic of Gilgamesh: A New Translation, *(New York: Barnes & Noble, 1999), 2–5, 7, 8, 15–17, 23–25, 39, 40, 42–44, 46, 55, 57–62, 70, 83–95, 98, 99 .*

---

### Discussion Questions

1. From what is Gilgamesh running and for what is he searching?
2. What themes dominate the epic and what values does it impress on the audience?
3. What is the relationship of humans to the gods?
4. What does the epic illustrate about the Mesopotamian view of life?

## THE EPIC OF GILGAMESH

*[The subjects of Gilgamesh complain to the gods of the tyranny of their superhuman king. The gods listen and respond by creating Enkidu as a rival to divert his attention and give them some rest. Enkidu is brought up in the wild by the animals until a hunter instructs a prostitute to reveal her charms in order to lure him away from his herd.]*

Surpassing all other kings, heroic in stature,
brave scion of Uruk, wild bull on the rampage!
Going at the fore he was the vanguard,
Going at the rear, one his comrades could trust!

. . . Who is there can rival his kingly standing,
and say like Gilgamesh, 'It is I am the king'?
Gilgamesh was his name from the day he was born,
two-thirds of him god and one third human.

. . . In Uruk-the-Sheepfold he *walks [back and forth,]*
like a wild bull lording it, head held aloft,
He has no equal when his weapons are brandished,
his companions are kept on their feet by his *contests.*

The young men of Uruk he harries without warrant,
Gilgamesh lets no son go free to his father.
By day and by night his tyranny grows harsher . . .

. . . '[Though powerful, pre-eminent,] expert [and *mighty,*]
[Gilgamesh] lets [no] girl go free to [her *bridegroom.*]'
The warrior's daughter, the young man's bride,
to their complaint the goddesses paid heed.

. . . The goddess Aruru, she washed her hands,
took a pinch of clay, threw it down in the wild.
In the wild she created Enkidu, the hero . . .

Coated in hair like the god of the animals,
with the gazelles he grazes on grasses,
*joining the throng* with the game at the water-hold,
his heart *delighting* with the beasts in the water.

*[The hunter speaks to the prostitute Shamhat:]*

. . . 'Spread your clothing so he may lie on you,
do for the man the work of a woman!
Let his passion caress and embrace you,
his herd will spurn him, though he grew up amongst it.'

Shamhat unfastened the cloth of her loins,
she bared her sex and he took in her charms.
She did not recoil, she took in his scent:
she spread her clothing and he lay upon her.

She did for the man the work of a woman,
his passion caressed and embraced her.
For six days and seven nights
Enkidu was erect, as he coupled with Shamhat.

When with her delights he was fully sated,
he turned his gaze to his herd.
The gazelles saw Enkidu, they started to run,
the beasts of the field shied away from his presence.

Enkidu had defiled his body so pure,
his legs stood still, though his herd was in motion.
Enkidu was weakened, could not run as before,
but now he had *reason*, and wide understanding.

[Shamhat persuades Enkidu to go with her to the city of Uruk. He is shocked when he hears how Gilgamesh exercises his royal right of "droit de seigneur" at wedding ceremonies, sleeping with the bride before the groom. Interrupting Gilgamesh as he is about to sleep with the bride, Enkidu fights Gilgamesh until Enkidu accepts Gilgamesh's supremacy, whereupon the two become trusted friends].

. . . Enkidu with his foot blocked the door of the wedding house,
not allowing Gilgamesh to enter.
They seized each other at the door of the wedding house,
in the street they joined combat, in the Square of the Land.

The door-jambs shook, the wall did shudder,
[in the street Gilgamesh and Enkidu joined combat, in the Square of the Land.]
[The door-jambs shook, the wall did shudder.]

Gilgamesh knelt, one foot on the ground,
his anger subsided, he broke off from the fight.
After he broke off from the fight,
said Enkidu to him, to Gilgamesh:

'As one unique your mother bore you,
the wild cow of the gold, the goddess Ninsun!
High over warriors you are exalted,
to be king of the people Enlil made it your destiny!'

. . . They kissed each other and formed a friendship.

*[The two friends decide to go on an adventure together in search of fame and glory. They journey to the Forest of Cedar where they encounter Humbaba, the ogre who guards it. Gilgamesh and Humbaba do battle and the god, Shamash, assists Gilgamesh in winning victory.][Enkidu dreams that the gods have decreed his death. He blames the prostitute, Shamhat, because she was responsible for introducing him to civilization. The god, Shamash, persuades him to change his attitude. Languishing on his deathbed, Enkidu laments the ignominy of his fate. After dreaming a vision of hell, Enkidu dies.]*

*[Enkidu speaks to Gilgamesh:]*

'My brother, this night what a dream [I dreamed!] The gods Anu, Enlil, Ea and celestial Shamash [held assembly], and Anu spoke unto Enlil: "These, because they slew the Bull of Heaven, and slew Humbaba that [guarded] the mountains dense-[wooded] with cedar," so said Anu, "between these two [let one of them die!]"

'And Enlil said: "Let Enkidu die, but let not Gilgamesh die!"

. . . Enkidu lay down before Gilgamesh, his tears [flowed] down like streams: 'O my brother, dear to me is my brother! They will [never] raise me up again for my brother. [Among] the dead I shall sit, the threshold of the dead [I shall cross,] never again [shall I set] eyes on my dear brother.'

. . . [After] he had cursed the hunter to his hearts content,
he decided [also] to curse Shamhat [the harlot:]
'Come, Shamhat, I will fix your destiny,
a doom to endure for all eternity:

'[I will] curse you with a mighty curse,
my curse shall afflict you now and forthwith!
A household to delight in [you shall not] acquire,
[never to] reside *in the [midst]* of a family!

'In the young women's [*chamber* you shall not] sit!
Your finest [garment] the ground shall defile!
Your festive gown [the drunkard] shall stain [in the dirt!]
Things of beauty [you shall never acquire!]

. . . 'Because [you made] me [weak, who was undefiled!]
Yes, in the wild [you weakened ] me, who was undefiled!'
Shamash heard what he had spoken,
straight away from the sky there cried out a voice:

'O Enkidu, why curse Shamhat the harlot,
who fed you bread that was fit for a god,
and poured you ale that was fit for a king,
who clothed you in a splendid garment,
and gave you as companion the handsome Gilgamesh?

'And now Gilgamesh, your friend and your brother,
[will] lay you out on a magnificent bed.
[On] a bed of honour he will lay you out,
[he will] place you on his left, on a seat of repose;
[the rulers] of the underworld will all kiss your feet.

Enkidu [heard] the words of Shamash the hero,
. . . his heart so angry grew calm,

. . . [his heart] so furious grew calm . . .

What was on his mind he told to his friend:
'My friend, in the course of the night I had such a dream!

'The heavens thundered, the earth gave echo,
and there was I, standing between them.
A man there was, grim his expression,
just like a Thunderbird his features were frightening.

'His hands were a lion's paws, his claws an eagle's talons,
he seized me by the hair, he overpowered me.
I struck him, but back he sprang like a skipping rope,
he struck me, and like a raft capsized me.

'Underfoot [he] crushed me, like a mighty wild bull,
[drenching] my body with poisonous slaver . . .

'[He bound] my arms like the wings of a bird,
to lead me captive to the house of darkness, seat of Irkalla:
to the house which none who enters ever leaves,
on the path that allows no journey back,

'to the house whose residents are deprived of light,
where soil is their sustenance and clay their food,
where they are clad like birds in coats of feathers,
and see no light, but dwell in darkness.

. . . The day he had the dream [his strength] was exhausted,
    Enkidu was cast down, he lay one day sick [and then a second.]
Enkidu [lay] on his bed, [his sickness *worsened.*]
    a third day and a fourth day, [the sickness of Enkidu *worsened.*]

*[Enkidu speaks to his friend Gilgamesh]*
. . . '[My *god*] has taken against me, my friend, . . . ,
    [*I do not die*] like one who [falls] in the midst of battle.
I was afraid of combat, and . . .
    My friend, one who [falls] in combat [*makes his name,*]
but I, [*I do not fall*] in [*combat, and shall make not my name.*]'

*[The description of Enkidu's final death . . . has not yet been recovered.]*

*[As he laments for Enkidu, Gilgamesh is struck by the realization of his own mortality. He leaves Uruk, wandering the earth in search of Uta-napishti, a man reputed to have the secret of everlasting life. After many adventures, Gilgamesh reaches the edge of the world where he encounters Uta-napishti, who reminds him that death is inevitable.]*

'How can I keep silent? How can I stay quiet?
    My friend, whom I loved, has turned to clay,
my friend Enkidu, [whom I loved, has turned to clay.]
    [Shall] I not be like him and also lie down,
never to rise again, through all [eternity?]' . . .

'Of slumber sweet my face had too little,
    I scourged myself by going sleepless.
I have filled my sinews with sorrow,
    and what have I achieved by my toil?

. . . Said Uta-napishti to him, to [Gilgamesh:]
    'Why, Gilgamesh, do you ever [chase] sorrow?
You, who are [built] from gods' flesh and human,
    whom the [gods did fashion] like your father and mother!

'[*Enkidu indeed*] they took to his doom.
    [But you,] you toiled away, and what did you achieve?
You exhaust yourself with ceaseless toil,
    you fill your sinews with sorrow,

'bringing forward the end of your days.
    Man is snapped off like a reed in a canebrake!
The comely young man, the pretty young woman –
    *all [too soon in]* their *[prime]* Death abducts them!

'No one at all sees Death,
    no one at all sees the face [of Death,]
no one at all [hears] the voice of Death,
    Death so savage, who hacks men down.

'Ever do we build our households,
    ever do we make our nests,

ever do brothers divide their inheritance,
    ever do feuds arise in *the land.*

'Ever the river has risen and brought us the flood,
    the mayfly floating on the water.
On the face of the sun its countenance gazes,
    then all of a sudden nothing is there!

. . . 'The Anunnaki, the great gods, held an assembly,
    Mammitum, maker of destiny, fixed fates with them:
both Death and Life they have established,
    but the day of Death they do not disclose.'

*[Uta-napishti tells Gilgamesh the story of the Flood, explaining how he obtained eternal life.]*

Said Gilgamesh to him, to Uta-napishti the Distant:
    . . . How did you find the life eternal?'

Said Uta-hapishti to him, to Gilgamesh:
    'Let me disclose, O Gilgamesh, a matter most secret,
to you I will tell a mystery of gods.

'The town of Shuruppak, a city well known to you,
    which stands on the banks of the river Euphrates:
this city was old – the gods once were in it –
    when the great gods decided to send down the Deluge. . . .

' "O man of Shuruppak, son of Ubar-Tutu,
    demolish the house, and build a boat!
Abandon wealth, and seek survival!
    Spurn property, save life!
Take on board the boat all living things' seed!

. . . 'By the fifth day I had set her hull in position,
    one acre was her area, ten rods the height of her sides.
At ten rods also, the sides of her roof were each the same length.
    I set in place her body, I drew up her design.

. . . 'For my workmen I butchered oxen,
    and lambs I slaughtered daily.
Beer and ale, oil and wine
    like water from a river [I gave my] workforce,
so they enjoyed a feast like the days of New Year.
'At sun-*[rise]* I set my hand [to] the oiling,
    [before] the sun set the boat was complete.

'[Everything I owned] I loaded aboard:
all the gold I owned I loaded aboard,
    all the living creatures I had I loaded aboard.
I sent on board all my kith and kin,
    the beasts of the field, the creatures of the wild, and members of every skill and craft.

. . . 'At the very first glimmer of brightening dawn,
there rose on the horizon a dark cloud of black,
and bellowing within it was Adad the Storm God.
The gods Shullat and Hanish were going before him,
bearing his throne over mountain and land.

'The god Errakal was uprooting the mooring-poles,
Ninurta, passing by, made the weirs overflow.
The Anunnaki gods carried torches of fire,
scorching the country with brilliant flashes.

'The stillness of the Storm God passed over the sky,
and all that was bright then turned into darkness.
[He] charged the land like a *bull [on the rampage,]*
he smashed [it] in pieces *[like a vessel of clay.]*

'For a day the gale [winds *flattened the country,*]
quickly they blew, and *[then came]* the *[Deluge.]*
Like a battle [the cataclysm] passed over the people.
One man could not discern another,
nor could people be recognized amid the destruction.

Story of Noah & the Ark

'Even the gods took fright at the Deluge,
they left and went up to the heaven of Anu,
lying like dogs curled up in the open.
The goddess cried out like a woman in childbirth,
Belet-ili wailed, whose voice is so sweet:

. . . The Anunnaki gods were weeping with her,
wet-faced with sorrow, they were weeping [with her,]
their lips were parched and stricken with fever.

'For six days and [seven] nights,
there blew the wind, the downpour,
the gale, the Deluge, it flattened the land.

'But the seventh day when it came,
the gale relented, the Deluge *ended.*
The ocean grew calm, that had thrashed like a woman in labour,
the tempest grew still, the Deluge ended.

. . . 'On the mountain of Nimush the boat ran aground,
Mount Nimush held the boat fast, allowed it no motion. . .

'The seventh day when it came,
I brought out a dove, I let it loose:
off went the dove but then it returned,
there was no place to land, so back it came to me.

When Noah checked to see if there was land after the flood.

'I brought out a swallow, I let it loose:
off went the swallow but then it returned,
there was no place to land, so back it came to me.

'I brought out a raven, I let it loose:
off went the raven, it saw the waters receding,
finding food, it was *swooping*, and *strutting*, it did not come back
to me.

. . . 'Then at once Enlil arrived, . . . to bless us:

' "In the past Uta-hapishti was a mortal man,
but now he and his wife shall become like us gods!

*[Uta-napishti directs Gilgamesh to a magical plant growing deep under the sea that has the power of rejuvenation. Gilgamesh ties rocks to his feet and sinks to the bottom of the sea and retrieves it, but on his return home a snake steals the precious plant while he is bathing at a refreshing pool. Gilgamesh realizes that all his labors have been in vain—that his only immortality rests in his life's lasting achievements.]*

moral lesson

# READING 2

## Ancient Mesopotamian Law

*This ancient compilation of earlier laws was issued by the great ruler of the Old Babylonian or Amorite dynasty, Hammurabi, in the eighteenth century B.C. It is likely that it reflects legal practices and social attitudes held by preceding Mesopotamian civilizations, including that of the Sumerians. The severe code is also significant for what it tells us about the importance of writing among elites in Babylonian society and about their ideals concerning justice. Notice how urban society has imposed certain minimal requirements of deference. These selections are taken from C H. W. Johns, ed.,* Babylonian and Assyrian Laws, Contracts and Letters, *Library of Ancient Inscriptions (New York: Charles Scribner's Sons, 1904), 44–67, passim.*

---

### For Discussion

1. What are the advantages of a written law code over one merely transmitted orally?
2. What seem to be the main principles of justice of this law code?
3. Does the code reflect social distinctions in Babylonian society?
4. How do they make it clear that Babylonia was a patriarchal society?
5. Why do you think the code was so severe?

## THE LAW CODE OF HAMMURABI

When the lofty *Anu,* king of the *Anunnaki,* and *Enlil,* lord of heaven and earth, who determine the destinies of the land, committed the rule of all mankind to *Marduk,* the first-born son of *Ea,* and made him great among the *Igigi;* . . . at that time Anu and Enlil named me, Hammurabi, the exalted prince, the worshipper of the gods, to cause righteousness to prevail in the land, to destroy the wicked and the evil, to prevent the strong from plundering the weak, to go forth like the sun over the black-headed race, to enlighten the land and to further the welfare of the people. Hammurabi, the shepherd, named by Enlil am I, who increased plenty and abundance; who made every thing complete for *Nippur,* the bond of heaven and earth; the exalted supporter of *Ekur;* the wise king, who restored *Eridu* to its place. . . . The ancient of royalty, the powerful king, the sun of Babylon, who caused light to go forth over the lands of Sumer and Akkad; the obedience; the favorite of *Inanna* am I. When Marduk sent me to rule the people and to bring help to the land, I established law and justice in the language of the land and promoted welfare of the people.

1. If a man has accused another of laying [a death spell] upon him, but has not proved it, he shall be put to death.

3. If a man has borne false witness in a trial, or has not established the statement he has made, if the cause be a capital crime that man shall be put to death.

6. If a man has stolen goods from a temple, or house, he shall be put to death; and he that has received the stolen property from him shall be put to death.

15. If a man has induced either a male or female slave from the house of a nobleman, or commoner, to leave the city, he shall be put to death.

16. If a man has harbored in his house a male or female slave from a nobleman's or commoner's house, and has not caused the fugitive to leave on demand of the officer over the slaves condemned to public forced labor, that householder shall be put to death.

22. If a man has committed highway robbery and has been caught, that man shall be put to death.

23. If the highwayman has not been caught, the man that has been shall state on oath what he has lost and the city or district governor in whose territory the robbery took place shall restore to him what he has lost.

25. If a fire has broken out in a man's house and the one who has to put it out has coveted the property of the householder and appropriated any of it, that man shall be cast into the self-same fire.

53. If a man has neglected to strengthen his dike and has not kept his dike strong, and a breach has broken out in his dike, and the waters have flooded the meadow, the man in whose dike the breach has broken out shall restore the corn he has caused to be lost.

54. If he be not able to restore the corn, he and his goods shall be sold, the owners of the meadow whose corn the water carried away shall share the money.

108. If the mistress of a beer-shop has not received corn as the price of beer or has demanded silver on an excessive scale, and has made the measure of beer less than the measure of corn, that beer-seller shall be prosecuted and drowned.

109. If the mistress of a beer-shop has assembled seditious slanderers in her house and those seditious persons have not been captured and have not been taken to the palace, that beer-seller shall be put to death.

127. If a man has caused a finger to be pointed at a votary, or a man's wife, and has not justified himself, that man shall be brought before the judges, and have his forehead branded.

128. If a man has taken a wife and has not executed a marriage contract, that woman is not a wife.

129. If a man's wife is caught lying with another, they shall be strangled and cast into the water. If the wife's husband would save his wife, the king can save his servant.

131. If a man's wife has been accused by her husband, and has not been caught lying with another, she shall swear her innocence, and return to her house.

132. If a man's wife has the finger pointed at her on account of another, but has not been caught lying with him, for her husband's sake she shall plunge into the sacred river.

138. If a man has divorced his wife, who has not borne him children, he shall pay over to her as much money as was given for her bride-price and the dowry which she brought from her father's house, and so shall divorce her.

141. If a man's wife, living in her husband's house, has persisted in going out, has acted the fool, has wasted her house, has belittled her husband, he shall prosecute her. If her husband has said, "I divorce her," she shall go her way; he shall give her nothing as her price of divorce. If her husband has said, "I will not divorce her," he may take another woman to wife and [his former] wife shall live as a slave in her husband's house.

145. If a man has married a votary, and she has not granted him children, and he is determined to marry a concubine, that man shall marry the concubine, and bring her into his house, but the concubine shall not place herself on an equality with the votary.

148. If a man has married a wife and a disease has seized her, if he is determined to marry a second wife, he shall marry her. He shall not divorce the wife whom the disease has seized. In the home they made together she shall dwell, and he shall maintain her as long as she lives.

157. If a nobleman has lain in the bosom of his mother after the death of his father, they both shall burn.

159. If a man, who has presented a gift to the house of his prospective father-in-law and has given the bride-price, has afterward looked upon another woman and has said to his father-in-law, "I will not marry your daughter," the father of the girl shall keep whatever he has brought as a present.

215. If a surgeon has operated with the bronze lancet on a nobleman for a serious injury, and has cured him, or has removed with a bronze lancet a cataract for a nobleman, and has cured his eye, he shall take ten shekels of silver.

215. If it be a commoner, he shall take five shekels of silver.

217. If it be a man's slave, the owner of that slave shall give two shekels of silver to the surgeon.

218. If a surgeon has operated with the bronze lancet on a nobleman for a serious injury, and has caused his death, or has removed a cataract for a nobleman, with a bronze lancet, and has made him lose his eye, his hands shall be cut off.

229. If a builder has built a house for a man, and has not made his work sound, and the house he built has fallen, and caused the death of its owner, that builder shall be put to death.

230. If it is the owner's son that is killed, the builder's son shall be put to death.

# LECTURE TOPIC 3

# Ancient Israel

I. What were the Origins of Ancient Israel?
   A. Mesopotamian Origin of Abraham: ca. 1900 B.C
   B. Hebrews or "Habiru" and the Hyksos?: ca. 1800 B.C.
II. What is the Historical interpretation of the story of Moses in Egypt?
   A. What was the Voelkerwanderungzeit of 1300 B.C?
III. United Kingdom under David (970–930 B.C) and Solomon (930–890 B.C)
IV. How was Israel Divided after Solomon?
   A. Judah in the South; Israel in the North
   B. Fall of Israel to Assyrians under Sargon II: 722 B.C.
   C. Judah Overrun by Chaldeans under Nebuchadnezzar II: 586 B.C.
V. Return to Homeland under Persians (538 B.C) and Rebuilding of Temple of Solomon: 515 B.C.
VI. Roman Hegemony and Diaspora
VII. What are the Philosophical and Religious Contributions of Ancient Judaism?
   A. Monotheism
   B. Fatherhood of God
   C. Sin and Moral Agency
   D. Idea of the Messiah
   E. Jewish Scriptures and Wisdom Literature
VIII. The Judaic Heritage
   A. Its Contributions to Christianity and Islam
   B. Its Remarkable Historical Integrity
   C. National Rebirth in the Modem Middle East

# READING 1

## The Judaic Account of Human Creation

*While biblical scholars no longer attribute authorship of the first five books of the Bible singly to Moses, he undoubtedly contributed significantly to their composition. The creation account provided here has become a part of the religious canon of three world religions: Judaism, Christianity and Islam. The selection is taken from the book of Genesis, Chapter 1:1–5; 26–31, Chapter 2:15–17, Chapter 3:1–19.*

### Discussion Questions

1. According to this account, what is the relationship between humans and their surroundings? How will these views impact the way humans perceive the world around them?
2. What kind of relationship exists between God and humans? How does this relationship differ from other ancient societies and their gods, for example in Mesopotamia?
3. Does Genesis portray Eve as the chief offender in defying the commandments of God and introducing sin into the world?

## THE BOOK OF GENESIS

1 In the beginning God created the heavens and the earth. [2]And the earth was without form and void, and darkness was upon the face of the deep; and the Spirit of God was moving over the face of the waters. [3]And God said, "Let there be light"; and there was light. [4]And God saw that the light was good; and God separated the light from the darkness. [5]God called the light Day, and the darkness he called Night . . .

[26]Then God said, "Let us make man in our image, after our likeness; and let them have dominion over the fish of the sea, and over the birds of the air, and over the cattle, and over all the earth, and over every creeping thing that creeps upon the earth." [27]So God created man in his own image, in the image of God he created him; male and female he created them. [28]And God blessed them, and God said to them, "Be fruitful and multiply, and fill the earth and subdue it; and have dominion over the fish of the sea and over the birds of the air and over every living thing that moves upon the earth." [29]And God said, "Behold, I have given you every plant yielding seed which is upon the face of all the earth, and every tree with seed in its fruit; you shall have them for food. [30]And to every beast of the earth, and to every bird of the air, and to everything that creeps on the earth, everything that has the breath of life, I have given every green plant for food." And it was so. [31]And God saw everything that he had made, and, behold, it was very good . . .

2 . . . [15]The LORD God took the man and put him in the garden of Eden to till it and keep it. [16]And the LORD God commanded the man, saying, "You may freely eat of every tree of the garden; [17]but of the tree of the knowledge of good and evil you shall not eat, for in the day that you eat of it you shall die." . . .

3 Now the serpent was more subtle than any other wild creature that the LORD God had made. He said to the woman, "Did God say, 'You shall not eat of any tree of the garden'?" [2]And the woman said to the serpent, "We may eat of the fruit of the trees of the garden; [3]but God said, 'You shall not eat of the fruit of the tree which is in the midst of the garden, neither shall you touch it, lest you die.'" [4]But the serpent said to the woman, "You will not die. [5]For God knows that when you eat of it your eyes will be opened, and you will be like God, know-

ing good and evil" [6]So when the woman saw that the tree was good for food, and that it was a delight to the eyes, and that the tree was to be desired to make one wise, she took of its fruit and ate; and she also gave some to her husband, and he ate. [7]Then the eyes of both were opened, and they knew that they were naked; and they sewed fig leaves together and made themselves aprons.

[8]And they heard the sound of the LORD God walking in the garden in the cool of the day, and the man and his wife hid themselves from the presence of the LORD God among the trees of the garden. [9]But the LORD God called to the man, and said to him, "Where are you?" [10]And he said, " I heard the sound of thee in the garden, and I was afraid, because I was naked; and I hid myself." [11]He said, "Who told you that you were naked? Have you eaten of the tree of which I commanded you not to eat?" [12]The man said, "The woman whom thou gavest to be with me, she gave me fruit of the tree, and I ate." [13]Then the LORD God said to the woman, "What is this that you have done?" The woman said, "The serpent beguiled me, and I ate." [14]The LORD God said to the serpent, "Because you have done this, cursed are you above all cattle, and above all wild animals; upon your belly you shall go, and dust you shall eat all the days of your life. [15]I will put enmity between you and the woman, and between your seed and her seed; he shall bruise your head, and you shall bruise his heel." [16]To the woman he said, "I will greatly multiply your pain in childbearing; in pain you shall bring forth children, yet your desire shall be for your husband, and he shall rule over you." [17]And to Adam he said, "Because you have listened to the voice of your wife, and have eaten of the tree of which I commanded you, 'You shall not eat of it,' cursed is the ground because of you; in toil you shall eat of it all the days of your life; [18]thorns and thistles it shall bring forth to you; and you shall eat the plants of the field. [19]In the sweat of your face you shall eat bread till you return to the ground, for out of it you were taken; you are dust, and to dust you shall return."

# READING 2

## Proverbs and Ecclesiastes

*Most historical societies accumulate what is called "wisdom literature." Such materials consist of homilies and proverbs intended to teach how to live a happier, more successful life. Jewish wisdom literature is more extensive than most. Many of their proverbs are yet common stock in contemporary Western society. The book of Proverbs, while containing advice that arose from Jewish experience, borrows heavily from non-Jewish sources, especially Phoenician and Canaanite. Some of these homilies date from the time of Solomon or earlier. The book itself did not take its present form, however, until at least 400 B.C. The book of Ecclesiastes is even more recent.*

---

Discussion Questions

1. What are the most common themes in this sampling of Jewish wisdom literature?
2. According to these sources, how are women perceived?
3. Can you discern the influence of Hellenistic skepticism in the tone of the book of Ecclesiastes?

### PROVERBS

---

*Chapter 3*

1. My son, forget not my law; but let thine heart keep my commandments:

2. For length of days, and long life, and peace, shall they add to thee.

3. . . . bind them about thy neck; write them upon the table of thine heart:

4. So shalt thou find favour and good understanding in the sight God and man.

5. Trust in the Lord with all thine heart; and lean not unto thine own understanding.

12. For whom the Lord loveth he correcteth; even as a father the son in whom he delighteth.

13. Happy is the man that findeth wisdom, and the man that getteth understanding.

14. For the merchandise of it is better than the merchandise of silver, and the gain thereof than fine gold.

*Chapter 5*

3. For the lips of a strange woman drop as an honeycomb, and her mouth is smoother than oil:

4. But her end is bitter as wormwood, sharp as a two edged sword.

5. Her feet go down to death; her steps take hold on hell.

*Chapter 6*

23. For the commandment is a lamp; and the law is light; and reproofs of instruction are the way of life:

24. To keep thee from the evil woman, from the flattery of the tongue of a strange woman.

25. Lust not after her beauty in thine heart; neither let her take thee with her eyelids.

*Chapter 8*

13. The fear of the Lord is to hate evil: pride, and arrogancy, and the evil way, and the forward mouth, do I hate.

*Chapter 10*

1. . . . A wise son maketh a glad father; but a foolish son is the heaviness of his mother.

7. The memory of the just is blessed: but the name of the wicked shall rot.

8. The wise in heart will receive commandments: but a prating fool shall fall.

12. Hatred stirreth up strifes: but love covereth all sins.

*Chapter 11*

2. When pride cometh, then cometh shame: but with the lowly is wisdom.

*Chapter 12*

4. A virtuous woman is a crown to her husband: but she that maketh ashamed is a rottenness in his bones.

*Chapter 13*

24. He that spareth his rod hateth his son: but he that loveth him chasteneth him betimes.

*Chapter 15*

1. A soft answer turneth away wrath: but grievous words stir up anger.

*Chapter 16*

32. He that is slow to anger is better than the mighty; and he that ruleth his spirit than he that taketh a city.

*Chapter 20*

1. Wine is a mocker, strong drink is raging: and whosoever is deceived thereby is not wise.

13. Love not sleep, lest thou come to poverty; open thine eyes, and thou shalt be satisfied with bread.

15. There is gold, and a multitude of rubies: but the lips of knowledge are a precious jewel.

19. He that goeth about as a talebearer revealeth secrets: therefore meddle not with him that flattereth with his lips.

20. Whoso curseth his father or his mother, his lamp shall be put out in obscure darkness.

*Chapter 21*

9. It is better to dwell in a corner of the housetop, than with a brawling woman in a wide house.

13. Whoso stoppeth his ears at the cry of the poor, he also shall cry himself, but shall not be heard.

17. He that loveth pleasure shall be a poor man: he that loveth wine and oil shall not be rich.

materialism = bad

*Chapter 22*

6. Train up a child in the way he should go: and when he is old, he will not depart from it.

7. The rich ruleth over the poor, and the borrower is servant to the lender.

*Chapter 23*

13. Withhold not correction from the child: for if thou beatest him with the rod, he shall not die.

14. Thou shalt beat him with the rod, and shalt deliver his soul from hell.

21. For the drunkard and the glutton shall come to poverty: and drowsiness shall clothe a man with rags.

*Chapter 25*

9. Debate thy cause with thy neighbour himself; and discover not a secret to another.

28. He that hath no rule over his own spirit is like a city that is broken down, and without walls.

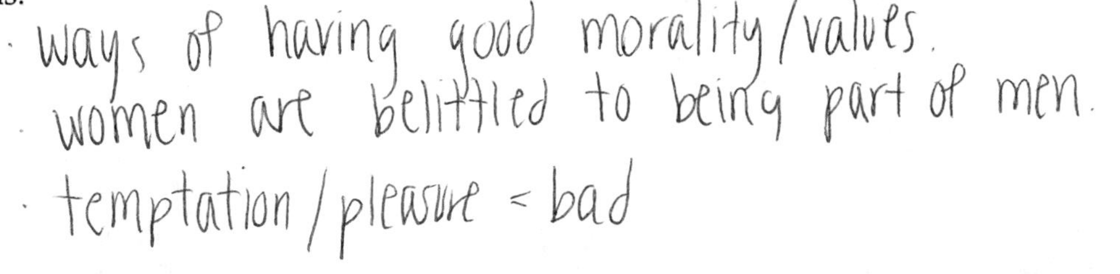

*Chapter 29*

3. Whoso loveth wisdom rejoiceth his father: but he that keepeth company with harlots spendeth his substance.

20. Seest thou a man that is hasty in his words? There is more hope of a fool than of him.

23. A man's pride shall bring him low: but honour shall uphold the humble in spirit.

## Ecclesiastes

*Chapter 1*

4. One generation passeth away, and another generation cometh: but the earth abideth forever.

9. The thing that hath been, it is that which shall be; and that which is done is that which shall be done: and there is no new thing under the sun.

18. For in much wisdom is much grief: and he that increaseth knowledge increaseth sorrow.

*Chapter 3*

1. To every thing there is a season, and a time to every purpose under the heaven: . . .

19. For that which befalleth the sons of men befalleth beasts; even one thing befalleth them: as the one dieth, so dieth the other; yea, they have all one breath; so that a man hath no preeminence above a beast: for all is vanity.

20. All go unto one place; all are of the dust, and dust again.

22. Wherefore I perceive that there is nothing better, than that a man should rejoice in his own works; for that is his portion: for who shall bring him to see what shall be after him?

*Chapter 7*

1. A good name is better than precious ointment; and the day of death than the day of one's birth.

15. All things have I seen in the days of my vanity: there is a just man that perisheth in his righteousness, and there is a wicked man that prolongeth his life in his wickedness.

*Chapter 9*

10. Whatsoever thy hand findeth to do, do it with thy might; for there is no work, nor device, nor knowledge, nor wisdom in the grave, whither thou goest.

11. I returned, and saw under the sun, that the race is not to the swift, nor the battle to the strong, neither yet bread to the wise, nor yet riches to men of understanding, nor yet favour to men of skill; but time and chance happeneth to them all.

morality & equality

# READING 3

## Josephus' Antiquities of the Jews

*Flavius Josephus lived during the first century A.D. He was a witness and participant in the Jewish revolt against Rome. Although he was later reconciled to Roman rule, he always remained a strong advocate of the accomplishments of his early forbearers. The following excerpts from his "Antiquities of the Jews", while extensively based on the biblical narrative, employ other sources as well—some that are now unavailable. The passages printed describe the Jewish account of Noah and the flood, Abraham's Mesopotamian origin, Solomon's achievements, and the Khaldean conquest of Judea in the sixth century B.C. The selections below are taken from, William Whiston, trans.,* The Works of Flavius Josephus, *(3 vols; New York: International Book Co., n.d.), I: 72–78, 85–86, 510–514, 630–633.*

---

### Discussion Questions

1. In light of the following excerpts by Josephus, do you agree with the Jewish claim that the Israelites are God's chosen people?
2. What is the relationship between God and the Israelites, and how does this relationship compare to that of other ancient societies and their gods?
3. Of what do you think the author is trying to convince the reader?

## CHAPTER III

---

*Concerning the Flood; and After What Manner Noah Was Saved In an Ark, With His Kindred, and Afterwards Dwelt In the Plain of Shinar.*

I. Now this posterity Seth continued to esteem God as the Lord of the universe, and to have an entire regard to virtue, for seven generations; but in process of time they were perverted, and forsook the practices of their forefathers . . . But for what degree of zeal they had formerly shown for virtue, they now showed by their actions a double degree of wickedness; whereby they made God to be their enemy . . . But Noah was very uneasy at what they did; and, being displeased at their conduct, persuaded them to change their dispositions and their acts for the better;—but, seeing that they did not yield to him, but were slaves to their wicked pleasures, he was afraid they would kill him, together with his wife and children, and those they had married; so he departed out of that land.

2. Now God loved this man for his righteousness; yet he not only condemned those other men for their wickedness, but determined to destroy the whole race of mankind, and to make another race that should be pure from wickedness . . . [Therefore] he turned the dry land into sea; and thus were all these men destroyed: but Noah alone was saved; for God suggested to him the following contrivance and way of escape:—That he should make an ark . . . Accordingly he entered into that ark, and his wife and sons, and their wives; and put into it not only other provisions, to support their wants there, but also sent in with the rest all sorts of living creatures, the male and his female, for the preservation of their kinds . . . and thus was Noah, with his family, preserved . . .

5. When God, gave the signal, and it began to rain, the water poured down forty entire days, till it became fifteen cubits higher than the earth; which was the reason why there was no greater number preserved, since they had no place to fly to. When the rain ceased, the water did but just begin to abate, after one hundred and fifty days (that is, on the seventeenth

day of the seventh month) it then ceasing to subside for a little while. After this the ark rested on the top of a certain mountain in Armenia; which, when Noah understood, he opened it; and seeing a small piece of land about it, he continued quiet, and conceived some cheerful hopes of deliverance; but a few days afterwards, when the water was decreased to a greater degree, he sent out a raven, as desirous to learn whether any other part of the earth were left dry by the water, and whether he might go out of the ark with safety; but the raven, finding all the land still overflowed, returned to Noah again. And after seven days he sent out a dove, to know the state of the ground; which came back to him covered with mud, and bringing an olive-branch. Hereby Noah learned that the earth was become clear of the flood. So after he had stayed seven more days, he sent the living creatures out of the ark; and both he and his family went out, when he also sacrificed to God, and feasted with his companions. However, the Armenians call this place (A_oßa_npiov) *The Place of Descent;* for the ark being saved in that place, its remains are shown there by the inhabitants to this day.

6. Now all the writers of barbarian histories make mention of this flood and of this ark; among whom is Berosus the Chaldean for when he is describing the circumstances of the flood, he goes on thus:—"It is said there is still some part of this ship in Armenia, at the mountain of the Cordyæans; and that some people carry off pieces of the bitumen, which they take away, and use chiefly as amulets for the averting of mischiefs." Hieronymus the Egyptian, also, who wrote the Phoenician Antiquities, and Mnaseas, and a great many more, make mention of the same. Nay; Nicolaus of Damascus, in his ninety-sixth book, hath a particular relation about them, where he speaks thus:—"There is a great mountain in Armenia, over Minyas, called Baris, upon which it is reported that many who fled at the time of the Deluge were saved; and that one who was carried in an ark came on shore upon the top of it; and that the remains of the timber were a great while preserved. This might be the man about whom Moses, the legislator of the Jews wrote."

7. But as for Noah, he was afraid, since God had determined to destroy mankind, lest he should drown the earth every year; so he offered burnt offerings, and besought God that Nature might hereafter go on in its former orderly course, and that he would not bring on so great a judgment any more, by which the whole race of creatures might be in danger of destruction; but that, having now punished the wicked, he would of his goodness spare the remainder . . . He also entreated God to accept of his sacrifice, and to grant that the earth might never again undergo the like effects of his wrath; that men might be permitted to go on cheerfully in cultivating the same—to build cities, and live happily in them; and that they might not be deprived of any of those good things which they enjoyed before the Flood; but might attain to the like length of days and old age which the ancient people had arrived at before.

8. When Noah had made these supplications, God, who loved the man for his righteousness, granted entire success to his prayers, and said, that it was not he who brought the destruction on a polluted world, but that they underwent that vengeance on account of their own wickedness . . . "[They] forced me to bring this punishment upon them; but I will leave off for the time to come to require such punishments, the effects of so great wrath, for their future wicked actions, and especially on account of thy prayers; but if I shall at any time send tempests of rain in an extraordinary manner, be not affrighted at the largeness of the showers, for the waters shall no more overspread the earth. However, I require you to abstain from shedding the blood of men, and to keep yourselves pure from murder; and to punish those that commit any such thing. I permit you to make use of all the other living creatures at your pleasure, and as your appetites lead you; for I have made you lords of them all, both of those that walk on the land, and those that swim in the waters, and of those that fly in the regions of the air on high—excepting their blood, for therein is the life: but I will give you a sign that I have left off my anger, by my bow" [whereby is meant the rainbow, for they determined that the rainbow was the bow of God]; and when God had said and promised thus, he went away.

## Chapter VII

*How Abram Our Forefather Went Out of the Land of the Chaldeans, and Lived In the Land Then Called Canaan, But Now Judea.*

I. Now Abram having no son of his own, adopted Lot, his brother Haran's son, and his wife Sarai's brother; and he left the land of Chaldea when he was seventy-five years old, and at the command of *God* went into Canaan, and therein he dwelt himself, and left it to his posterity. He was a person of great sagacity, both for understanding all things and persuading his hearers, and not mistaken in his opinions; for which reason he began to have higher notions of virtue than others had, and he determined to renew and to change the opinion all men happened then to have concerning *God;* for he was the first that ventured to publish this notion, That there was but one *God,* the Creator of the universe; and that, as to other [gods], if they contributed a thing to the happiness of men, that each of them afforded only according to his appointment, and not by their own power. . . . For which doctrines, when the Chaldeans and other people of Mesopotamia raised a turn against him, he thought fit to leave that country and the command, and by the assistance of God, he came and lived in the land of Canaan. And when he was there settled, he built an altar, and performed a sacrifice to God.

2. Berosus mentions our father Abram without naming him, when he says thus:—"In the tenth generation after the Flood, there was among the Chaldeans a man righteous and great, and skillful in the celestial science." But Hecatæus does more than barely mention him; for he composed and left behind him a book concerning him. And Nicolaus of Damascus, in the fourth book of his history, says thus:—"Abram reigned at Damascus, being a foreigner who came with an army out of the land above Babylon, called the land of the Chaldeans. But after a long time he got him up, and removed from that country also with his people, and went into the land then called the land of Canaan, but now the land of Judea, and this when posterity were become a multitude; as to which posterity of his, we relate their history in another work. Now the name of Abram is even still famous in the country of Damascus; and there is shown a village named from him, *The Habitation of Abram.*

## Chapter VI

*How Solomon Entertained the Queen of Egypt and of Ethiopia.*

There was then a woman, queen of Egypt and Ethiopia; she was inquisitive into philosophy, and one that on other accounts also was to be admired. When this queen heard of the virtue and prudence of Solomon . . . so she resolved to come to him, and that especially, in order to have a trial of his wisdom, while she proposed questions of very great difficulty, and entreated that he would solve their hidden meaning. Accordingly she came to Jerusalem with great splendor and rich furniture; for she brought with her camels laden with gold, with several sorts of sweet spices, and with precious stones. Now, upon the king's kind reception of her, he both showed a great desire to please her, and easily comprehending in his mind the meaning of the curious questions she propounded to him, he resolved them sooner than any body could have expected. So she was amazed at the wisdom of Solomon, and discovered that it was more excellent upon trial than what she had heard by report beforehand; and especially she was surprised at the fineness and largeness of his royal palace, and not less so at the good order of the apartments, for she observed that the king had therein shown great wisdom; but she was beyond measure astonished at the house which was called the *Forest of Lebanon,* as also at the magnificence of his daily table, and the circumstances of its preparation and ministration, with the apparel of his servants that waited, and the skillful and decent management of their attendance: nor was she less affected with those daily sacrifices which were offered to

God, and the careful management which the priests and Levites used about them. When she saw this done every day, she was in the greatest admiration imaginable, insomuch that she was not able to contain the surprise she was in, but openly confessed how wonderfully she was affected . . . "Accordingly, I esteem the Hebrew people, as well as thy servants and friends, to be happy, who enjoy the presence and hear thy wisdom every day continually. One would therefore bless God, who hath so loved his country, and those that inhabit therein."

## CHAPTER VIII

*How the King of Babylon Took Jerusalem and Burnt the Temple, and Removed the People of Jerusalem and Zedekiah to Babylon.*

I. Now the king of Babylon was very intent and earnest upon the siege of Jerusalem . . . However, those that were within bore the siege with courage and alacrity, for they were not discouraged, either by the famine or by the pestilential distemper, but were of cheerful minds in the prosecution of the war, although those miseries within oppressed them also; and they did not suffer themselves to be terrified, either by the contrivances of the enemy, or by their engines of war, but contrived still different engines to oppose all the other withal . . . and this siege they endured for eighteen months, until they were destroyed by the famine, and by the darts which the enemy threw at them from the towers.

2. Now the city was taken on the ninth day of the fourth month, in the eleventh year of the reign of Zedekiah . . . when the city was taken about midnight, and the enemy's generals were entered into the temple, and when Zedekiah was sensible of it, he took his wives and his children, and his captains and friends, and with them fled out of the city, through the fortified ditch, and through the desert; and when certain of the deserters had informed the Babylonians of this, at break of day, they made haste to pursue after Zedekiah, and overtook him not far from Jericho . . . so the enemy took Zedekiah alive, when he was deserted by all but a few, with his children and his wives, and brought him to the king. When he was come, Nebuchadnezzar began to call him a wicked wretch, and a covenant breaker, and one that had forgotten his former words, when he promised to keep the country for him. He also reproached him for his ingratitude, that when he had received the kingdom from him, who had taken it from Jehoiachin, and given it him, he had made use of the power he gave him against him that gave it: "but," said he, "God is great, who hateth that conduct of thine, and hath brought thee under us." And when he had used these words to Zedekiah, he commanded his sons and his friends to be slain, while Zedekiah and the rest of the captains looked on; after which he put out the eyes of Zedekiah, and bound him, and carried him to Babylon. And these things happened to him, as Jeremiah and Ezekiel had foretold to him, that he should be caught, and brought before the king of Babylon, and should speak to him face to face, and should see his eyes with his own eyes; and thus far did Jeremiah prophesy. But he was also made blind, and brought to Babylon but did not see it, according to the prediction of Ezekiel.

3. We have said thus much because it was sufficient to show the nature of God to such as are ignorant of it that it is various and acts many different ways, and that all events happen after a regular manner, in their proper season, and that it foretells what must come to pass. It is also sufficient to show the ignorance and incredulity of men, whereby they are not permitted to foresee any thing, that is future, and are, without any guard, exposed to calamities, so that it is impossible for them to avoid the experience of those calamities.

4. And after this manner have the kings of David's race ended their lives, being in number twenty-one, until, the last king, who all together reigned five hundred and fourteen years, and six months, and ten days: of whom Saul, who was their first king, retained the government twenty years, though he was not of the same tribe with the rest.

5. And now it was that the king of Babylon sent Nebuzaradan, the general of his army, to Jerusalem, to pillage the temple; who had it also in command to bum it and the royal palace, and to lay the city even with the ground, and to transplant the people into Babylon. Accordingly he came to Jerusalem, in the eleventh year of king Zedekiah, and pillaged the temple, and carried out the vessels of God, both gold and silver, and particularly that large laver which Solomon dedicated, as also the pillars of brass, and their chapiters, with the golden tablets and the candlesticks: and when he had carried these off, he set fire to the temple . . . But the general of the Babylonian king now overthrew the city to the very foundations, and removed all the people, and took for prisoners the high-priest . . . So the kin commanded the heads of the high-priest and of the rulers to be cut off there.

# LECTURE TOPIC 4

# *Ancient Egypt*

I. The Old Kingdom: 3100–2181 B.C. Was it the Most Glorious?
  A. Inundations of the Nile
  B. How Did Upper and Lower Egypt Become United?
    1. Aho or Menes or Narmer
    2. Capital at Memphis
    3. Nomarchs
  C. Who Built the First Pyramids?
    1. Cheops, Kheferen and Mycerinas
    2. Egyptian Engineering
  D. What about Religion and the Social Hierarchy?
    1. Polytheistic and Mythopoeic
    2. Divine Kingship and the Pharaoh
    3. A Social Ladder from Gods to Slaves
    4. What was the Egyptian View of Women?
  E. Early Triumphs of Egyptian Science
    1. Edwin Smith Papyrus
    2. Embalming
    3. Hieroglyphic Writing on Papyrus
  F. What Caused the Decline of the Old Kingdom?
II. The First Intermediate Period: 2181–2050 B.C.
  A. "A Time of Troubles"
  B. Description of Ipuwer
III. Middle Kingdom: 2050–1786 B.C.
  A. Who Restored Order and Prosperity?
    1. Amenemhets and Senuserts
    2. Pushing Back the Nubians
  B. What Is the Idea of *Ma'at?*
  C. Domestication of Cats?
  D. Decline of Middle Kingdom
    1. Nubian Independence
    2. Invasion by the Hyksos
      a) Horses; Chariots
      b) Bronze; Composite Bow
IV. The Second Intermediate Period: 1786–1585 B.C.
  A. Pattern of Invasion and Assimilation
  B. Expulsion of the Hyksos
V. The New Kingdom: 1585–1087 B.C.
  A. Ahmose (1585–1557 B.C.): The Savior of Egypt
  B. Three Thutmoses and Hatshepsut: (1490–1456 B.C.)
    1. How Did A Female Pharaoh Come to Power?
      a) Incestuous Marriages

            b) The Queen Elizabeth of Ancient Egypt
            c) Trade and Monument Building
                (1) Expedition to Punt
                (2) Obelisks and Temples at Karnak
        2. Imperial Expansion under Thutmose III
        3. Hatshepsut: the Mystery Pharaoh
    C. What Was the Amarna Revolution?
        1. Amenhotep IV/ Akhenaton (1375–1358 B.C.)
            a) World's First Monotheists?
            b) Court Life at Amarna
            c) Naturalistic Art
        2. What Was the Role of Nefertiti?
        3. Thutankhamon (fl. 1352–1344 B.C.)
            a) Military Reverses and Collapsing Borders
            b) Opposition from Priests and Army
                (1) Overthrow by Haremhab (ca. 1340–1309 B.C.)
                (2) Was Thutankhamon Murdered?
            c) Twentieth-Century Rediscovery: Howard Carter: 1922
    D. Nineteenth Dynasty Revival
        1. Renewed Building Program at Karnak
        2. Military Defeats and Decline of Empire
            a) Hittites at Kadesh: 1287 B.C.
            b) Merneptah (1236–1223 B.C.) and the Israelites under Moses
    E. Continued Decline
        1. Vassalage to Assyria and Persia
        2. Vassalage to Macedonia and Rome
VI. Conclusions
    A. Continuing Fascination with Egypt
    B. Napoleon's Invasion: 1799
        1. Rosetta Stone
        2. Champollion (1778–1867)
    C. Controversy: Egyptian Contribution to Classical/Western Civilization
        1. The Bernal Thesis
        2. *Not Out of Africa*

# READING 1

## Hymn to the Nile

*Herodotus wrote, "Egypt is the gift of the Nile." The famous Greek historian recognized that without the Nile the large population of laborers and surpluses necessary to create the flourishing civilization of Ancient Egypt might never have developed. From the fifth millennia B.C. when people fled the emerging deserts of northern Africa, the Nile continued to attract people in times of drought or hardship because of its irrigated and therefore habitable land. The Nile was sacred to the Egyptians, and many hymns were written to it. The following is an example of one such hymn written about 2100 BC and taken from Oliver J. Thatcher, ed.,* The Library of Original Sources *(Milwaukee: University Research Extension Co., 1907), Vol. I: The Ancient World, pp. 79–83.*

---

Discussion Questions

1. Describe the characteristics and the Egyptian perception of the Nile, one of their chief deities.
2. What was the Egyptian view of the proper relationship between humans and this deity?
3. What does this document illustrate about Egyptian life?

### HYMN TO THE NILE

---

Adoration to the Nile!<br>
Hail to thee, O Nile!<br>
Who manifesteth thyself over this land<br>
And comest to give life to Egypt!<br>
Mysterious is thy issuing forth from the darkness,<br>
On this day whereon it is celebrated!<br>
Watering the orchards created by Ra<br>
To cause all the cattle to live,<br>
Thou givest the earth to drink, inexhaustible one! . . .

Lord of the fish, during the inundation,<br>
No bird alights on the crops.<br>
Thou createst the corn, thou bringest forth the barley,<br>
Assuring perpetuity to the temples.<br>
If thou ceasest thy toil and thy work,<br>
Then all that exists is in anguish.<br>
If the gods suffer in heaven<br>
Then the faces of men waste away.

He brings the offerings, as chief of provisioning;<br>
He is the creator of all good things,<br>
As master of energy, full of sweetness in his choice.<br>
If offerings are made it is thanks to him.<br>
He brings forth the herbage for the flocks,<br>
And sees that each god receives his sacrifices.

All that depends on him is a precious incense.
He spreads himself over Egypt,
Filling the granaries, renewing the marts,
Watching over the goods of the unhappy. . . .

When thou shinest in the royal city,
The rich man is sated with good things,
The poor man even disdains the lotus;
All that is produced is of the choicest;
All the plants exist for thy children.
If thou hast refused [to grant] nourishment,
The dwelling is silent, devoid of all that is good
The country falls exhausted. . . .

O inundation of the Nile,
Offerings are made unto thee,
Oxen are immolated to thee,
Great festivals are instituted for thee.

# READING 2

## The Great Pyramid

*Historical evidence indicates that for about a thousand years the Ancient Egyptians built pyramids in the desert west of the Nile as tombs for their kings. Considered a marvel of the ancient world, the pyramids have stimulated human imagination throughout their history and remain today one of mankind's greatest feats of engineering. The Great Pyramid was built by the Egyptian pharaoh Khufu (Cheops ) around the year 2560 B.C. and is located at the city of Giza, a necropolis* of ancient Memphis, and today part of Greater Cairo. Historians used to believe that the pyramids were built by slave labor, but the consensus today is that they were probably public-works projects to aid the unemployed. There was no large military police force, which would have been necessary if the workers had been slaves, and historians emphasize that during the flooding of the Nile many thousands of workers would have been available for work. Instead of monuments to brutal dictators, the pyramids were more likely the result of an early socialism. Almost twenty-five centuries ago, the famous Greek traveler, Herodotus, visited Egypt. Like all tourists, he was greatly impressed by the Great Pyramid, which was already two thousand years old. The account of Herodotus which follows is taken from George Rawlinson, ed.,* History of Herodotus, *vol. 1, (London, J. M. Dent & Sons Ltd. & New York, E. P. Dutton & Co.), pg. 177–179, also Book II, Chapters 124, 125.*

---

### Discussion Questions

1. Do you think the Egyptians brought with them the idea of the pyramid when they migrated into the valley of the Nile, and if so, where might the idea have originated?
2. According to Herodotus, did the Egyptians use machines in building the pyramids?
3. What does the position of the pyramids imply about the astronomical knowledge at that time?

## HERODOTUS

. . . He [Khufu or Cheops] closed the temples, and forbade the Egyptians to offer sacrifice, compelling them instead to labour, one and all, in his service. Some were required to drag blocks of stone down to the Nile from the quarries in the Arabian range of hills; others received the blocks after they had been conveyed in boats across the river, and drew them to the range of hills called the Libyan. A hundred thousand men laboured constantly, and were relieved every three months by a fresh lot. It took ten years' oppression of the people to make the causeway for the conveyance of the stones, a work not much inferior, in my judgment, to the pyramid itself. . . . The pyramid itself was twenty years in building. It is a square, eight hundred feet each way, and the height the same, built entirely of polished stone, fitted together with the utmost care. The stones of which it is composed are none of them less than thirty feet in length. The pyramid was built in steps, battlement-wise, as it is called, or, according to others, altar-wise. After laying the stones for the base, they raised the remaining stones to their places by means of machines formed of short wooden planks. The first machine raised them from the ground to the top of the first step. On this there was another machine, which received the stone upon its arrival, and conveyed it to the second step, whence a third machine

* a large, elaborate and usually ancient cemetery.

advanced it still higher. Either they had as many machines as there were steps in the pyramid, or possibly they had but a single machine, which, being easily moved, was transferred from tier to tier as the stone rose—both accounts are given, and therefore I mention both, The upper portion of the pyramid was finished first, then the middle, and finally the part which was lowest and nearest the ground. There is an inscription in Egyptian characters on the pyramid which records the quantity of radishes, onions, and garlic consumed by the labourers who constructed it; and I perfectly well remember that the interpreter who read the writing to me said that the money expended in this way was *1600* talents of silver. If this then is a true record, what a vast sum must have been spent on the iron tools used in the work, and on the feeding and clothing of the labourers, considering the length of time the work lasted, which has already been stated, and the additional time—no small space, I imagine—which must have been occupied by the quarrying of the stones, their conveyance, and the formation of the underground apartments.

· how Egyptians created pyramids
· time & effort it required.

# READING 3

## Herodotus Describes Egypt

*Herodotus, who was the source for Reading 2 above, also provides us with the following. These passages also deal with what he saw and experienced in Egypt. Give particular attention to the deference he pleaded that Greeks owed to the Egyptians. The selection comes from Henry Cary, trans., Herodotus.* A New and Literal Version. . . . *(New York: Harper and Bros., 1863), pp. 108–109, 116, 120–121, 124–127.*

---

### Discussion Questions

1. What do you find to be the most striking similarities and differences between the ancient Egyptians and ourselves?
   A. Their toilet habits?
   B. Their funerary practices?
   C. Something else?
2. What did they do with the body of a person seized by a crocodile?

I now proceed to give a more particular account of Egypt. It possesses more wonders than any other country, and exhibits works greater than can be described in comparison with all other regions; therefore more must be said about it. The Egyptians, besides having a climate peculiar to themselves, and a river differing in its nature from all other rivers, have adopted customs and usages in almost every respect different from the rest of mankind. Among them the women attend markets and traffic, but the men stay at home and weave . . . . The men carry burdens on their heads; the women, on their shoulders. The women stand when they make water, but the men sit down, they ease themselves in their houses, but eat out of doors; alleging that whatever is indecent, though necessary, ought to be done in private; but what is not indecent, openly. No woman can serve the office for any god or goddess; but men are employed for both offices. Sons are not compelled to support their parents unless they choose, but daughters are compelled to do so whether they choose or not.

In other countries the priests of the gods wear long hair; in Egypt they have it shaved. With other men it is customary in mourning for the nearest relations to have their heads shorn; the Egyptians, on occasions of death, let the hair grow both on the head and face, though till then used to shave. Other men live apart from beasts; but the Egyptians live with them. Others feed on wheat and barley, but it is a very great disgrace for an Egyptian to make food of them; but they make bread from spelt, which some call zea. They knead the dough with their feet, but mix clay and take up dung with their hands. Other men leave their private parts as they are formed by nature, except those who have learned otherwise from them; but the Egyptians are circumcised. Every man wears two garments; the women, but one. Other men fasten the rings and sheets of their sails outside; but the Egyptians, inside. The Grecians write and cipher moving the hand from left to right; but the Egyptians, from right to left; and doing so, they say they do it right-ways, and the Greeks left-ways. They have two sorts of letters, one of which is called sacred, the other common . . .

Although the domesticated animals are many, they would be much more numerous were it not for the following accidents which befall the cats. When the females have littered, they no longer seek the company of the males, and they, being desirous of having intercourse with them, are not able to do so, wherefore they have recourse to the following artifice: having taken the young from the females, and carried them away secretly, they kill them, though, when they have killed them, they do not eat them. The females, being deprived of their young, and desirous of others, again seek the company of the males; for this animal is very fond of its young. When a conflagration takes place, a supernatural impulse seizes on the cats; for the Egyptians, standing at a distance, take care of the cats, and neglect to put out the fire; but the cats, making their escape, and leaping over the men, throw themselves into the fire; and when this happens, great lamentations are made among the Egyptians. In whatever house a cat dies of a natural death, all the family shave their eyebrows only; but if a dog die, they shave the whole body and the head. All cats that die are carried to certain sacred houses, where, being first embalmed, they are buried in the city of Bubastis. All persons bury their dogs in sacred vaults within their own city; and ichneumons are buried in the same manner as the dogs; but field-mice and hawks they carry to the city of Buto; the ibis to Hermopolis; the bears, which are few in number, and the wolves, which are not much larger than foxes, they bury wherever they are found lying. . . .

. . . the Egyptians . . . cultivate the memory of past events more than any other men, are the best informed of all with whom I have had intercourse. Their manner of life is this. They purge themselves every month, three days successively, seeking to preserve health by emetics and clysters; for they suppose that all diseases to which men are subject proceed from the food they use. And, indeed, in other respects, the Egyptians, next to the Libyans, are the most healthy people in the world, as I think, on account of the seasons, because they are not liable to change; for men are most subject to disease at periods of change, and, above all others, at the change of the seasons . . . . At their convivial banquets, among the wealthy classes, when they have finished supper, a man carries round in a coffin the image of a dead body carved in wood, made as like as possible in color and workmanship, and in size generally about one or two cubits in length; and showing this to each of the company, he says, "Look upon this, then drink and enjoy yourself; for when dead you will be like this." This practice they have at their drinking parties . . .

Their manner of mourning and burying is as follows. When in a family a man of any consideration dies, all the females of that family besmear their heads and faces with mud, and then leaving the body in the house, they wander about the city, and beat themselves, having their clothes girt up, and exposing their breasts, and all their relations accompany them. On the other hand, the men beat themselves, being girt up, in like manner. When they have done this, they carry out the body to be embalmed.

There are persons who are appointed for this very purpose; they, which the dead body is brought to them, show to the bearers wooden models of corpses, made exactly like by painting. And they show that which they say is the most expensive manner of embalming, the name of which I do not think its right to mention on such an occasion; they then show the second, which is inferior and less expensive; and then the third, which is the cheapest. Having explained them all, they learn from them in what way they wish the body to be prepared; then the relations, when they have agreed on the price, depart; but the embalmers remaining in the work-shops thus proceed to embalm in the most expensive manner. First they draw out the brains through the nostrils with an iron hook, taking part of it out in this manner, the rest by the infusion of drugs. Then with a sharp Ethiopian stone they make an incision in the side, and take out all the bowels; and having cleansed the abdomen and rinsed it with palm-wine, they next sprinkle it with pounded perfumes. Then, having filled the belly with pure myrrh pounded, and cassia, and other perfumes, frankincense excepted, they sew it up again; and when they have done this, they steep it in natrum, leaving it under for seventy days; for a longer time than this it is not lawful to steep it. At the expiration of the seventy days they wash the corpse, and wrap the whole body in bandages of flaxen cloth, smearing it with gum, which the Egyptians commonly use instead of glue. After this the relations, having taken the body back again, make a wooden case in the shape of a man, and having made it, they enclose the body; and thus, having fastened it up, they store it in a sepulchral chamber, setting it upright against the wall. In this manner they prepare the bodies that are embalmed in the most expensive way.

Those who, avoiding great expense, desire the middle way, they prepare in the following manner. When they have charged their syringes with oil made from cedar, they fill the abdomen of the corpse without making any incision or taking out the bowels, but inject it at the fundament; and having prevented the injection from escaping, they steep the body in natrum for the prescribed number of days, and on the last day they let out from the abdomen the oil of cedar which they had before injected, and it has such power that it brings away the intestines and vitals in a state of dissolution; the natrum dissolves the flesh, and nothing of the body remains but the skin and the bones. When they have done this they return the body without any farther operation.

The third method of embalming is this, which is used only for the poorer sort: having thoroughly rinsed the abdomen in syrmaea, they steep it with natrum for the seventy days, and then deliver it to be carried away. But the wives of considerable persons, when they die, they do not immediately deliver to be embalmed, nor such women as are very beautiful and of celebrity, but when they have been dead three or four days they then deliver them to the embalmers; and they do this for the following reason, that the embalmers may not abuse the bodies of such women; for they say that one man was detected in abusing a body that was fresh, and that a fellow-workman informed against him.

Should any person, whether Egyptian or stranger, no matter which, be found to have been seized by a crocodile, or drowned in the river, to whatever city the body may be carried, the inhabitants are by law compelled to have the body embalmed, and having adorned it in the handsomest manner, to bury it in the sacred vaults. Nor is it lawful for anyone else, whether relations or friends, to touch him; but the priests of the Nile bury the corpse with their own hands, as being something more than human.

# READING 4

## Opportunity in Ancient Egypt

*This remarkable account of a commoner's rise and favor in the employment of Old Kingdom pharaohs is taken from Egyptian hieroglyphic inscriptions carved in limestone. In addition to providing a view of the lives and projects of early Egyptian god-kings, it also resembles the Jewish story of Joseph, sold into Egypt by his brothers, that dates centuries later. The printing here comes from Miriam Lichtheim,* Ancient Egyptian Literature: A Book of Readings, *3 vols. (Berkeley: University of California Press, 1973–1980), I: pp. 18–22.*

---

Discussion Questions

1. Based on Weni's autobiography, how would you describe the social structure of ancient Egypt?
2. What does this reading tell us about the perceived nature of the Pharaoh?

### THE AUTOBIOGRAPHY OF WENI

(1/2) [The Count, Governor of Upper Egypt, Chamberlain], Warden of Nekhen, Mayor of Nekheb, Sole Companion, honored by Osiris Foremost-of-the-Westerners, Weni [says]: [I was] a fillet-wearing [youth] under the majesty of King Teti, my office being that of custodian of the storehouse, when I became

inspector of [tenants] of the palace———. [When I had become] overseer of the robing-room under the majesty of King Pepi, his majesty gave me the rank of companion and inspector of priests of his pyramid town.

While my office was that of—his majesty made me senior warden of Nekhen, his heart being filled with me beyond any other servant of his. I heard cases alone with the chief judge and vizier, concerning all kinds of secrets. [I acted] in the name of the king for the royal harem and for the six great houses, because his majesty's heart was filled with me beyond any official of his, any noble of his, any servant of his.

(5/6) When 1 begged of the majesty of my lord that there be brought for me a sarcophagus of white stone from Tura, his majesty had a royal seal-bearer cross over with a company of sailors under his command, to bring me this sarcophagus from Tura. It came with him in a great barge of the court, together with its lid, a doorway, lintel, two doorjambs and a libation-table. Never before had the like been done for any servant—but I was excellent in his majesty's heart; I was rooted in his majesty's heart; his majesty's heart was filled with me.

While I was senior warden of Nekhen, his majesty made me a sole companion and overseer of the [royal tenants]. I replaced four overseers of [royal tenants] who were there. I acted for his majesty's praise in guarding, escorting the king, and attending. I acted throughout (10/11) so that his majesty praised me for it exceedingly.

When there was a secret charge in the royal harem against Queen Weretyamtes, his majesty made me go in to hear (it) alone. No chief judge and vizier, no official was there, only I alone; because I was worthy, because I was rooted in his majesty's heart; because his majesty had filled his heart with me. Only I put (it) in writing together with one other senior warden of Nekhen, while my rank was (only) that of overseer of [royal tenants]. Never before had one like me heard a secret of the king's harem; but his majesty made me hear it, because I was worthy in his majesty's heart beyond any official of his, beyond any noble of his, beyond any servant of his.

When his majesty took action against the Asiatic Sand-dwellers, his majesty made an army of many tens of thousands from all of Upper Egypt . . .

His majesty sent me at the head of this army, there being counts, royal sealbearers, sole companions of the palace, chieftains and mayors of towns of Upper and Lower Egypt, companions, scoutleaders, chief priests of Upper and Lower Egypt, and chief district officials at the head of the troops of Upper and Lower Egypt, from the villages and towns that they governed and from the Nubians of those foreign lands. I was the one who commanded them—while my rank was that of overseer of [royal tenants]—because of my rectitude, so that no one attacked his fellow, (20/21) so that no one seized a loaf or sandals from a traveler, so that no one took a cloth from any town, so that no one took a goat from anyone . . .

His majesty praised me for it beyond anything. His majesty sent me to lead this army five times, to attack the land of the Sand-dwellers as often as they rebelled, with these troops. I acted so that his majesty praised me [for it beyond anything] . . .

When I was chamberlain of the palace and sandal-bearer, King Mernere, my lord who lives forever, made me Count and Governor of Upper Egypt, from Yebu in the south to Medenyt in the north, because I was worthy in his majesty's heart, because I was rooted in his majesty's heart, because his majesty's heart was filled with me . . .

I governed Upper Egypt for him in peace, so that no one attacked his fellow. I did every task. I counted everything that is countable for the residence in this Upper Egypt two times, and every service that is countable for the residence in this Upper Egypt two times. I did a perfect job in this Upper Egypt. Never before had the like been done in this Upper Egypt. I acted throughout so that his majesty praised me for it . . .

His majesty sent me to Hatnub to bring a great altar of alabaster of Hatnub. I brought this altar down for him in seventeen days. After it was quarried at Hatnub, I had it go downstream in this barge I had built for it, a barge of acacia wood of sixty cubits in length and thirty cubits in width. Assembled in seventeen days, in the third month of summer, when there was no (45/46) water on the sandbanks, it landed at the pyramid "Mernere-appears-in-splendor" in safety. It came about through me entirely in accordance with the ordinance commanded by my lord.

His majesty sent me to dig five canals in Upper Egypt, and to build three barges and four tow-boats of acacia wood of Wawat. Then the foreign chiefs of Irtjet, Wawat, Yam, and Medja cut the timber for them. I did it all in one year. Floated, they were loaded with very large granite blocks for the pyramid "Mernere-appears-in-splendor." Indeed I made a [saving] for the palace with all these five canals. As King Mernere who lives forever is august, exalted, and mighty more than any god, so everything came about in accordance with the ordinance commanded by his *ka*.

I was one beloved of his father, praised by his mother, (50/51) gracious to his brothers. The count, true governor of Upper Egypt, honored by Osiris, Weni.

# READING 5

## Egyptian Love Poem

*Poetry and songs celebrating the thrill of new-found love exist in nearly every society known to man. This tender poem, dating from nineteenth-dynasty, New Kingdom Egypt, illustrates that such emotions are also very old. It is taken from Miriam Lichtheim,* Ancient Egyptian Literature: A Book of Readings, *3 vols. (Berkeley: University of California Press, 1973–1980), II: pp. 190–191.*

---

### Discussion Questions

1. With what occupation is the poet occupied at the beginning of the poem?
2. What is interfering with her work?
3. Where and how does the tone of the poem shift?
4. How does it end?

Beginning of the delightful, beautiful songs of your beloved sister as she comes from the fields.

*2*

The voice of the wild goose shrills,
It is caught by its bait;
My love of you pervades me,
I cannot loosen it.
I shall retrieve my nets,
But what do I tell my mother,
To whom I go daily,
Laden with bird catch?
I have spread no snares today,
I am caught in my love of you!

lots of love!

forbidden love?

*3*

The wild goose soars and swoops,
It alights on the net;
Many birds swarm about,
I have work to do.
I am held fast by my love,
Alone, my heart meets your heart,
From your beauty I'll not part!

*6*

The voice of the dove is calling,
It says: "It's day! Where are you?"
O bird, stop scolding me!
I found my brother on his bed,
My heart was overjoyed;
Each said: "I shall not leave you,
My hand is in your hand;
You and I shall wander

In all the places fair."
He makes me the foremost of women,
He does not aggrieve my heart.

*7*

My gaze is fixed on the garden gate,
My brother will come to me;
Eyes on the road, ears straining,
I wait for him who neglects me.
I made my brother's love my sole concern,
About him my heart is not silent;
It sends me a fleet-footed messenger
Who comes and goes to tell me:
"He deceives you, in other words,
He found another woman,
She is dazzling to his eyes."
Why vex another's heart to death?

focused on loving someone else & forgot her own needs; expresses the way she feels.

*8*

My heart thought of my love of you,
When half of my hair was braided;
I came at a run to find you,
And neglected my hairdo.
Now if you let me braid my hair,
I shall be ready in a moment.

# LECTURE TOPIC 5

# *Ancient India*

I. Geography
   A. A Land of Mountains, Jungle and Desert
      1. Himalayas and the Deccan; Indus; Punjab; Ganges
II. Another Very Ancient Civilization: Indus Valley: ca. 2500 B.C.
   A. Mohenjo-daro and Harappa
   B. Indus Valley Script
   C. Religion: Mother Goddess
III. What Happened to this Remarkable People?
   A. Aryan Invaders: 1500–500 B.C.
      1. Indo-Europeans from the Northwest
      2. Dravidians Forced South
   B. What Were the Origins of the Caste System?
      1. Brahman
      2. Kashatriya
      3. Vaisya
      4. Shudra
      5. Outcasts/Untouchables
IV. India: The Mother of Many Religions
   A. Hinduism
      1. Sanscrit and the *Rig Veda:* Hymns to Aryan Heroes; They become Their Gods
      2. Many Become Gods of Nature
      3. Ritual and Meditation/ Yoga
      4. *Samsura* and *Karma*
      5. Asceticism and Escape from Reincarnation
      6. The *Upanishads*: ca. 500 B.C.
         a) *Atman* and *Brahma*
         b) *Dharma* or the moral law
            (1) Honesty, Honorable Labor in One's Caste
         c) *Moksha* or Release
   B. Jainism
      1. Vardhamana Mahavira (540–468 B.C.)
         a) *Ahimsa* and the Hierarchy of Life
   C. How Did Buddhism Originate and What Are its Basic Principles?
      1. Siddhartha Gautama (563–483 B.C.)
         a) "The Enlightened One"
         b) Path to *Nirvana*
         c) Rejection of Caste
         d) Hinayana/Mahayana Divisions
V. Alexander the Great Invades from the West: 4th Century B.C.
VI. Mauryan Empire: 322–232 B.C.
   A. Chandragupta Maurya (d. 286 B.C.)

(use this for notes)

- B. Ashoka (269–232 B.C.)
  - 1. Victory over Kalinga and Conversion to Buddhism
- VII. Kushan Rule: 250 B.C.–200 A.D.
  - A. Hellenistic Influences
  - B. Why Was Buddhism Exported to China During this Period?
- VIII. Conclusions
  - A. India's Rich Religious Legacy

# READING 1

## Hinduism

*Aryan invaders of the second millennium B.C. were authors of the more than one thousand poems and hymns collectively referred to as the Rig Veda. While the Upanishads, a later body of commentary, would make significant contributions to Hindu belief and ritual, the Vedic texts provided the basis for all subsequent Hindu development. The passages below are from, Ralph T. H. Griffith, trans., The* Hymns of the Rgveda, *The Chowkhamba Sanskrit Studies (Varanase, India, 1971), Vol. I: pp. 43–45; II: pp. 575–576.*

---

### Discussion Questions

1. What do you find to be the dominant theme and tone of this poem about Indra? Can we safely project these values onto India's Aryan invaders generally?
2. Do you feel that this society clearly explains the creation of the world? How is the overall tone similar or different to other ancient myths?

## THE RIG VEDA

---

*Indra (32)*

I will declare the manly deeds of *Indra*, the first that he achieved, the Thunder wielder.
He slew the Dragon, then disclosed the waters, and cleft the channels of the mountain torrents.
He slew the Dragon lying on the mountain; his heavenly bolt of thunder *Tvashtar* fashioned.
Like lowing kine in rapid flow descending the waters glided downward to the ocean.
Impetuous as a bull, he chose the *Soma*, and in three sacred beakers drank the juices. [Indra the Generous] grasped the thunder for his weapon, and smote to death this firstborn of the dragons.
When, Indra, thou hadst slain the dragons, first born, and overcome the charms of the enchanters,
Then, giving life to Sun and Dawn and Heaven, thou foundest not one foe to stand against thee.
Indra with his own great and deadly thunder smote into pieces *Vritra*, worst of Vritras.
As trunks of trees, what time the axe felled them, Iowan the earth so lies the prostrate dragon.
He, like a mad weak warrior, challenged Indra, the great impetuous many slaying Hero.
He, brooking not the clashing of the weapons, crushed-Indra's foe-the shattered forts in failing.
Footless and handless still he challenged Indra, who smote him with his bolt between the shoulders.

Emasculate yet claiming many vigors, thus Vritra lay with scattered limbs dissevered.
There he lies like a bank-bursting river, the waters taking courage flow above him.
The Dragon lies beneath the feet of torrents which Vritra with his greatness had encompassed.
Then humbled was the strength of Vritra's mother: Indra hath cast his deadly bolt against her.
The mother was above, the son was under, and like a cow beside her calf lay *Danu.*
Rolled in the midst of never-ceasing currents flowing without a rest for ever onward.
The waters bear off Vritra's nameless body: the foe of Indra sank to enduring darkness . . .
Indra is King of all that moves and moves not, of creatures tame and homed, the thunder-wielder.
Over all living men he rules as Sovereign, containing all as spokes within the belly.

### *On Creation (129)*

Then was not non-existence: there was no realm of air, no sky beyond it.
What covered it, and where? And what gave shelter?
Was water there, unfathomed depths of water?
Death was not then, nor was there aught immoral: no sign was there, the day and night's divider.
That One Thing, breathless breathed by its own nature: apart from it was nothing whatsoever.
Darkness there was: at first concealed in darkness this All was indiscriminate chaos.
All that existed then was void and formless: by the great power of Warmth was that Unit.
Therefore rose Desire in the beginning, Desire, the primal seed and germ of Spirit . . .
Who verily knows and who can declare it, whence it was born and whence comes this creation?
The Gods are later than this world's production. Who knows then whence it first came into being?
He, the first origin of this creation, whether he formed it all or did not form it,
Whose eye controls the world in highest heaven, he verily knows it,
Or perhaps he knows not.

# READING 2

## *Jainism*

*Dating from the sixth and fifth centuries B.C., Jainists ascribe the origin of their sect to Mahavira, an ancient Indian sage. In addition to belief in the necessity of freeing one's soul from its material prison, Jainism also emphasizes the universal presence of life, urging ahimsa or nonviolence toward all things. This reading is from, Hermann Jacobi, trans.,* The Gaina Sutras, Part Two, The Uttaradhyayana Sutra, in The Sacred Books of the East, *ed. F. Max Muller (Oxford: Clarendon Press, 1895), vol. 45 passim.*

---

Discussion Questions

1. What modern religion or philosophy, if any, resembles Jainism?
2. What sort of life does Mahavira challenge his followers to lead?

### THE JAINIST SUTRAS OR BOOK OF SERMONS

---

Earth and water, fire and wind,
Grass, trees, and plants, and all creatures that move,
Born of the egg, born of the womb, born of dung, born of liquids
These are the classes of living beings.
Know that they all seek happiness.
In hurting them men hurt themselves,
And will be born again among them. . . .
But [Mahavira] has said, "Their principles are base
Who hurt for their own pleasure."
The man who lights a fire kills living things,
While he who puts it out kills the fire;
Thus a wise man who understands the Law
Should never light a fire.
There are lives in earth and lives in water,
Hopping insects leap into the fire,
And worms dwell in rotten wood.
All are burned when a fire is lighted.
Even plants are beings, capable of growth,
Their bodies need food, they are individuals.
The reckless cut them for their own pleasure
And slay many living things in doing so.
He who carelessly destroys plants, whether sprouted or full grown,
Provides a rod for his own back.
He has said, "Their principles are ignoble
Who harm plants for their own pleasure." . . .
One should know what binds the soul, and, knowing, break free from bondage. What bondage did the Hero [Mahavira] declare,
And what knowledge did he teach to remove it? . . .
If a man kills living things, or slays by the hand of another, or consents to another

slaying, his sin goes on increasing . . .
All his wealth and relations cannot save him from sorrow. Only if he knows the nature of life, will he get rid of karma . . .

# READING 3

## Buddhism

*Buddhism is another world religion that had its origin as a by-product of Hinduism. Siddhartha Gautama (563–483 B.C.), its founder, admonished followers to seek escape from suffering by a disciplined selflessness. The Buddha's "first sermon," reproduced below in part, is from C.F. Horne, ed.,* The Sacred Books and Early Literature of the East *(New York: Parke, Austin, Lipscomb, 1917), Vol. 10 passim.*

---

### Discussion Questions

1. What did Buddha see in this sermon as being the source of all human suffering?
2. What does he advise as the only way to escape it?

## THE SERMON AT BENARES

There are two extremes, oh *Bhikkus,* (devout followers) which a holy man should avoid—the habitual practice of . . . self-indulgence, which is vulgar and profitless . . . and the habitual practice of self-mortification, which is painful and equally profitless.

There is a middle path . . . a path which opens the eyes, and bestows understanding, which leads to peace of mind, to the higher wisdom, to full enlightenment, to *Nirvana.* Verily! it is this noble eightfold path; that is to say: Right views; Right aspirations; Right speech; Right conduct; Right livelihood; Right effort; Right mindfulness; and, Right contemplation.

This, oh Bhikkus, is that middle path, avoiding these two extremes . . . that path which opens the eyes, and bestows understanding, which leads to peace of mind, to the higher wisdom, to full enlightenment, to Nirvana!

Now this, oh Bhikkus, is the noble truth concerning suffering. Birth is attended with pain, decay is painful, disease is painful, death is painful. Union with the unpleasant is painful, painful is separation from the pleasant; and any craving that is unsatisfied, that too is painful. In brief, these [components of individuality] are painful.

This, then, oh Bhikkus, is the noble truth concerning suffering.

Now this, oh Bhikkus, is the noble truth concerning the origin of suffering.

Verily, it is that thirst, causing the renewal of existence, accompanied by sensual delight, seeking satisfaction now here, now there—that is to say, the craving for the gratification of the passions, or the craving for a future life, or the craving for success in this present life.

This, oh Bhikkus, is the noble truth concerning the origin of suffering.

Now this, oh Bhikkus, is the noble truth concerning the destruction of suffering. Verily, it is the destruction, in which no passion remains, of this very thirst; the laying aside of, the getting rid of, the being free from, the harboring no longer of this thirst.

This then, oh Bhikkus, is the noble truth concerning the destruction of suffering.

Now this, oh Bhikkus, is the noble truth concerning the way which leads to the destruction of sorrow. Verily! it is this noble eightfold path; that is to say: Right views; Right aspirations; Right speech; Right conduct; Right livelihood; Right effort; Right mindfulness; and, Right contemplation.

This then, oh Bhikkus, is the noble truth concerning the destruction of sorrow.

That this was the noble truth concerning sorrow, was not, oh Bhikkus, among the doctrines handed down, but there arose within me the eye to perceive it, there arose the knowledge of its nature, there arose the understanding of its cause, there arose the wisdom to guide in the path of tranquillity, there arose the light to dispel darkness from it.

. . . That I had become versed in the way which leads to the destruction of sorrow, though the noble truth concerning it was not among the doctrines handed down, there arose within me the eye, there arose the knowledge, there arose the understanding, there arose the wisdom, there arose the light . . .

And now this knowledge and this insight has arisen within me. Immovable is the emancipation of my heart. This is my last existence. There will now be no rebirth for me!

reached enlightenment

# READING 4

## Edicts of Asoka

*The Mauryan emperor Asoka was, perhaps, the greatest of all Indian military strategists. After successfully unifying most of India under his rule, he converted from Hinduism to Buddhism, pledging that he would never fight again. He devoted the balance of his life to establishing a government of righteousness and peace throughout his kingdom. His edicts, urging justice and kindness, were inscribed on stone stelae throughout the land. The following are to be read in Vincent A. Smith,* Asoka, The Buddhist Emperor of India, *2nd edn. (New Delhi, India: S. Chand, n.d.), pp. 159–161, 166–167, 170–175.*

---

### Discussion Questions

1. Do you think Asoka was influenced by Jainism?
2. What do you think of Asoka's claim that all sects deserve respect and toleration? Do you think he would have tolerated religious terrorists?

### EDICT FOUR

For a long time past, even for many hundred years, [there has been an] increase in the sacrificial slaughter of living creatures, the killing of animate beings, [which is] unseemly behavior to relatives, and unseemly behavior to *Brahmins* and ascetics.

But now, by reason of His Sacred Majesty the King's [Asoka's] practice of piety, the reverberation of the war-drums—or rather, the reverberation of the Law of Piety—is heard, bringing with it the display to the people of processional cars, elephants, illuminations, and other heavenly spectacles.

As for many hundred years before has not happened, now at this time, by reason of His Sacred Majesty the King's instruction in the Law of Piety, have increased abstention from the [sacrificial] slaughter of living creatures . . .

Thus, and in many other ways, the practice of piety has increased, and His Sacred Majesty the King will cause such practice of piety to increase still more.

The sons, grandsons, and great-grandsons of His Sacred Majesty the King will promote the increase in the practice of such piety . . .

For this very purpose has this been caused to be written, in order that in this matter, men may strive for increase and not behold decrease.

This has been written by command of His Sacred and Gracious Majesty the King . . .

### EDICT ELEVEN

Thus saith His Sacred and Gracious Majesty the King:

There is no such almsgiving as the almsgiving of the Law of Piety

. . . Herein does it consist—in proper treatment of slaves and servants, hearkening to father and mother, giving to friends, comrades, relations, ascetics, and Brahmins, and sparing of living creatures. Therefore a father, son, brother, master, friend, comrade, nay, even a neighbor, ought to say, "This is meritorious, this ought to be done."

He who acts thus both gains this world and in the other world begets infinite merit, by means of this very almsgiving of piety.

## Edict Twelve

His Sacred and Gracious Majesty the King does reverence to men of all sects, whether ascetics or householders, by gifts and various forms of reverence. . . . a man must not do reverence to his own sect or disparage that of another man without reason . . . because the sects of other people all deserve reverence for one reason or another.

By thus acting, a man exalts his own sect, and at the same time does service to the sects of other people. By acting contrary, a man hurts his own sect, and does disservice to the sects of other people. For he who does reverence to his own sect while disparaging the sects of others wholly from attachment to his own, with intent to enhance the splendor of his own sect, in reality by such conduct inflicts the severest injury on his own sect.

. . . For this is the desire of His Sacred Majesty that all sects should hear much teaching and hold sound doctrine.

Wherefore the adherents of all sects, whatever they may be, must be informed that His Sacred Majesty cares not so much for gifts or external reverence as that there should be growth in the essence of the matter and respect for all sects . . .

## Edict Thirteen

The Kalingas were conquered by His Sacred and Gracious Majesty the King when he had been consecrated eight years. One hundred and fifty thousand persons were thence carried away captive, one hundred thousand were there slain, and many times that number perished.

Directly after the annexation of the Kalingas, began his Sacred Majesty's zealous protection of the Law of Piety, his love of the Law, and his giving instruction in that Law [of dharma]. Thus arose His Sacred Majesty's remorse for having conquered the Kalingas, because the conquest of a country previously unconquered involves the slaughter, death, and carrying away captive of the people. That is a matter of profound sorrow and regret to His Sacred Majesty.

There is, however, another reason for His Sacred Majesty feeling still more regret, inasmuch as in such a country dwell Brahmins or ascetics, or men of various denominations, or householders, upon whom is laid this duty of hearkening to superiors, hearkening to father and mother, hearkening to teachers, and proper treatment of friends, acquaintances, comrades, relatives, slaves, and servants, with fidelity of attachment. To such people in such a country befalls violence, or slaughter, or separation from their loved ones. Or misfortune befalls the friends, acquaintances, comrades, and relatives of those who are themselves well protected, while their affection is undiminished. Thus for them also that is a mode of violence. All these several happenings to men are matter of regret to His Sacred Majesty; because it is never the case that people have not faith in some one denomination or other.

Thus of all the people who were then slain, done to death, or carried away captive in the Kalingas, if the hundredth or the thousandth part were to suffer the same fate, it would now be matter of regret to His Sacred Majesty. Moreover, should anyone do him wrong, that too must be borne with. Even upon the forest folk in his dominions His Sacred Majesty looks kindly and he seeks their conversion, for [if he did not] repentance would come upon His Sacred Majesty. They are bidden to turn from evil ways that they be not chastised. For His Sacred Majesty desires that all animate beings should have security, self-control, peace of mind, and joyousness . . .

# LECTURE TOPIC 6

# *Ancient China*

I. Geography: A Vast and Isolated Land
   A. Yellow and Yangtze Rivers
   B. Natural Boundaries
II. Who Were China's First Rulers? The Shang: 1523–1027 B.C.
   A. Capital at Anyang
   B. King and Warrior Aristocracy
   C. Agriculture and Metalwork
      1. Silk
      2. Bronze
   D. Religion: Divine Kingship Again
      1. Ancestor Worship
   E. Writing
      1. The Shang Oracle Bones
      2. Pictographic
III. Chou or Zhou Dynasty: 1027–221 B.C.
   A. Chou Rebellion Against the Shang and "The Mandate of Heaven"
   B. Feudal Tendencies
   C. Cast Iron
   D. Philosophical Developments: What Impact Did They Have on China?
      1. K'ung Fu-tzy (551–479 B.C.) and Confucianism
         a) *Analects*
            (1) Order and Universal Law
            (2) Moderation and Propriety
            (3) Reverence for Elders
            (4) Learning
         b) Civil Service Examinations: Literary and Recitational Emphasis: Unconcerned with Practical or Technical Competence
      2. Lao-tzu (6th Cent. B.C.) and Taoism
         a) What is "The Way" and How Does Taoism Contrast to Other Chinese Philosophies?
         b) Importance of Fidelity to Nature
         c) Retreat from Government and Social Obligation
         d) A Philosophy of Consolation
IV. Ch'in or Qin Dynasty: 221–206 B.C.
   A. Totalitarian and Centralized
   B. What Motivated the Chinese to Build The Great Wall?
   C. "Legalist" and Anti-Confucian
V. Han Dynasty: 206 B.C.–220 A.D.
   A. Peace and Prosperity
   B. Expansion of Borders
   C. Confucian Revival

D. What Were the Advances in Scholarship and Medicine in this Period?
   1. Ssu-ma Ch'ien (145–86 B.C.): *Records of the Grand Historian*
   2. Surgery and Anesthesia
   3. Silk Culture
   4. Paper
   5. Iron Work

E. Barbarian Invasions; Disorder; Local Revolt; and Disintegration

VI. Conclusion

A. Independent Magnificence of the Chinese Achievement

# READING 1

## The Book of T'ang From the Book of History

*This early Chinese text, presumably gathered and edited by Confucius in the sixth century B.C., but originating even earlier, illustrates Chinese emphases on respect for order and correct behavior. Addressing what leaders must do if they wished to be given the "mandate of heaven," policies that were both equitable and peaceful were praised. The brief extract below is taken from James Legge, trans.,* The Shu King, The Sacred Books of The East, *ed. F. Max Muller (Oxford: Clarendon Press, 1879), Vol. 3: pp. 15–27.*

### Discussion Questions

1. Do you agree with Confucius that personal virtue is necessary to be a good leader?
2. What do you think of his contention that the private character of a ruler can transform his subjects?

## THE BOOK OF T'ANG

Examining into antiquity, we find that the emperor Yao was called Fang-hsun. He was reverential, intelligent, accomplished, and thoughtful—naturally and without effort. He was sincerely courteous, and capable of all complaisance. The display of these qualities reached to the four extremities of the empire, and extended from earth to heaven. He was able to make the able and virtuous distinguished, and thence proceeded to the love of the nine classes of his kindred, who all became harmonious. He also regulated and nourished the people of his domain, who all became brightly intelligent. Finally, he united and harmonized the myriad states of the empire; and lo! the black-haired people were transformed. The result was universal concord . . .

# READING 2

## The Analects of Confucius

*Much of classical Chinese thought and culture is traceable to the influence of Confucius (551–479 B.C). He taught his followers both courtesy and the importance of acquiring knowledge—not only for its usefulness but for the pleasure and enlarging consequences it brings. These excerpts are from James Legge, trans.,* The Analects, The Sacred Books of China: The Texts of Confucianism, In The Sacred Books of the East, *ed. F. Max Muller (Oxford: Clarendon Press, 1861), Vol. I: 139ff.*

---

### Discussion Questions

1. Did Confucius believe that proper behavior and order in families resulted in a properly governed society generally?
2. Do you agree or disagree? Why?

## BOOK ONE

1. The Master said, "Is it not pleasant to learn with a constant perseverance and application? Is it not delightful to have friends coming from distant quarters? Is he not a man of complete virtue, who feels no discomposure though men may take no note of him?"

2. "The superior man bends his attention to what is radical. That being established, all practical courses naturally grow up. Filial piety and fraternal submission!—are they not the root of all benevolent actions?"

3. The Master said, "Fine words and an insinuated appearance are seldom associated with true virtue."

## BOOK TWO

1. The Master said, "He who exercises government by means of his virtue may be compared to the north polar star, which keeps its place and all the stars turn towards it"

4. The Master said, "At fifteen, I had my mind bent on learning. At thirty, I stood firm. At forty, I had no doubts. At fifty, I knew the decrees of Heaven. At sixty, my ear was an obedient organ for the reception of truth. At seventy, I could follow what my heart desired, without transgressing what was right"

5. *Mang-I [Tzu]* asked what filial piety was. The Master said, "It is not being disobedient"

Soon after, as Fan Ch'ih was driving him, the Master told him, saying, "Mang-I asked me what filial piety was, and I answered him,—'not being disobedient'"

Fan Ch'ih said, "What did you mean?" The Master replied, "That parents, when alive, should be served according to propriety; that, when dead, they should be buried according to propriety; and that they should be sacrificed to according to propriety."

21. Some one addressed Confucius, saying, "Sir, why are you not engaged in the government?"

The Master said, "What does the *Book of History* say of filial piety?—'You are filial, you discharge your brotherly duties. These qualities are displayed in government' This then also constitutes the exercise of government. Why must there be THAT—making one be in the government?"

# READING 3

## *The* Tao Te *Ching of* Lao Tzu

*Lao Tzu, like other pivotal religious thinkers and reformers of the ancient world, lived during the sixth or early fifth centuries B.C. And, as with other great philosophers, the writings ascribed to him are most likely the work of later followers. The Tao, or "eternal way of the universe," is apprehended more by intuition than reason or analysis. Renunciation of self and desire, balance between yin and yang, and passive surrender to nature's harmonies were important ingredients of Taoist teaching. The more structured, obligatory requirements of Confucian thought obviously conflicted with Taoist belief. The writings reproduced here are from Arthur Waley, trans.,* The Way and Its Power *(London: George Allen and Unwin Ltd., 1934), pp. 141–193 passim.*

---

### Discussion Questions

1. Would Taoists think good citizenship important?
2. Contrast Taoist and Confucian teaching.
3. Can you see the reliance Taoism places on recognition of the universal presence of opposites?

### ONE

The Way that can be told is not an Unvarying Way;
The names that can be named are not unvarying names.
It was from the nameless that Heaven and Earth sprang;
The named is but the mother that rears the ten thousand creatures, each after its kind.

### TWO

It is because everyone under heaven recognizes beauty as beauty, that the idea of ugliness exists.

And equally if every one recognized virtue as virtue, this would merely create a fresh concept of wickedness.
For truly "Being and Not-being grow out of one another";
Difficult and easy complete one another.
Long and short test one another;
High and low determine one another.
Pitch and mode give harmony to one another.
Front and back give sequence to one another.
Therefore the Sage relies on actionless activity.

### TWENTY-FIVE

There was something formless yet complete,
That existed before Heaven and Earth;
Without sound, without substance,

Dependent on nothing, unchanging,
All pervading, unfailing.
One may think of it as the mother of all things under heaven.
Its true name we do not know;
"Way" is the by-name that we give it . . .
Forty
In Tao the only motion is returning;
The only useful quality, weakness.
For though all creatures under heaven are the product of Being,
Being itself is the product of Not-being.

## FORTY-ONE

When the man of highest capacities hears Tao
He does his best to put it into practice.
When the man of middling capacity hears Tao
He is in two minds about it.
When the man of low capacity hears Tao
He laughs loudly at it.
If he did not laugh, it would not be worth the name of Tao.
Therefore the proverb has it:
The way out into the light often looks dark,
The way that goes ahead often looks as if it went back.
The way that is least hilly often looks as if it went up and down,
The "power" that is really loftiest looks like an abyss,
What is sheerest white looks bluffed.
The "power" that is the most sufficing looks inadequate.
The "power" that stands firmest looks flimsy.
What is in its natural, pure state looks faded;
The largest square has no corners,
The greatest vessel takes the longest to finish,
Great music has the faintest notes,
The Great Form is without shape.
For Tao is hidden and nameless.
Yet Tao alone supports all things and brings them to fulfillment.

# LECTURE TOPIC 7

# Cretan, Mycenaean and Archaic Greek Civilization

I. Who Were The First Greeks? Ancient Minoan Civilization: 2600–1150 B.C.
   A. Sir Arthur Evans
   B. Architecture, Athletics, and Women
   C. Writing: Linear A
   D. Religion in Ancient Minoan Society
   E. Agriculture and Commerce
   F. Destruction and Decline
II. Mycenaean Civilization: 2000–800 B.C.
   A. The World's Most Famous Story
      1. Heinrich Schliemann and Homer's *Iliad* and *Odyssey*
      2. The Old Story: Troy, Priam, Menelaus, Alexander and Helen
      3. Agamemnon, Achilles, Hector and Odysseus
   B. Schliemann's Discovery in the Troad
   C. Further Work on the Greek Mainland
      1. Mycenaean Cities: Mycenae, Pylos, Athens, Tiryns, Sparta
      2. Characteristics of Mycenaean Civilization
         a) Megalithic Architecture
         b) Monarchies
         c) Viking-like
         d) Slavery and Women
         e) Writing: Linear B
III. Mycenaean Decline
   A. Dorian Invasion: 1100–800 B.C.
   B. Greece's Dark Age
      1. Lack of Information
      2. Introduction of the Phoenician Alphabet
IV. The Archaic Period: 800–600 B.C.
   A. Hesiod (fl. 8th cent. B.C.) and Greek Cosmology
      1. *Theogony*
         a) Gaea (Earth)
         b) Uranus (Heaven)
         c) Cronos
         d) Titans including Jove
      2. *Works and Days*
V. Rise of the *Hoi Polloi*
   A. Emergence of the Polis: Monarchy to Democracy
   B. Heroes to Hoplites
   C. Colonization

D. Lyric Poetry
  1. Sappho of Lesbos (fl. 7th Cent. B.C.)

VI. Philosophy: Challenges to the Magic World View
  A. Ionia and the "Presocratics"
    1. Thales of Miletus (624–545 B.C.)
    2. Pythagoras (fl. 6th Cent. B.C.)
  B. Rational and Empirical vs. Mythopoeic
  C. Significance of the "Presocrataics" for Western Civilization

VII. Conclusion: An Age of Profound Change
  A. Political, Social and Intellectual Transformation
  B. Homer as the Bible of the Greeks
    1. *Areté:* Individual Excellence
    2. Foundation of Classical Literature

# READING 1

## The Trojan War

*Few poets have enjoyed more fame or have been more widely read than Homer (8th cent. B.C). The ancient Greeks regarded Homer as their greatest poet, and modern readers concur. Yet, he is clouded by mystery, uncertainty, and controversy. Who was Homer? When did he live? Did he really compose two of the world's masterpieces? Did he dictate them or teach them to others who passed them on? We lack conclusive evidence and scholars disagree. His accounts of the Trojan War and Ulysses' long, difficult journey home after the war were a major source of historical and religious instruction among the ancient Greeks. The selection here, from Book XII of* The Iliad, *not only illustrates the poem's preoccupation with heroic combat but provides good examples of their concern with martial ceremony. One should also notice the extent to which Homer involves the gods in the trials and adventures of his heroes. One of the noblest characters in* The Iliad *was the Trojan hero Hector. The following account of the intervention of the goddess Minerva in the fight between Hector and the Greek warrior Achilles is taken from Louise R. Loomis, ed., The Iliad of Homer, translated by Samuel Butler (Roslyn, N. Y.: Walter J. Black, Inc., 1942), pp. 340–345.*

The Odyssey *is the tale of Odysseus' (Ulysses') return home after the Trojan War. Because the Greek heroes forget to thank the gods, they are forced to wander for ten years throughout the Mediterranean before at last reaching their homeland. The poem tells of the many trials and adventures Odysseus experienced as he searched for the way home. Finally, the poem suggests that sailors have always loved to tell tall tales to amaze their audiences. The excerpt below is taken from Book 12 of* The Odyssey, *as found in:* The Iliad of Homer and The Odyssey Rendered into English Prose *by Samuel Butler (Chicago: Encyclopedia Britannica, Inc., 1952), vol. 4:* Great Books of the Western World, *pp. 251–252.*

---

### Discussion Questions

1. How do Homer's accounts of ancient events differ from the way a modern writer would portray them?
2. Can you give examples from Homer's poem that illustrate mythopoeic thought?

### THE ILIAD BY HOMER
### THE DEATH OF HECTOR

---

. . . All the gods watched them, and the sire of gods and men was the first to speak.

"Alas," said he, "my eyes behold a man who is dear to me being pursued round the walls of Troy. My heart is full of pity for Hector, who has burned the thighbones of many a heifer in my honor, at one while on the crests of many-valleyed Ida, and again on the citadel of Troy; and now I see noble Achilles in full pursuit of him round the city of Priam. What say you? Consider among yourselves and decide whether we shall now save him or let him fall, valiant though he be, before Achilles, son of Peleus."

Then Minerva said, "Father, wielder of the lightning, lord of cloud and storm, what mean you? Would you pluck this mortal whose doom has long been decreed out of the jaws of death? Do as you will, but we others shall not be of a mind with you."

And Jove answered, "My child, Trito-born, take heart. I did not speak in full earnest, and I will let you have your way. Do without let or hindrance as you are minded."

Thus did he urge Minerva who was already eager, and down she darted from the topmost summits of Olympus.

Achilles was still in full pursuit of Hector, as a hound chasing a fawn which he has started from its covert on the mountains, and hunts through glade and thicket. The fawn may try to elude him by crouching under cover of a bush, but he will scent her out and follow her up until he gets her—even so there was no escape for Hector from the fleet son of Peleus. Whenever he made a set to get near the Dardanian gates and under the walls, that his people might help him by showering down weapons from above, Achilles would gain on him and head him back towards the plain, keeping himself always on the city side. As a man in a dream who fails to lay hands upon another whom he is pursuing—the one cannot escape nor the other overtake—even so neither could Achilles come up with Hector, nor Hector break away from Achilles. Nevertheless, he might even yet have escaped death had not the time come when Apollo, who thus far had sustained his strength and nerved his running, was now no longer to stay by him. Achilles made signs to the Achaean host and shook his head to show that no man was to aim a dart at Hector, lest another might win the glory of having hit him and he might himself come in second. Then, at last, as they were nearing the fountains for the fourth time, the father of all balanced his golden scales and placed a doom in each of them, one for Achilles and the other for Hector. As he held the scales by the middle, the doom of Hector fell down deep into the house of Hades—and then Phoebus Apollo left him. Thereon Minerva went close up to the son of Peleus and said, "Noble Achilles, favored of heaven, we two shall surely take back to the ships a triumph for the Achaeans by slaying Hector, for all his lust of battle. Do what Apollo may as he lies groveling before his father, aegis-bearing Jove, Hector cannot escape us longer. Stay here and take breath, while I go up to him and persuade him to make a stand and fight you."

Thus spoke Minerva. Achilles obeyed her gladly, and stood still, leaning on his bronze-pointed ashen spear, while Minerva left him and went after Hector in the form and with the voice of Deiphobus. She came close up to him and said, "Dear brother, I see you are hard pressed by Achilles who is chasing you at full speed round the city of Priam; let us await his onset and stand on our defense."

And Hector answered, "Deiphobus, you have always been dearest to me of all my brothers, children of Hecuba and Priam, but henceforth I shall rate you yet more highly, inasmuch as you have ventured outside the wall for my sake when all the others remain inside."

Then Minerva said, "Dear brother, my father and mother went down on their knees and implored me, as did all my comrades, to remain inside, so great a fear has fallen upon them all; but I was in an agony of grief when I beheld you. Now, therefore, let us two make a stand and fight, and let there be no keeping our spears in reserve, that we may learn whether Achilles shall kill us and bear off our spoils to the ships, or whether he shall fall before you."

Thus did Minerva inveigle him by her cunning, and when the two were now close to one another great Hector was first to speak. "I will no longer fly you, son of Peleus," said he, "as I have been doing hitherto. Three times have I fled round the mighty city of Priam, without daring to withstand you, but now, let me either slay or be slain, for I am in the mind to face you. Let us, then, give pledges to one another by our gods, who are the fittest witnesses and guardians of all covenants; let it be agreed between us that if Jove vouchsafes me the longer stay and I take your life, I am not to treat your dead body in any unseemly fashion, but when I have stripped you of your armor, I am to give up your body to the Achaeans. And do you likewise."

Achilles glared at him and answered: "Fool, prate not to me about covenants. There can be no covenants between men and lions; wolves and lambs can never be of one mind, but hate each other out and out all through. Therefore there can be no understanding between you and me, nor may there be any covenants between us, till one or other shall fall and glut grim Ares with his life's blood. Put forth all your strength; you have need now to prove yourself indeed a bold soldier and man of war. You have no more chance, and Pallas Minerva will forthwith vanquish you by my spear: you shall now pay me in full for the grief you have caused me on account of my comrades whom you have killed in battle."

He poised his spear as he spoke and hurled it. Hector saw it coming and avoided it; he watched it and crouched down so that it flew over his head and stuck in the ground beyond; Minerva then snatched it up and gave it back to Achilles without Hector's seeing her; Hector thereon said to the son of Peleus: "You have missed your aim, Achilles, peer of the gods, and Jove has not yet revealed to you the hour of my doom, though you made sure that he had done so. You were a false-tongued liar when you deemed that I should forget my valor and quail before you. You shall not drive your spear into the back of a runaway—drive it, should heaven so grant you power, drive it into me as I make straight towards you; and now for your own part avoid my spear if you can—would that you might receive the whole of it into your body. If you were once dead the Trojans would find the war an easier matter, for it is you who have harmed them most."

He poised his spear as he spoke and hurled it. His aim was true for he hit the middle of Achilles' shield, but the spear rebounded from it, and did not pierce it. Hector was angry when he saw that the weapon had sped from his hand in vain, and stood there in dismay for he had no second spear. With one loud cry he called Deiphobus and asked him for one, but there was no man; then he saw the truth and said to himself, "Alas! the gods have lured me on to my destruction. I deemed that the hero Deiphobus was by my side, but he is within the wall, and Athene has inveigled me; death is now indeed exceedingly near at hand and there is no way out of it—for so Jove and his son Apollo, the far-darter, have willed it, though heretofore they have been ever ready to protect me. My doom has come upon me; let me not then die ingloriously and without a struggle, but let me first do some great thing that shall be told among men hereafter."

As he spoke he drew the keen blade that hung so great and strong by his side, and gathering himself together he sprang on Achilles like a soaring eagle which swoops down from the clouds on to some lamb or timid hare—even so did Hector brandish his sword and spring upon Achilles. Achilles mad with rage, darted toward him, with his wondrous shield before his breast, and his gleaming helmet, made with four layers of metal, nodding fiercely forward. . . . He eyed his [Hector's] fair flesh over and over to see where he could best wound it, but all was protected by the goodly armor of which Hector had spoiled Patroclus after he had slain him, save only the throat where the collarbones divide the neck from the shoulders, and this is a most deadly place. Here then did Achilles strike him as he was coming on towards him, and the point of his spear went right through the fleshy part of the neck, but it did not sever his windpipe so that he could still speak.

Hector fell headlong, and Achilles vaunted over him saying: "Hector, you deemed that you should come off scatheless when you were spoiling Patroclus, and recked not of myself who was not with him. Fool that you were: for I, his comrade, mightier far than he, was still left behind him at the ships, and now I have laid you low. The Achaeans shall give him all due funeral rites, while dogs and vultures shall work their will upon yourself."

Then Hector said, as the life ebbed out of him, "I pray you by your life and knees, and by your parents, let not dogs devour me at the ships of the Achaeans, but accept the rich treasure of gold and bronze which my father and mother will offer you, and send my body home, that the Trojans and their wives may give me my dues of fire when I am dead."

Achilles glared at him and answered, "Dog, talk not to me neither of knees nor parents; would that I could be as sure of being able to cut your flesh into pieces and eat it raw, for the ill you have done me, as I am that nothing shall save you from the dogs—it shall not be, though they bring ten or twenty-fold ransom and weigh it out for me on the spot, with promise of yet more hereafter. Though Priam, son of Dardanus, should bid them offer me your weight in gold, even so your mother shall never lay you out and make lament over the son she bore, but dogs and vultures shall eat you utterly up."

Hector with his dying breath then said: "I know you what you are, and was sure that I should not move you, for your heart is hard as iron; look to it that I bring not heaven's anger upon you on the day when Paris and Phoebus Apollo, valiant though you be, shall slay you at the Scaean gates."

When he had thus said the shrouds of death enfolded him, whereon his soul went out of him and flew down to the house of Hades, lamenting its sad fate that it should enjoy youth and strength no longer. But Achilles said, speaking to the dead body, "Die; for my part I will accept my fate whensoever Jove and the other gods see fit to send it."

As he spoke he drew his spear from the body and set it on one side; then he stripped the blood-stained armor from Hector's shoulders while the other Achaeans came running up to view his wondrous strength and beauty; and no one came near him without giving him a fresh wound. Then would one turn to his neighbor and say, "It is easier to handle Hector now than when he was flinging fire on to our ships"—and as he spoke he would thrust his spear into him anew.

## THE ODYSSEY
## HOMER

Then, being much troubled in mind, I said to my men, "My friends, it is not right that one or two of us should know the prophecies that Circe has made me, I will therefore tell you about them, so that whether we live or die we may do so with our eyes open. First she said we were to keep clear of the Sirens, who sit and sing most beautifully in a field of flowers; but she said I might hear them myself so long as no one else did. Therefore, take me and bind me to the cross-piece half way up the mast; bind me as I stand upright, with a bond so fast that I cannot possibly break away, and lash the rope's ends to the mast itself. If I beg and pray you to set me free, then bind me more tightly still."

I had hardly finished telling everything to the men before we reached the island of the two Sirens, for the wind had been very favorable. Then all of a sudden it fell dead calm; there was not a breath of wind nor a ripple upon the water, so the men furled the sails and stowed them; then taking to their oars they whitened the water with the foam they raised in rowing. Meanwhile I took a large wheel of wax and cut it up small with my sword. Then I kneaded the wax in my strong hands till it became soft, which it soon did between the kneading and the rays of the sun-god son of Hyperion. Then I stopped the ears of all my men, and they bound me hands and feet to the mast as I stood upright on the crosspiece; but they went on rowing themselves. When we had got within earshot of the land, and the ship was going at a good rate, the Sirens saw that we were getting close in shore and began with their singing.

"'Come here,' they sang, 'renowned Odysseus, honor to the Achaean name, and listen to our two voices. No one ever sailed past us without staying to hear the enchanting sweetness of our song—and he who listens will go on his way not only charmed, but wiser, for we know all the ills that the gods laid upon the Argives and Trojans before Troy, and can tell you everything that is going to happen over the whole world.'

"They sang these words most musically, and as I longed to hear them further I made signs by frowning to my men that they should set me free; but they quickened their stroke, and Eurylochus and Perimedes bound me with still stronger bonds till we had got out of hearing of the Sirens' voices. Then my men took the wax from their ears and unbound me.

"Immediately after we had got past the island I saw a great wave from which spray was rising, and I heard a loud roaring sound. The men were so frightened that they loosed hold of their oars, for the whole sea resounded with the rushing of the waters, but the ship stayed where it was, for the men had left off rowing. I went round, therefore, and exhorted them man by man not to lose heart.

"'My friends,' said I, 'this is not the first time that we have been in danger, and we are in nothing like so bad a case as when the Cyclops shut us up in his cave; nevertheless, my courage and wise counsel saved us then, and we shall live to look back on all this as well. Now, therefore, let us all do as I say, trust in Jove and row on with might and main. As for you, coxswain, these are your orders—attend to them, for the ship is in your hands: turn her head away from these steaming rapids and hug the rock, or she will give you the slip and be over yonder before you know where you are, and you will be the death of us.'

"So they did as I told them; but I said nothing about the awful monster Scylla, for I knew the men would not go on rowing if I did, but would huddle together in the hold. In one thing only did I disobey Circe's strict instructions—I put on my armor. Then seizing two strong spears I took my stand on the ship's bows, for it was there that I expected

first to see the monster of the rock, who was to do my men so much harm; but I could not make her out anywhere, though I strained my eyes with looking the gloomy rock all over and over.

"Then we entered the Straits [the Straits of Messina] in great fear of mind, for on the one hand was Scylla, and on the other dread Charybdis kept sucking up the salt water. As she vomited it up, it was like the water in a cauldron when it is boiling over upon a great fire, and the spray reached the top of the rocks on either side. When she began to suck again, we could see the water all inside whirling round and round, and it made a deafening sound as it broke against the rocks. We could see the bottom of the whirlpool all black with sand and mud, and the men were at their wits ends for fear. While we were taken up with this, and were expecting each moment to be our last, Scylla pounced down suddenly upon us and snatched up my six best men. I was looking at once after both ship and men, and in a moment I saw their hands and feet ever so high above me, struggling in the air as Scylla was carrying them off, and I heard them call out my name in one last despairing cry. As a fisherman, seated, spear in hand, upon some jutting rock throws bait into the water to deceive the poor little fishes, and spears them with the ox's horn with which his spear is shod, throwing them gasping on to the land as he catches them one by one—even so did Scylla land these panting creatures on her rock and munch them up at the mouth of her den, while they screamed and stretched out their hands to me in their mortal agony. This was the most sickening sight that I saw throughout all my voyages.

# READING 2

## Poets of the Lyric Age

*In the years between the eighth and fifth centuries B. C., Greek poetry departed from the heroic, long-lined epic productions illustrated by Homer. Verse became more "lyrical," more sing-song in its meter, reflecting ordinary, personal emotions such as romantic love, disappointment and loss. The poems of Sappho (7th cent. B.C.), in their preoccupation with amorous delight, are a preeminent example of this. Archilochus (7th cent. B.C.) and Alcaeus (fl. ca. 600 B.C.) provide other specimens of the genre. The poems given here are from T. F. Higham and C. M. Bowra, eds.,* The Oxford Book of Greek Verse in Translation *(Oxford: At The Clarendon Press, 1938), pp. 184–186, 201–202, 205–206, 210.*

---

### Discussion Questions

1. In what specific ways do the poems in this section reflect more democratic sentiment than the Iliad and Odyssey of Homer?
2. In your opinion are the love poems of Sappho erotic?

### SAPPHO

---

*To Aphrodite*

Immortal on thy many-splendoured throne
Hear, Aphrodite Queen, that art
Jove's witching daughter; and with pain and moan
Break not my heart!

But come, if ever thou hast caught of old
My distant cry and heard my plea,
And left thy father's palaces of gold
To visit me;

And yoked thy chariot, and from heaven forth
Driven thy sparrows fleet and fair
With whirr of wings above the swarthy earth
Through middle air.

How fast they came! Then, Blessed One, didst thou
With lips divinely smiling ask:
'What new mischance is come upon thee now?

Unto what task

'Have I been called? what is the dearest aim
Of thy mad heart? who is to be
Persuaded to thy passion? Sappho, name
Thine enemy!

'For whoso flies thee now shall soon pursue;
Who spurns thy gifts shall give anon;
And whose loves thee not, whate'er she do,
Shall love thee soon.'

Ah, come then, and release me from alarms
That crush me: all I long to see
Fulfilled, fulfil! A very mate-in-arms
Be thou to me.
SIR WILLIAM MARRIS

*To a Bride*

Blest beyond earth's bliss, with heaven I deem him
Blest, the man that in thy presence near thee
Face to face may sit, and while thou speakest,
Listening may hear thee,

And thy sweet-voiced laughter:—In my bosom
The rapt heart so troubleth, wildly stirred:
Let me see thee, but a glimpse—and straightway
Utterance of word

Fails me; no voice comes; my tongue is palsied;
Thrilling fire through all my flesh hath run;
Mine eyes cannot see, mine cars make dinning
Noises that stun;

cannot speak
filled w/passion

The sweat streameth down,—my whole frame seized with

Shivering,—and wan paleness o'er me spread,
Greener than the grass; I seem with faintness
Almost as dead.
WALTER HEADLAM

*Mother, I Cannot Mind My Wheel*

Sweet mother, let the weaving be,
My hand is faint to move.
Frail Aphrodite masters me; I long for my young love.
T. F. HIGHAM

associates love of young woman with aphrodite

## ARCHILOCHUS

*The Poet's Shield*

A perfect shield bedecks some Thracian now;
I had no choice: I left it in a wood.
Ah, well, I saved my skin, so let it go!
Anew one's just as good.
SIR WILLIAM MARRIS

## Alcaeus

### *Drinking Songs*

(iii)
Drink! Why wait for lamps? The day
Has not another inch to fall.
Fetch the biggest beakers—they
Hang on pegs along the wall.

pesuading to drink & enjoy oneself.

Bacchus, son of Semele
And of Jove, discovered wine
Giving it to man to be
Care's oblivious anodyne.

Pour in water two to one,
Fill them full to overflowing;
When the first is drained and done,
Set another cup a-going!

(iv)
Soak your lungs with wine, for now
The Dog Star's at the turn.
How the summer wounds, and how
All must thirst and bum.

In the bushes, strong and clear
Now the cricket sings,
And sweet music fills the air
From beneath his wings.

Now is all the earth at song

In the summer's fire,
And the girasole is strong.
Now does wild desire

Make the girls most amorous.
But the men won't please;
For the fire of Sirius
Withers heads and knees.

(v)
On my long-suffering head let the sweet myrrh flow,
Let it flow on my breast where the white hairs show.
C. M. Bowra

READING 3

# The Presocratic Philosophers

*Those thinkers referred to as the "Presocratics" are of the greatest importance in human thought, especially in the history of the Western mind. It was they who bent both observation and intellect to understand nature in ways that would lead, eventually, to the modern scientific temper. The conclusions at which they arrived were less important than their departure from traditional mythopoeic explanations. With their concern for precision of language, developmental relationships and logical formulation, they were unprecedented. The fragments we have from these pioneers are few and, often, preserved to us only as paraphrase by other authors. Those used here are taken from Philip Wheelwright,* The Presocratics *(New York: Odyssey Press, Inc., 1966), pp. 44–45, 60, 69–71, 230–231.*

---

### Discussion Questions

1. Do you find contradictions in the thinking of some of the Presocratics?
2. Do you agree with Heraclitus in his comment on Homer that if all strife disappeared, nature would cease to exist?

## THALES (640?–546 B.C.)

*Main Propositions of Thales as Stated By Aristotle*

1. The first principle and basic nature of all things is water.
2. The earth rests upon water.
3. All things are full of gods.
4. The magnetic stone has soul because it sets the iron in motion.

## ANAXIMENES (6TH CENT. B.C.)

*Fragment*

1. As our souls, being air, hold us together, so breath and air embrace the entire universe.

## HERACLITUS (641–575? B.C.)

*Fragments*

1. Although this Logos is eternally valid, yet men are unable to understand it—not only before hearing it, but even after they have heard it for the first time. That is to say, although all things come to pass in accordance with this Logos, men seem to be quite without any experience of it—at least judged in the light of such words and deeds as I am here setting forth. My own method is to distinguish each thing according to its nature, and to specify how it behaves; other men, on the contrary, are as neglectful of what they do when awake as they are when asleep.

2. We should let ourselves be guided by what is common to all. Yet, although the Logos is common to all, most men live as if each of them had a private intelligence of his own.

3. Men who love wisdom should acquaint themselves with a great many particulars.

4. Seekers after gold dig up much earth and find little.

5. Let us not make arbitrary conjectures about the greatest matters.

6. Much learning does not teach understanding, otherwise would have taught Hesiod and Pythagoras, Xenophanes and Hectaeus.

7. Of those whose discourses I have heard there is not one who attains to the realization that wisdom stands apart from all else.

8. I have searched myself.

9. It pertains to all men to know themselves and to be temperate.

10. To be temperate is the greatest virtue. Wisdom consists in speaking and acting the truth, giving heed to the nature of things.

11. The things of which there can be sight, hearing, and learning—these are what I especially prize.

12. Eyes are more accurate witnesses than ears.

13. Eyes and ears are bad witnesses to men having barbarian souls.

14. One should not act or speak as if he were asleep.

15. The waking have one world in common, whereas each sleeper turns away to a private world of his own.

16. Whatever we see when awake is death; when asleep, dreams.

17. Nature loves to hide.

18. The lord whose oracle is at Delphi neither speaks nor conceals, but gives signs.

19. Unless you expect the unexpected you will never find [truth], for it is hard to discover and hard to attain.

20. Everything flows and nothing abides; everything gives way and nothing stays fixed.

21. You cannot step twice into the same river, for other waters and yet others go ever flowing on.

22. Cool things become warm, the warm grows cool; the moist dries, the parched becomes moist.

23. It is in changing that things find repose.

24. Time is a child moving counters in a game; the royal power is a child's.

25. War is both father and king of all; some he has shown forth as gods and others as men, some he has made slaves and others free.

26. It should be understood that war is the common condition, that strife is justice, and that all things come to pass through the compulsion of strife.

27. Homer was wrong in saying, "Would that strife might perish from amongst gods and men." For if that were to occur, then all things would cease to exist.

28. There is exchange of all things for fire and of fire for all things, as there is of wares for gold and of gold for wares.

29. This universe, which is the same for all, has not been made by any god or man, but it always has been, is, and will be—an ever-living fire, kindling itself by regular measures and going out by regular measures.

30. [The phases of fire are] craving and satiety.

31. It throws apart and then brings tog ether again; it advances and retires.

# LECTURE TOPIC 8

# Athens and Sparta: Different Ways of Life in Ancient Greece

I. Athens: The Democratic Model
   A. Government
      1. Dracon (early 7th Cent. B.C.) and the Tyrannoi
      2. Solon (638–559 B.C.)
   B. Athenian Democracy
      1. Ecclesia
      2. Strategoi
      3. Bureaucratic Offices
II. Who Was Pericles and How Did He Usher In the Golden Age of Greece?
III. Athenian Society
   A. Citizens
   B. Metics
   C. Slaves
   D. Women
IV. How Did the Greeks View Sexuality?
   A. Prostitutes/ Hetairi
   B. Pederasty
V. Sparta: The Totalitarian Model
   A. First and Second Messenian Wars (735, 650 B.C.)
      1. Lycurgan Reforms
   B. Spartan Government
      1. Kings and Elders
      2. Apella
VI. Sparta as a Garrison State
   A. Messenian Helots
   B. Krypteia
VII. Life of Spartan Citizens
   A. The Syssition and Male Society
   B. Spartan Women
VIII. Conclusions: How Did Athens and Sparta Contrast?
   A. Athens and Sparta: Two Contrasting Ways of Life
   B. Corresponding Appeal to Different Needs of Human Nature

# READING 1

## Plutarch's "Pericles" and "Lycurgus"

*Because he sometimes depended on no more than unsubstantiated tradition, and because his purpose was explicitly didactic, Plutarch is not entirely reliable. Still, there is much in his biographies that is useful to the historian and, in many cases, the information he provides is all that is available. The first sketch is of Pericles, perhaps the most famous citizen and leader of fifth-century B.C. Athens. The second deals with the legendary architect of Sparta's harsh, military-like society. Both are from Plutarch's Lives of the Noble Greeks and Romans. The translation from the Greek that is used here is by John Dryden, revised by Arthur Hugh Clough, under title of* Plutarch: The Lives of the Noble Grecians and Romans *(New York: Modern Library, n.d.), pp. 58–64, 68–71, 185–189, 191–192, 194.*

---

### Discussion Questions

1. Based on the descriptions of Plutarch, can you identify ways in which the personalities of Pericles and Lycurgus agree? In what ways are they different?
2. What other civilizations have we studied or are you aware of that were/are similar to ancient Sparta?

### "PERICLES"

. . . Pericles entertained an extraordinary esteem and admiration, and filling himself with this lofty and, as they call it, up-in-the-air sort of thought, derived hence not merely, as was natural, elevation of purpose and dignity of language, raised far above the base and dishonest buffooneries of mob eloquence, but, besides this, a composure of countenance, and a serenity and calmness in all his movements, which no occurrence whilst he was speaking could disturb, a sustained and even tone of voice, and various other advantages of similar kind, which produced the greatest effect on his bearers. Once, after being reviled and ill-spoken of all day long in his own hearing by some vile and abandoned fellow in the open market-place, where he was engaged in the despatch of some urgent affair, he continued his business in perfect silence, and in the evening returned home composedly, the man still dogging him at the heels, and pelting him all the way with abuse and foul language; and stepping into his house, it being by this time dark, he ordered one of his servants to take a light, and to go along with the man and see him safe home . . .

. . . in all the time he had to do with the public, which was not a little, he was never known to have gone to any of his friends to a supper, except that once when his near kinsman Euryptolemus married, he remained present till the ceremony of the drink-offering, and then immediately rose from table and went his way. For these friendly meetings are very quick to defeat any assumed superiority, and in intimate familiarity an exterior of gravity is hard to maintain. . .

. . . A saying also of Thucydides, the son of Melesias, stands on record, spoken by him by way of pleasantry upon Pericles's dexterity. Thucydides was one of the noble and distinguished citizens, and had been his greatest opponent; and, when Archidamus, the King of the Lacedcemonians, asked him whether he or Pericles were the better wrestler, he made this answer: "When I," said he, "have thrown him and given him a fair fall, by persisting that he had no fall, he gets the better of me, and makes the bystanders, in spite of their own eyes, believe him."

## "LYCURGUS"

Lycurgus would never reduce his laws into writing; nay there is a Rhetra expressly to forbid it. For he thought that the most material points, and such as most directly tended to the public welfare, being imprinted on the hearts of their youth by a good discipline, would be sure to remain, and would find a stronger security, than any compulsion would be, in the principles of action formed in them by their best lawgiver, education . . .

In order to the good education of their youth (which, as I said before, he thought the most important and noblest work of a lawgiver), he went so far back as to take into consideration their very conception and birth, by regulating their marriages. For Aristotle is wrong in saying, that, after he had tried all ways to reduce the women to more modesty and sobriety, he was at last forced to leave them as they were, because that in the absence of their husbands, who spent the best part of their lives in the wars, their wives, whom they were obliged to leave absolute mistresses at home, took great liberties and assumed the superiority; and were treated with overmuch respect and called by the title of lady or queen. The truth is, he took in their case, also, all the care that was possible; he ordered the maidens to exercise themselves with wrestling, running, throwing the quoit, and casting the dart, to the end that the fruit they conceived might, in strong and healthy bodies, take firmer root and find better growth, and withal that they, with this greater vigour, might be the more able to undergo the pains of childbearing. And to the end he might take away their overgreat tenderness and fear of exposure to the air, and all acquired womanishness, he ordered that the young women should go naked in the processions, as well as the young men, and dance, too, in that condition, at certain solemn feasts, singing certain songs, whilst the young men stood around, seeing and bearing them. On these occasions they now and then made, by jests, a befitting reflection upon those who had misbehaved themselves in the wars; and again sang encomiums upon those who had done any gallant action, and by these means inspired the younger sort with an emulation of their glory. Those that were thus commended went away proud, elated, and gratified with their honour among the maidens; and those who were rallied were as sensibly touched with it as if they had been formally reprimanded; and so much the more, because the kings and the elders, as well as the rest of the city, saw and heard all that passed. Nor was there anything shameful in this nakedness of the young women; modesty attended them, and all wantonness was excluded . . .

In their marriages, the husband carried off his bride by a sort of force; nor were their brides ever small and of tender years, but in their full bloom and ripeness. After this, she who superintended the wedding comes and clips the hair of the bride close round her head, dresses her up in man's clothes, and leaves her upon a mattress in the dark; afterwards, comes the bridegroom, in his everyday clothes, sober and composed, as having supped at the common table, and, entering privately into the room where the bride lies, unties her virgin zone, and takes her to himself; and, after staying some time together, he returns composedly to his own apartment, to sleep as usual with the other young men. And so he continues to do, spending his days, and, indeed, his nights, with them, visiting his bride in fear and shame, and with circumspection, when he thought he should not be observed; she, also, on her part, using her wit to help and find favourable opportunities for their meeting, when company was out of the way. In this manner they lived a long time, insomuch that they sometimes had children by their wives before ever they saw their faces by daylight. Their interviews, being thus difficult and rare, served not only for continual exercise of their self-control, but brought them together with their bodies healthy and vigorous, and their affections fresh and lively, unsated and undulled by easy access and long continuance with each other; while their partings were always early enough to leave behind unextinguished in each of them some remaining fire of longing and mutual delight. After guarding marriage with this modesty and reserve, he was equally careful to banish empty and womanish jealousy. For this object, excluding all licentious disorders, he made it, nevertheless, honourable for men to give the use of their wives to those whom they should think fit, that so they might have children by them; ridiculing those in whose opinion such favours are so unfit for participation as to fight and shed blood and go to war about it. Lycurgus allowed a man who was advanced in years and had a young wife to recommend some virtuous and approved young man, that she might have a child by him, who might inherit the good qualities of the father, and be a son to himself. On the other side, an honest man who had love for a married woman upon account of her modesty and the well-favouredness of her children, might, without formality, beg her company of her husband, that he might raise, as it were, from this plot. Of good ground, worthy and well-allied children for himself. And indeed, Lycurgus was of a persuasion that children were not so much the property of their parents as of the whole commonwealth, and, therefore, would not have his citizens begot by the first-comers, but by the best men that could be found; the laws of other nations seemed to him very absurd and inconsistent, where people would be so solicitous for their dogs and horses as to exert interest and to pay money to procure fine breeding, and yet kept their wives shut up, to be made mothers only by themselves, who might be foolish, infirm, or diseased; as if it were not apparent that children of a bad breed would prove their bad qualities first upon those who kept and were rearing them, and well-born children, in like manner, their good qualities. These regulations, founded on natural and social grounds, were certainly so far from that scandalous liberty which was afterwards charged upon their women, that they knew not what adultery meant. It is told, for instance, of Geradas, a very ancient Spartan, that, being asked by a stranger what punishment their law had appointed for adulterers, he answered, "There are no adulterers in our country." "But," replied the stranger, "suppose there were?" "Then," answered he, "the offender would have to give the plaintiff a bull with a neck so long as that he might drink from the top of Taygetus of the Eurotas river below it." The man, surprised at this, said, "Why, 'tis impossible to find such a bull" Geradas smilingly replied, "'Tis as possible as to find an adulterer in Sparta." So much I had to say of their marriages.

# READING 2

## Xenophon's Sketch of an Athenian Lady and Gentleman

*Xenophon (434–355 B.C.), a student of the famous philosopher Socrates, sketched the life of a well-born Athenian lady and gentleman in the following passage. It took the form of a contrived dialogue between Socrates and an Athenian citizen named Ischomachus as they visited near the market place in downtown Athens. The selection is taken from a translation of Xenophon's "Economist," contained in William Stearns Davis,* Readings in Ancient History *(Boston, New York and Chicago: Allyn and Bacon, 1912), 265–71.*

---

### Discussion Questions

1. Do you know of any modern societies where men have exercised patriarchal authority in the ways displayed in Ischomachus' training of his wife in her duties, as described below?
2. Are you surprised at the limited freedoms possessed by women in "democratic" ancient Athens?

## XENOPHON'S "ECONOMIST"

It chanced one day that I [Socrates] saw my friend Ischomachus . . . and as he seemed to be at leisure I went up to him, and sitting down by his side, accosted him: "How is this? As a rule, when I see you, you are doing something, or at any rate not sitting idle in the market place." . . .

. . . I Certainly [he said] . . . do not spend my days indoors, if for no other reason than because my wife can manage all our domestic affairs without my aid."

"Ah!" said I, "and that is just what I dearly want to learn about. Did you educate your wife yourself, to be all that a wife should be, or [when you married her] was she already proficient?"

"Well skilled?" he replied,—"Why, what skill was she likely to bring with her? Not yet fifteen when she married me, and during her whole previous life most carefully trained to see and hear as little as possible, and to ask the fewest questions. Shouldn't anybody be satisfied, if at marriage her whole experience consisted in knowing how to take wool and make a dress and see that her mother's handwomen had their daily spinning tasks assigned? For (he added) as regards control of appetite and self-indulgence, she had the soundest education, and that I take it is the chief thing in the bringing up of man or woman."

"Then all else, (said I) you taught your wife yourself, Ischomachus, until you had made her capable of attending carefully to her proper duties?"

"That I did not do (he replied) until I had offered sacrifice, and prayed that I might teach, and she might learn all that could conduce to the happiness of us twain." . . .

[Ischomachus then told how his wife asked what her particular duties were to be. Her husband answered as follows]

"You will need to stay indoors, and dispatch to their toils such of your servants whose work lies outside the house. Those whose duties are indoors you will manage. It will be your task to receive the stuffs brought in, to apportion part for daily use, and to make provision for the rest, to guard and garner it so that the outgoings destined for a year may not be expended in a month. It will be your duty when the wools are brought in, to see that clothing is made for those who have need. You must also see that the dried corn is made fit and serviceable for food. Then, too, there is something else not altogether pleasing. If any of the household fall sick, it will be your care to see and tend them to the recovery of their health." . . .

[Ischomachus adds that at another time he told his wife not to use cosmetics, nor to think that she made her face more handsome with white enamel or rouge, and to leave off high-heeled shoes; she promised to comply, but asked her husband if he could advise her how she might become not a false show, but really fair to look upon? To which he replied:]

Do not be forever seated like a slave, but, with heaven's help, to assume the attitude of a true mistress standing before the loom, and where your knowledge gives you the superiority, there give the aid of your instruction, and where your knowledge fails, as bravely try to learn. I counsel you to oversee the baking woman as she makes the bread; to stand beside the housekeeper as she measures out her stores; to go on tours of inspection to see if all things are in order as they should be. For, as it seems to me, this will be at once walking exercise and supervision. And [as] an excellent gymnastic I urge you to knead the dough, and roll the paste; to shake the coverlets and make the beds; and if you train yourself in exercise of this sort you will enjoy your food, grow vigorous in health, and your complexion will in very truth be lovelier. The very look and aspect of the wife, the mistress, seen in rivalry with that of her attendants, being as she is at once more fair and more becomingly adorned, has an attractive charm, and not the less because her acts are acts of grace, not services enforced . . .

[Ischomachus concludes by saying to Socrates], And I would have you to know that still to-day my wife is living in a style as that which I taught her . . . [Ischomachus then told Socrates how he spent his own time in the morning, describing the life of a prosperous and successful Athenian gentleman]:

"Why . . . Socrates, my habit is to rise from bed betimes, when I may still expect to find at home this, that, or the other friend whom I may wish to see. Then, if anything has to be done in town, I set off to transact the business and make that my walk; or if there is no business to transact in town, my serving boy leads on my horse to the farm; I follow, and so make the country road my walk, which suits my purpose quite as well or better, Socrates, perhaps, than pacing up and down the colonnade [in the city]. Then when I have reached the farm, where mayhap some of my men are planting trees, or breaking fallow, sowing, or getting in the crops, I inspect their various labors with an eye to every detail, and whenever I can improve upon the present system, I introduce reform.

After this, usually I mount my horse and take a canter. I put him through his paces, suiting these, so far as possible, to those inevitable in war,—in other words, I avoid neither steep slope, nor sheer incline, neither trench nor runnel, only giving my uttermost heed the while so as not to lame my horse while exercising him. When that is over, the boy gives the horse a roll, and leads him homeward, taking at the same time from the country to town whatever we may chance to need. Meanwhile I am off for home, partly walking, partly running, and having reached home I take a bath and give myself a rub,—and then I breakfast,—a repast that leaves me neither hungry nor overfed, and will suffice me through the day."

# LECTURE TOPIC 9

# The Persian Wars

- I. How Came Persia To Conquer All But Greece?
  - A. Cyrus (fl. 549–529 B.C.) and Persian Society
    - 1. Satraps and Religious Diversity
    - 2. Mithraism
  - B. Roads and Postal Service
  - C. Education of Youth
- II. The Advance Under Cambyses (fl. 529–522 B.C.)
- III. How Does Herodotus Explain Why the Hellenes Won?
  - A. Expansion under Darius I (fl. 558–486 B.C.)
    - 1. Battle of Marathon: 490 B.C.
      - a) Miltiades (540–489 B.C.)
      - b) Pheidippides
    - 2. The Significance of the Battle of Marathon
      - a) The Inspiration of Marathon to the Greeks
      - b) The "Marathonomacoi"
  - B. Xerxes (519–465 B.C.) and the Invasion Across the Hellespont
    - 1. Story of Demaratus
    - 2. Battle of Thermopylae: 480 B.C.
      - a) Leonidus and the 300
      - b) Defeat Becomes a Moral Victory
    - 3. The Burning of Athens
    - 4. Battle of Salamis: 480 B.C.
      - a) Themistocles (527–460 B.C.)
      - b) Persian Retreat
    - 5. Battle of Plataea: 479 B.C.
      - a) Combined Forces
      - b) Spartan Leadership
      - c) Greek Victory
  - C. The Consequences of Victory
    - 1. *Eluceria*: The Concept of Freedom
    - 2. The Illustration of *The Persians* by Aeschylus

## READING 1

# The Customs of the Persians

*Herodotus, who has been called the "father of history," wrote an account of the conflicts between Greece and Persia in the fifth century B.C. A marvelous story teller, though given to extensive diversion in his narrative, He remains a major source for our knowledge of the ancient Mediterranean world. Despite gullibility and a tendency to exaggerate, his descriptions enjoy a measure of credibility because he was a contemporary of much that he wrote. In the following excerpt he describes life among the Persians when they and the Greeks were at war. This passage is taken from* The History of Herodotus, *George Rawlinson trans. (London and Toronto: J.M. Dent & Sons, Ltd; New York: E.P. Dutton & Co., 1910), Bk. 1, 131–140.*

---

### Discussion Questions

1. How do you explain why the Persians looked upon all other nations as their inferiors?
2. Are you impressed with the way ancient Persians educated their young men? And what about their practice of weighing an accused person's past behavior against his alleged crime before determining judgment?
3. What do you think Herodotus is referring to when he says the Persians borrowed from the Greeks a taste for "unnatural lust"?

## THE HISTORY OF HERODOTUS

---

The customs which I know the Persians to observe are the following. They have no images of the gods, no temples nor altars, and consider the use of them a sign of folly. This comes, I think, from their not believing the gods to have the same nature with men, as the Greeks imagine. Their wont, however, is to ascend the summits of the loftiest mountains, and there to offer sacrifice to Jupiter, which is the name they give to the whole circuit of the firmament. They likewise offer to the sun and moon, to the earth, to fire, to water, and to the winds. These are the only gods whose worship has come down to them from ancient times. At a later period they began the worship of Urania, which they borrowed from the Arabians and Assyrians. Mylitta is the name by which the Assyrians know this goddess, whom the Arabians call Alitta, and the Persians Mitra.

To these gods the Persians offer sacrifice in the following manner: they raise no altar, light no fire, pour no libations; there is no sound of the flute, no putting on of chaplets, no consecrated barley-cake; but the man who wishes to sacrifice brings his victim to a spot of ground which is pure from pollution, and there calls upon the name of the god to whom he intends to offer. It is usual to have the turban encircled with a wreath, most commonly of myrtle. The sacrificer is not allowed to pray for blessings on himself alone, but he prays for the welfare of the king, and of the whole Persian people, among whom he is of necessity included. He cuts the victim in pieces, and having boiled the flesh, he lays it out upon the tenderest herbage that he can find, trefoil especially. When all is ready, one of the Magi comes forward and chants a hymn, which they say recounts the origin of the gods. It is not lawful to offer sacrifice unless there is a Magus present. After waiting a short time the sacrificer carries the flesh of the victim away with him, and makes whatever use of it he may please.

Of all the days in the year, the one which they celebrate most is their birthday. It is customary to have the board furnished on that day with an ampler supply than common. The richer Persians cause an ox, a horse, a camel, and an ass to be baked whole and so served up to them: the poorer classes use instead the smaller kinds of cattle. They eat little solid food but abundance of dessert, which is set on table a few dishes at a time; this it is which makes them say that "the Greeks, when they eat, leave off hungry, having nothing worth mention served up to them after the meats; whereas, if they had more put before them, they would not stop eating." They are very fond of wine, and drink it in large quantities. To vomit or obey natural calls in the presence of another, is forbidden among them. Such are their customs in these matters.

It is also their general practice to deliberate upon affairs of weight when they are drunk; and then on the morrow, when they are sober, the decision to which they came the night before is put before them by the master of the house in which it was made; and if it is then approved of, they act on it; if not, they set it aside. Sometimes, however, they are sober at their first deliberation, but in this case they always reconsider the matter under the influence of wine.

When they meet each other in the streets, you may know if the persons meeting are of equal rank by the following token; if they are, instead of speaking, they kiss each other on the lips. In the case where one is a little inferior to the other, the kiss is given on the cheek; where the difference of rank is great, the inferior prostrates himself upon the ground. Of nations, they honour most their nearest neighbours, whom they esteem next to themselves; those who live beyond these they honour in the second degree; and so with the remainder, the further they are removed, the less the esteem in which they hold them. The reason is, that they look upon themselves as very greatly superior in all respects to the rest of mankind, regarding others as approaching to excellence in proportion as they dwell nearer to them; whence it comes to pass that those who are the farthest off must be the most degraded of mankind . . .

. . . As soon as they hear of any luxury, they instantly make it their own: and hence, among other novelties, they have learnt unnatural lust from the Greeks. Each of them has several wives, and a still larger number of concubines.

Next to prowess in arms, it is regarded as the greatest proof of manly excellence, to be the father of many sons. Every year the king sends rich gifts to the man who can show the largest number: for they hold that number is strength. Their sons are carefully instructed from their fifth to their twentieth year, in three things alone—to ride, to draw the bow, and to speak the truth. Until their fifth year they are not allowed to come into the sight of their father, but pass their lives with the women. This is done that, if the child die young, the may not be afflicted by its loss.

To my mind it is a wise rule, as also is the following—that the king shall not put any one to death for a single fault, and that none of the Persians shall visit a single fault in a slave with any extreme penalty; but in every case the services of the offender shall be set against his misdoings; and, if the latter be found to outweigh the former, the aggrieved party shall then proceed to punishment.

The Persians maintain that never yet did any one kill his own father or mother; but in all such cases they are quite sure that, if matters were sifted to the bottom, it would be found that the child was wither a changeling or else the fruit of adultery; for it is not likely they say that the real father should perish by the hands of his child.

. . . They never defile a river with the secretions of their bodies, nor even wash their hands in one; nor will they allow others to do so, as they have a great reverence for rivers . . .

Thus much I can declare of the Persians with entire certainty, from my own actual knowledge. There is another custom which is spoken of with reserve, and not openly, concerning their dead. It is said that the body of a male Persian is never buried, until it has been torn either by a dog or a bird of prey.

# READING 2

## The Battle of Marathon

*Again, we are in debt to Herodotus for this account of Athens' surprising victory over the Persians (to whom he referred as the "barbarians"). Fought in 490 B.C., it was memorialized for centuries as evidence of Athenian greatness. As Herodotus points out, however, the Athenians received at least some help from the Plataeans. The passage here is from the translation of George Rawlinson, Bk. VI, 105–106, 111–113, 117.*

---

### Discussion Questions

1. Can you think of a comparable military event where Americans won a military battle against overwhelming odds?
2. Do you think free men fight more fiercely than those enrolled to defend a totalitarian regime?

## THE HISTORY OF HERODOTUS

And first, before they left the city, the generals sent off to Sparta a herald, one Philippides, who was by birth an Athenian, and by profession and practice a trained runner. This man, according to the account which he gave to the Athenians on his return, when he was near Mount Parthenium, above Tegea, fell in with the god Pan, who called him by name, and bade him ask the Athenians, "Why they neglected him so entirely, when he was kindly disposed towards them, and had often helped them in times past, and would do so again in time to come?" The Athenians, entirely believing in the truth of this report, as soon as their affairs were once more in good order, set up a temple to Pan under the Acropolis, and, in return for the message which I have recorded, established in his honour yearly sacrifices and a torch-race.

On the occasion of which we speak, when Philippides was sent by the Athenian generals, and, according to his own account, saw Pan on his journey, he reached Sparta on the very next day after quitting the city of Athens. Upon his arrival he went before the rulers, and said:

"men of Lacedaemon, the Athenians beseech you to hasten to their aid, and not allow that state, which is the most ancient in all Greece, to be enslaved by the barbarians . . . "

Thus did Philippides deliver the message committed to him. And the Spartans wished to help the Athenians, but were unable to give them any present aid, as they did not like to break their established law. It was the ninth day of the month, and they could not march out of Sparta on the ninth, when the moon had not reached the full. So they waited for the full of the moon . . .

[Athenian soldiers then proceeded without Spartan assistance to gather] in order to do battle . . . when they were joined by the Plataeans, who came in full force to their aid . . .

Then at length . . . the Athenian battle was set in array, and this was the order of it . . . as they marshaled the host upon the field of Marathon, in order that the Athenian front might be of equal length with the Median, the ranks of the centre were diminished, and it became the weakest part of the line, while the wings were both made strong with a depth of many ranks.

So when the battle was set in array, and the victims showed themselves favourable, instantly the Athenians, so soon as they were let go, charged the barbarians at a run. Now the distance between the two armies was little short of a mile. The Persians, therefore, when they saw the Greeks coming on at speed, made ready to receive them, although it seemed to them that the Athenians were bereft of their senses, and bent upon their own destruction; for they saw a mere handful of men coming on at a run without either horsemen or archers. Such was the opinion of the barbarians; but the Athenians in close array fell upon them, and fought in a manner worthy of being recorded. They were the first of the Greeks, so far as I know, who introduced the custom of charging the enemy at a run, and they were likewise the first who dared to look upon the Median garb, and to face men clad in that fashion. Until this time the very name of the Medes had been a terror to the Greeks to hear.

The two armies fought together on the plain of Marathon for a length of time; and in the mid battle, where the Persians themselves and the Sacae had their place, the barbarians were victorious, and broke and pursued the Greeks into the inner country; but on the two wings the Athenians and the Plataeans defeated the enemy. Having so done, they suffered the routed barbarians to fly at their ease, and joining the two wings in one, fell upon those who had broken their own centre, and fought and conquered them. These likewise fled, and now the Athenians hung upon the runaways and cut them down, chasing them all the way to the shore, on reaching which they laid hold of the ships and called aloud for fire . . .

There fell in this battle of Marathon, on the side of the barbarians, about 6,400 men; on that of the Athenians, 192. Such was the number of the slain on the one side and the other.

# READING 3

## The Battle of Thermopylae

*Amazingly, in the fifth century B.C. the Greek city-states had stopped the Persians at Marathon, despite the latter's overwhelming numbers and were able to prevent a Persian conquest. With the death of the Persian king, Darius, the Greeks gained a ten-year respite. In 480 B.C., Xerxes, the new Persian king, led a full-scale invasion into Greece. At the pass of Thermopylae, 300 Spartans under the leadership of their king, Leonidas, assisted by some auxiliary troops, held the pass against the whole of the Persian army until they were betrayed. The story of Leonidas and the heroic resistance of the Greeks at Thermopylae is a remarkable and heroic episode, which reverberated throughout the rest of Greek history. The eventual defeat of the Greeks was transformed into a moral victory, while the Persians were demonized and turned into a monstrous enemy. The Persians finally did push through the pass and burned the city of Athens, but they lost their fleet to the Athenian navy. The following year, the Greeks defeated Persia on land and sea, and Persia was forced to withdraw from Greece. The story of the battle of Thermopylae by Herodotus is taken from E. H. Blakeney, ed.,* The History of Herodotus, *Vol. II, translated by George Rawlinson (London & Toronto: J. M. Dent & Sons Ltd. ; New York: E. P. Dutton & Co., 1916), pp. 201–208.*

---

Discussion Questions

1. In the passage below, how do you account for the fact that a Greek, Demaratus, was serving as a counselor to King Xerxes?
2. In your opinion, were the Lacedemonians (Spartans) foolish to persist with defense of the pass at Thermopylae when it became obvious that they were likely to be overwhelmed by the Persian forces?

### HERODOTUS

The Greek forces at Thermopylae, when the Persian army drew near to the entrance of the pass, were seized with fear; and a council was held to consider about a retreat. It was the wish of the Peloponnesians generally that the army should fall back upon the Peloponnese, and there guard the Isthmus. But Leonidas . . . gave his voice for remaining where they were, while they sent envoys to the several cities to ask for help, since they were too few to make a stand against an army like that of the Medes[Persians]. . . .

While this debate was going on, Xerxes sent a mounted spy to observe the Greeks, and note how many they were, and see what they were doing. He had heard, before he came out of Thessaly, that a few men were assembled at this place, and that at their head were certain Lacedaemonians, under Leonidas, a descendant of Hercules. The horseman rode up to the camp, and looked about him, but did not see the whole army. . . .It chanced that at this time the Lacedaemonians. . .were seen by the spy, some of them engaged in gymnastic exercises, others combing their long hair. At this the spy greatly marveled, but he counted their number, and when he had taken accurate note of everything, he rode back quietly; for no one pursued after him, nor paid any heed to his visit. So he returned, and told Xerxes all that he had seen.

[Xerxes sent for Demaratus, the son of Ariston, told him all that he had heard, and questioned him about the meaning of such behavior on the part of the Spartans.] Then Demaratus said—

"I spake to thee, O King! concerning these men long since, when we had just begun our march upon Greece; thou, however, didst only laugh at my words, when I told thee of all this, which I saw would come to pass. Earnestly do I struggle at all times to speak truth to thee, sire; and now listen to it once more. These men have come to dispute the pass with us; and it is for this that they are now making ready.... Be assured, however, that if thou canst subdue the men who are here and the Lacedaemonians who remain in Sparta, there is no other nation in all the world which will venture to lift a hand in their defence. Thou hast now to deal with the first kingdom and town in Greece, and with the bravest men."...

But Xerxes was not persuaded any the more. Four whole days he suffered to go by, expecting that the Greeks would run away. When, however, he found on the fifth that they were not gone, thinking that their firm stand was mere impudence and recklessness, he grew wroth, and sent against them the Medes and Cissians, with orders to take them alive and bring them into his presence. Then the Medes rushed forward and charged the Greeks, but fell in vast numbers: others however took the places of the slain.... The struggle continued during the whole day.

Then the Medes, having met so rough a reception, withdrew from the fight; and their place was taken by the band of Persians under Hydarnes... they, it was thought, would soon finish the business. But when they joined battle with the Greeks, 'twas with no better success than the Median detachment—things went much as before—the two armies fighting in a narrow space, and the barbarians using shorter spears than the Greeks, and having no advantage from their numbers. The Lacedaemonians fought in a way worthy of note, and showed themselves far more skilful in fight than their adversaries, often turning their backs, and making as though they were all flying away, on which the barbarians would rush after them with much noise and shouting, when the Spartans at their approach would wheel round and face their pursuers, in this way destroying vast numbers of the enemy. Some Spartans likewise fell in these encounters, but only a very few. At last the Persians, finding that all their efforts to gain availed nothing... withdrew to their own quarters....

Now, as the King was in a great strait, and knew not how he should deal with the emergency, Ephialtes, the son of Eurydemus, a man of Malis, came to him and was admitted to a conference. Stirred by the hope of receiving a rich reward at the King's hands, he had come to tell him of the pathway which led across the mountain to Thermopylae; by which disclosure he brought destruction on the bank of Greeks who had there withstood the barbarians....

The Greeks at Thermopylae received the first warning of the destruction which the dawn would bring on them from the seer Megistias, who read their fate in the victims as he was sacrificing. After this deserters came in, and brought the news that the Persians were marching round by the hills: it was still night when these men arrived. Last of all, the scouts came running down from the heights, and brought in the same accounts, when the day was just beginning to break. Then the Greeks held council to consider what they should do, and here opinions were divided: some were strong against quitting their post, while others contended to the contrary. So when the council had broken up, part of the troops departed and went their ways homeward to their several states; part however resolved to remain, and to stand by Leonidas to the last.

It is said that Leonidas himself sent away the troops who departed, because he tendered their safety, but thought it unseemly that either he or his Spartans should quit the post which they had been especially sent to guard.... He therefore commanded them to retreat, but said that he himself could not draw back with honour; knowing that, if he stayed, glory awaited him, and that Sparta in that case would not lose her prosperity....

At sunrise Xerxes made libations... and then began his advance.... The barbarians under Xerxes began to draw nigh; and the Greeks under Leonidas, as they now went forth determined to die, advanced much further than on previous days, until they reached the more open portion of the pass. Hitherto they had held their station within the wall, and from this had gone forth to fight at the point where the pass was narrowest. Now they joined battle beyond the defile, and carried slaughter among the barbarians, who fell in heaps. Behind them the captains of the squadrons, armed with whips, urged their men forward with continual blows. Many were thrust into the sea, and there perished; a still greater number were trampled to death by their own soldiers; no one heeded the dying. For the Greeks, reckless of their own safety and desperate, since they knew that, as the mountain had been crossed, their destruction was nigh at hand, exerted themselves with the most furious valour against the barbarians.

By this time the spears of the greater number were all shivered, and with their swords they hewed down the ranks of the Persians; and here, as they strove, Leonidas fell fighting bravely, together with many other famous Spartans, whose names I have taken care to learn on account of their great worthiness, as indeed I have those of all the three hundred. . . .

. . .And now there arose a fierce struggle between the Persians and the Lacedaemonians over the body of Leonidas, in which the Greeks four times drove back the enemy, and at last by their great bravery succeeded in bearing off the body. . . .They defended themselves to the last, such as still had swords using them, and the others resisting with their hands and teeth; till the barbarians. . . encircled them on every side, overwhelmed and buried the remnant which was left beneath showers of missile weapons.

# LECTURE TOPIC 10

# Religion, Philosophy, and Art in Classical Greece

I. What Were The Ancient Greeks' Religious Beliefs?
  A. Cosmology
  B. Polytheism and the Greek Pantheon
  C. The Practice of Religion
    1. The Act of Sacrifice
    2. Pan-Hellenic Festivals
      a) Olympian
      b) Isthmian
      c) Nemaean
      d) Pythian
    3. Shrines and Mystery Cults
      a) Delphi
      b) Eleusis
II. Philosophy: How Some Greeks Doubted The Gods
  A. The Sophists: Pragmatic Relativists
    1. Protgoras (481–411 B.C.)
    2. Antiphon (480–411 B.C.)
  B. Idealism: Reality Is In The Mind
    1. Socrates (469–399 B.C.)
      a) Allegory of the Cave
      b) The Doctrine of the Meno
    2. Plato (429–347 B.C.)
      a) The Academy: 385 B.C.–529 A.D.
      b) *Dialogues*
  C. Materialism: The *Only* Reality Is In Matter
    1. Leucippus (5th Cent. B.C.) and Democritus (460–370 B.C.)
    2. Atomic Theory of Matter
III. The Place of Drama in Classical Civilization
  A. Origins
    1. Dionysian Celebrations
    2. Thespis; Skene; Persona; Chorus
  B. Fifth Century Tragedies
    1. Simplicity of Structure
    2. The Quality of Performance
      a) Masks and Costumes
      b) Poetry
    3. Religious Context
    4. Transgressive Nature

a) Catharsis: Cleansing
b) Illustration of *Antigone* and the *Orestia* by Sophocles
C. Comedy: Aristophanes (450–380 B.C.) and *Lysistrata*
IV. How Did The Greeks Build Their Temples?
A. Greek Marble and Its Many Employments
1. Temples and Their Columns
a) Doric
b) Ionic
c) Corinthian
2. Example of the Parthenon
B. Would You Believe They Painted Them Bright Colors?
V. Greek Statuary Art: Gods And Mortals
A. Hellenic Characteristics
1. Heroic Pretension
2. Balance and Cross Tensions
3. Idealistic
B. Famous Sculptors
1. Polycleitus (5th Cent. B.C.)
a) Doryphorus statue (Spear-bearer)
b) Mathematical Proportions
2. Myron (5th Cent. B.C.)
a) Discobolus (discus-thrower)
b) Careful Proportion and Rhythm
3. Phidias of Athens ( c. 493–430 B.C.)
a) Statue of Athena and Zeus
b) Commissioned to Direct Construction of the Parthenon.
4. Praxiteles (4th Cent. B.C.)
a) Aphrodite of Knidos (Cnidos)
b) Hermes with the Infant Dionysus.
VI. What Were The Commonplace Values of Hellenic Greece?
A. *Politeia* vs. *Idiotai*
B. *Sophrosyne;* or *metron ariston*: "The Golden Mean"
C. *"Mens Sana in Corpore Sano"*: A Healthy Mind in a Healthy Body
D. The Persistence of Homeric *Aret_*
1. Protagoras and the Humanistic Imperative: "Man is the Measure of All Things"

# READING 1

## Protagoras the Sophist (5th Cent. B.C.)

*The Sophists were more important and profound than we generally believe. We in the modern world give the words "sophist" and "sophistry" pejorative meanings. Because of their skills, the ancient sophists were commonly employed as teachers and lawyers. More significantly, their relativism and pliability resulted in giving their views a distinctly humanistic cast. The following are taken from Philip Wheelwright, ed.,* The Presocratics *(New York: The Odyssey Press, Inc., 1966), pp. 239–240.*

---

### Discussion Questions

1. Would you describe these sayings from Protagoras as advocating a "pragmatic" approach to life?
2. Is he more or less like secular thinkers in the modern world?

### FRAGMENTS FROM PROTAGORAS

1\. Man is the measure of all things . . .

2\. All matter is in a state of flux . . .

6\. As for the gods, I have no way of knowing either that they exist or that they do not exist; nor, if they exist, of what form they are. For the obstacles to that sort of knowledge are many, including the obscurity of the matter and the brevity of human life.

# READING 2

## *Plato* (427–347 B.C.)

*Plato and his mentor Socrates probably had greater influence on Western thought than all other personalities and writers, with the exception of Christianity, put together. In the following famous passage, Plato illustrates, through a contrived dialogue involving Socrates, the limited and illusory nature of sensory knowledge. The following is taken from* The Dialogues of Plato, Book VII, *translated by B. Jowett, M.A. (Oxford University Press American Branch, 1892), pp. 214–218.*

---

### Discussion Questions

1. Do you believe that Plato's allegory of the Cave is applicable to all forms of knowledge, including religious, moral, and artistic thought?
2. Can you disprove Plato's view that all knowledge already exists within you?

## ALLEGORY OF THE CAVE

And now, I said, let me show in a figure how far our nature is enlightened or unenlightened; — Behold! human beings living in an underground den, which has a mouth open towards the light and reaching all along the den; here they have been from their childhood, and have their legs and necks chained so that they cannot move, and can only see before them, being prevented by the chains from turning round their heads. Above and behind them a fire is blazing at a distance, and between the fire and the prisoners there is a raised way; and you will see, if you look, a low wall built along the way, like the screen which marionette players have in front of them, over which they show the puppets.

I see.

And do you see, I said, men passing along the wall carrying all sorts of vessels, and statues and figures of animals made of wood and stone and various materials, which appear over the wall? Some of them are talking, others silent.

You have shown me a strange image, and they are strange prisoners.

Like ourselves, I replied; and they see only their own shadows, or the shadows of one another, which the fire throws on the opposite wall of the cave?

True, he said; how could they see anything but the shadows if they were never allowed to move their heads?

And of the objects which are being carried in like manner they would only see the shadows?

Yes, he said.

And if they were able to converse with one another, would they not suppose that they were naming what was actually before them?

Very true.

And suppose further that the prison had an echo which came from the other side, would they not be sure to fancy when one of the passers-by spoke that the voice which they heard came from the passing shadow?

No question, he replied.

To them, I said, the truth would be literally nothing but the shadows of the images.

That is certain.

And now look again, and see what will naturally follow if the prisoners are released and disabused of their error. At first, when any of them is liberated and compelled suddenly to stand up and turn his neck round and walk and look towards the light, he will suffer sharp pains; the glare will distress him, and he will be unable to see the realities of which in his former state he had seen the shadows; and then conceive some one saying to him, that what he saw before was an illusion, but that now, when he is approaching nearer to being and his eye is turned towards more real existence, he has a clearer vision —what will be his reply? And you may further imagine that his instructor is pointing to the objects as they pass and requiring him to name them,—will he not be perplexed? Will he not fancy that the shadows which he formerly saw are truer than the objects which are now shown to him?

Far truer.

And if he is compelled to look straight at the light, will he not have a pain in his eyes which will make him turn away to take refuge in the objects of vision which he can see, and which he will conceive to be in reality clearer than the things which are now being shown to him?

True, he said.

And suppose once more, that he is reluctantly dragged up a steep and rugged ascent, and held fast until he is forced into the presence of the sun himself, is he not likely to be pained and irritated? When he approaches the light his eyes will be dazzled, and he will not be able to see anything at all of what are now called realities.

Not all in a moment, he said.

He will require to grow accustomed to the sight of the upper world. And first he will see the shadows best, next the reflections of men and other objects in the water, and then the objects themselves; then he will gaze upon the light of the moon and the stars and the spangled heaven; and he will see the sky and the stars by night better than the sun or the light of the sun by day?

Certainly.

Last of all he will be able to see the sun, and not mere reflections of him in the water, but he will see him in his own proper place, and not in another; and he will contemplate him as he is.

Certainly.

He will then proceed to argue that this is he who gives the season and the years, and is the guardian of all that is in the visible world, and in a certain way the cause of all things which he and his fellows have been accustomed to behold?

Clearly, he said, he would first see the sun and then reason about him.

And when he remembered his old habitation, and the wisdom of the den and his fellow prisoners, do you not suppose that he would felicitate himself on the change, and pity them?

Certainly, he would.

And if they were in the habit of conferring honours among themselves on those who were quickest to observe the passing shadows and to remark which of them went before, and which followed after, and which were together; and who were therefore best able to draw conclusions as to the future, do you think that he would care for such honours and glories, or envy the possessors of them? Would he not say with Homer,

*"Better* to *be poor servant of a poor master,"* and to endure anything, rather than think as they do and live after their manner?

Yes, he said, I think that he would rather suffer anything than entertain these false notions and live in this miserable manner.

Imagine once more, I said, such an one coming suddenly out of the sun to be replaced in his old situation; would he not be certain to have his eyes full of darkness?

To be sure, he said.

And if there were a contest, and he had to compete in measuring the shadows with the prisoners who had never moved out of the den, while his sight was still weak, and before his eyes had become steady (and the time which would be needed to acquire this new habit of sight might be very considerable), would he not be ridiculous? Men would say of him that up he went and down he came without his eyes, and that it was better not even to think of ascending; and if anyone tried to loose another and lead him up to the light, let them only catch the offender, and they would put him to death.

No question, he said.

This entire allegory, I said, you may now append, dear Glaucon, to the previous argument; the prison-house is the world of sight, the light of the fire is the sun, and you will not misapprehand me if you interpret the journey upwards to be the ascent of the soul into the intellectual world according to my poor belief, which, at your desire, I have expressed—whether rightly or wrongly God knows. But, whether true or false, my opinion is that in the world of knowledge the idea of good appears last of all, and is seen only with an effort; and, when seen, is also inferred to be the universal author of all things beautiful and right, parent of light and of the lord of light in this visible world, and the immediate source of reason and truth in the intellectual; and that this is the power upon which he who would act rationally either in public or private life must have his eye fixed.

I agree, he said, as far as I am able to understand you.

Moreover, I said, you must not wonder that those who attain to the beatific vision are unwilling to descent to human affairs; for their souls are ever hastening into the upper world where they desire to dwell; which desire of theirs is very natural, if our allegory may be trusted.

Yes, very natural indeed.

And is there anything surprising in one who passes from divine contemplations to the evil state of man, misbehaving himself in a ridiculous manner; if, while his eyes are blinking and before he has become accustomed to the surrounding darkness, he is compelled to fight in courts of law, or in other places, about the images or the shadows of images of justice, and is endeavouring to meet the conceptions of those who have never yet seen absolute justice?

Anything but surprising, he replied.

Anyone who has common sense will remember that the bewilderments of the eyes are of two kinds, and arise from two causes, either from coming out of the light or from going into the light, which is true of the mind's eye, quite as much as of the bodily eye; and he who remembers this when he sees anyone whose vision is perplexed and weak, will not be too ready to laugh; he will first ask whether that soul of man has come out of the brighter life, and is unable to see because unaccustomed to the dark, or having turned from darkness to the day is dazzled by excess of light. And he will count the one happy in his condition and state of being, and he will pity the other; or, if he have a mind to laugh at the soul which comes from below into the light, there will be more reason in this than in the laugh which greets him who returns from above out of the light into the den.

That, he said, is a very just distinction.

But then, if I am right, certain professors of education must be wrong when they say they can put a knowledge into the soul which was not there before, like sight into blind eyes.

They undoubtedly say this, he replied.

Whereas, our argument shows that the power and capacity of learning exists

in the soul already; and that just as the eye was unable to turn from darkness to light without the whole body, so too the instrument of knowledge can only by the movement of the whole soul be turned from the world of becoming into that of being, and learn by degrees to endure the sight of being, and of the brightest and best of being, or in other words, of the good.

Very true.

READING 3

# Plato on the Death of Socrates

*In the Phaedo we have Plato at his literary and philosophical best. Not only does the book contain a moving account of the execution of Socrates, carried out by his own hand, but a recapitulation of the great philosopher's theory of innate knowledge. Other passages reveal his views on death and the nature of the soul. These excerpts come from Benjamin Jowett, trans.,* Dialogues of Plato. . . , *rev. edn. (New York: Wiley Book Co., 1899), pp. 77–80, 92–94, 102–105, 139–142.*

---

### Discussion Questions

1. Are you persuaded by Socrates' argument for reincarnation?
2. Compare the relationship described in this dialogue between Socrates and his wife with that between Socrates and his friends.
3. Are you impressed with the equanimity displayed by Socrates in the face of impending death?

PERSONS OF THE DIALOGUE

PHAEDO, *who is the narrator of the dialogue to* ECHECRATES *of Phlius*
Socrates
ATTENDANT OF THE PRISON
AROLLODORUS
SIMMIAS
CEBES
CRITO

Scene: *The Prison of Socrates*
Place of the Narratlon: *Phlius*

## THE PHAEDO

*Echecrates.* Were you yourself, Phaedo, in the prison with Socrates on the day when he drank the poison?

*Phaedo.* Yes, Echecrates, I was.

*Ech.* I wish that you would tell me about his death. What did he say in his last hours? We were informed that he died by taking poison, but no one knew anything more; for no Phliasian ever goes to Athens now, and a long time has elapsed since any Athenian found his way to Phlius, and therefore we had no clear account. . . .

What was the manner of his death, Phaedo? What was said or done? And which of his friends had he with him? Or were they not allowed by the authorities to be present? And did he die alone?

*Phaed.* No; there were several of his friends with him.

*Ech.* If you have nothing to do, I wish that you would tell me what passed; as exactly as you can.

*Phaed.* I have nothing to do, and will try to gratify your wish. For to me, too, there is no greater pleasure than to have Socrates brought to my recollection, whether I speak myself or hear another speak of him.

*Ech.* You will have listeners who are of the same mind with you, and I hope that you will be as exact as you can,

*Phaed.* I remember the strange feeling which came over me at being with him. For I could hardly believe that I was present at the death of a friend, and therefore I did not pity him, Echecrates; his mien and his language were so noble and fearless in the hour of death that to me he appeared blessed. I thought that in going to the other world he could not be without a divine call, and that he would be happy, if any man ever was, when he arrived there; and therefore I did not pity him as might seem natural at such a time. But neither could I feel the pleasure which I usually felt in philosophical discourse (for philosophy was the theme of which we spoke). I was pleased, and I was also pained, because I knew that he was soon to die, and this strange mixture of feeling was shared by us all; we were laughing and weeping by turns, especially the excitable Apollodorus—you know the sort of man?

*Ech.* Yes.

*Phaed.* He was quite overcome; and I myself, and all of us were greatly moved. . . . On entering we found Socrates just released from chains, and Xanthippe, whom you know, sitting by him, and holding his child in her arms. When she saw us she uttered a cry and said, as women will: "O Socrates, this is the last time that either you will converse with your friends, or they with you." Socrates turned to Crito and said: "Crito, let some one take her home." Some of Crito's people accordingly led her away, crying out and beating herself. And when she was gone, Socrates, sitting up on the couch, began to bend and rub his leg, saying, as he rubbed: How singular is the thing called pleasure, and how curiously related to pain, which might be thought to be the opposite of it; for they never come to a man together, and yet he who pursues either of them is generally compelled to take the other. They are two, and yet they grow together out of one head or stem; and I cannot help thinking that if AEsop had noticed them, he would have made a fable about God trying to reconcile their strife, and when he could not, he fastened their heads together; and this is the reason why when one comes the other follows, as I find in my own case pleasure comes following after the pain in my leg, which was caused by the chain. . . .

Now, said Socrates, I will analyze one of the two pairs of opposites which I have mentioned to you, and also its intermediate processes, and you shall analyze the other to me. The state of sleep is opposed to the state of waking, and out of sleeping waking is generated, and out of waking, sleeping; and the process of generation is in the one case falling asleep, and in the other waking up. Are you agreed about that?

Quite agreed.

Then, suppose that you analyze life and death to me in the same manner. Is not death opposed to life?

Yes.

And they are generated one from the other?

Yes.

What is generated from life?

Death.

And what from death?

I can only say in answer—life.

Then the living, whether things or persons, Cebes, are generated from the dead?

That is clear, he replied.

Then the inference is, that our souls are in the world below?

That is true.

And one of the two processes or generations is visible—for surely the act of dying is visible?

Surely, he said.

And may not the other be inferred as the complement of nature, who is not to be supposed to go on one leg only? And if not, a corresponding process of generation in death must also be assigned to her?

Certainly, he replied.

And what is that process?

Revival.

And revival, if there be such a thing, is the birth of the dead into the world of the living?

Quite true.

Then here is a new way in which we arrive at the inference that the living come from the dead, just as the dead come from the living; and if this is true, then the souls of the dead must be in some place out of which they come again. And this, as I think, has been satisfactorily proved.

Yes, Socrates, he said; all this seems to flow necessarily out of our previous admissions. . . .

Cebes added: Your favorite doctrine, Socrates, that knowledge is simply recollection, if true, also necessarily implies a previous time in which we learned that which we now recollect. But this would be impossible unless our soul was in some place before existing in the human form; here, then, is another argument of the soul's immortality.

But tell me, Cebes, said Simmias, interposing, what proofs are given of this doctrine of recollection? I am not very sure at this moment that I remember them.

One excellent proof, said Cebes, is afforded by questions. If you put a question to a person in a right way, he will give a true answer of himself; but how could he do this unless there were knowledge and right reason already in him? And this is most clearly shown when he is taken to a diagram or to anything of that sort. . . .

And were we not saying long ago that the soul when using the body as an instrument of perception, that is to say, when using the sense of sight or hearing or some other sense (for the meaning of perceiving through the body is perceiving through the senses)—were we not saying that the soul too is then dragged by the body into the region of the changeable, and wanders and is confused; the world spins round her, and she is like a drunkard when under their influence?

Very true.

But when returning into herself she reflects; then she passes into the realm of purity, and eternity, and immortality, and unchangeableness, which are her kindred, and with them she ever lives, when she is by herself and is not let or hindered; then she ceases from her erring ways, and being in communion with the unchanging is unchanging. And this state of the soul is called wisdom?

That is well and truly said, Socrates, he replied.

And to which class is the soul more nearly alike and akin, as far as may be inferred from this argument, as well as from the preceding one?

I think, Socrates, that, in the opinion of everyone who follows the argument, the soul will be infinitely more like the unchangeable—even the most stupid person will not deny that.

And the body is more like the changing?

Yes.

Yet once more consider the matter in this light: When the soul and the body are united, then nature orders the soul to rule and govern, and the body to obey and serve.

Now which of these two functions is akin to the divine? and which to the mortal? Does not the divine appear to you to be that which naturally orders and rules, and the mortal that which is subject and servant?

True.

And which does the soul resemble?

The soul resembles the divine, and the body the mortal—there can be no doubt of that, Socrates.

Then reflect, Cebes: is not the conclusion of the whole matter this—that the soul is in the very likeness of the divine, and immortal, and intelligible, and uniform, and indissoluble, and unchangeable; and the body is in the very likeness of the human, and mortal, and unintelligible, and multiform, and dissoluble, and changeable. Can this, my dear Cebes, be denied?

No, indeed.

But if this is true, then is not the body liable to speedy dissolution? and is not the soul almost or altogether indissoluble?

Certainly. . . .

And are we to suppose that the soul, which is invisible, in passing to the true Hades, which like her is invisible, and pure, and noble, and on her way to the good and wise God, whither, if God will, my soul is also soon to go—that the soul, I repeat, if this be her nature and origin, is blown away and perishes immediately on quitting the body, as the many say? That can never be, my dear Simmias and Cebes. The truth rather is that the soul which is pure at departing draws after her no bodily taint, having never voluntarily had connection with the body, which she is ever avoiding, herself gathered into herself (for such abstraction has been the study of her life). And what does this mean but that she has been a true disciple of philosophy, and has practised how to die easily? And is not philosophy the practice of death?

Certainly.

That soul, I say, herself invisible, departs to the invisible world—to the divine and immortal and rational: thither arriving, she lives in bliss and is released from the error and folly of men, their fears and wild passions and all other human ills, and forever dwells, as they say of the initiated, in company with the gods. Is not this true, Cebes?

Yes, said Cebes, beyond a doubt.

But the soul which has been polluted, and is impure at the time of her departure, and is the companion and servant of the body always, and is in love with and fascinated by the body and by the desires and pleasures of the body, until she is led to believe that the truth only exists in a bodily form, which a man may touch and see and taste and use for the purposes of his lusts—the soul, I mean, accustomed to hate and fear and avoid the intellectual principle, which to the bodily eye is dark and invisible, and can be attained only by philosophy—do you suppose that such a soul as this will depart pure and unalloyed?

That is impossible, he replied.

She is engrossed by the corporeal, which the continual association and constant care of the body have made natural to her.

Very true.

And this, my friend, may be conceived to be that heavy, weighty, earthy element of sight by which such a soul is depressed and dragged down again into the visible world, because she is afraid of the invisible and of the world below — prowling about tombs and sepulchres, in the neighborhood of which, as they tell us, are seen certain ghostly apparitions of souls which have not departed pure, but are cloyed with sight and therefore visible.

That is very likely, Socrates.

Yes, that is very likely, Cebes; and these must be the souls, not of the good, but of the evil, who are compelled to wander about such places in payment of the penalty of their former evil way of life; and they continue to wander until the desire which haunts them is satisfied and they are imprisoned in another body. And they may be supposed to be fixed in the same natures which they had in their former life.

What natures do you mean, Socrates?

I mean to say that men who have followed after gluttony, and wantonness, and drunkenness, and have had no thought of avoiding them, would pass into asses and animals of that sort. What do you think?

I think that exceedingly probable.

And those who have chosen the portion of injustice, and tyranny, and violence, will pass into wolves, or hawks, and kites; whither else can we suppose them to go?

Yes, said Cebes; that is doubtless the place of natures such as theirs.

And there is no difficulty, he said, in assigning to all of them places answering to their several natures and propensities?

There is not, he said.

Even among them some are happier than others; and the happiest both in themselves and their place of abode are those who have practised the civil and social virtues which are called temperance and justice, and are acquired by habit and attention without philosophy and mind.

Why are they the happiest?

Because they may be expected to pass into some gentle, social nature which is like their own, such as that of bees or ants, or even back again into the form of man, and just and moderate men spring from them.

That is not impossible.

But he who is a philosopher or lover of learning, and is entirely pure at departing, is alone permitted to reach the gods. And this is the reason, Simmias and Cebes, why the true votaries of philosophy abstain from all fleshly lusts, and endure and refuse to give themselves up to them—not because they fear poverty or the ruin of their families, like the lovers of money, and the world in general; nor like the lovers of power and honor, because they dread the dishonor or disgrace of evil deeds.

No, Socrates, that would not become them, said Cebes.

No, indeed, he replied; and therefore they who have a care of their souls, and do not merely live in the fashions of the body, say farewell to all this; they will not walk in the ways of the blind: and when Philosophy offers them purification and release from evil, they feel that they ought not to resist her influence, and to her they incline, and whither she leads they follow her. . . .

I do not mean to affirm that the description which I have given of the soul and her mansions is exactly true—a man of sense ought hardly to say that. But I do say that, inasmuch as the soul is shown to be immortal, he may venture to think, not improperly or unworthily, that something of the kind is true. The venture is a glorious one, and he ought to comfort himself with words like these, which is the reason why I lengthen out the tale. Wherefore, I say, let a man be of good cheer about his soul, who has cast away the pleasures and ornaments of the body as alien to him, and rather hurtful in their effects, and has followed after the pleasures of knowledge in this life who has adorned the soul in her own proper jewels, which are temperance, and justice, and courage, and nobility, and truth—in these arrayed she is ready to go on her journey to the world below, when her time comes. You, Simmias and Cebes, and all other men, will depart at some time or other. Me already, as the tragic poet would say, the voice of fate calls. Soon I must drink the poison; and I think that I had better repair to the bath first, in order that the women may not have the trouble of washing my body after I am dead.

When he had done speaking, Crito said: And have you any commands for us, Socrates—anything to say about your children, or any other matter in which we can serve you?

Nothing particular, he said: only, as I have always told you, I would have you to look to yourselves; that is a service which you may always be doing to me and mine as well as to yourselves. And you need not make professions; for if you take no thought for yourselves, and walk not according to the precepts which I have given you, not now for the first time, the warmth of your professions will be of no avail.

We will do our best, said Crito. But in what way would you have us bury you?

In any way that you like; only you must get hold of me, and take care that I do not walk away from you. Then he turned to us, and added with a smile: I cannot make Crito believe that I am the same Socrates who have been talking and conducting the argument; he fancies that I am the other Socrates whom he will soon see, a dead body—and he asks, How shall he bury me? And though I have spoken many words in the endeavor to show that when I have drunk the poison I shall leave you and go to the joys of the blessed—these words of mine, with which I comforted you and myself, have had, as I perceive, no effect upon Crito. And therefore I want you to be surety for me now, as he was surety for me at the trial: but let the promise be of another sort; for he was my surety to the judges that I would remain, but you must be my surety to him that I shall not remain, but go away and depart; and then he will suffer less at my death, and not be grieved when he sees my body being burned or buried. I would not have him sorrow at my hard lot, or say at the burial, Thus we layout Socrates, or, Thus we follow him to the grave or bury him; for false words are not only evil in themselves, but they infect the soul with evil. Be of good cheer, then, my dear Crito, and say that you are burying my body only, and do with that as is usual, and as you think best.

When he had spoken these words, he arose and went into the bath chamber with Crito, who bade us wait; and we waited, talking and thinking of the subject of discourse, and also of the greatness of our sorrow; he was like a father of whom we were being bereaved, and we were about to pass the rest of our lives as orphans. When he had taken the bath his children were brought to him—(he had two young sons and an elder one); and the women of his family also came, and he talked to them and gave them a few directions in the presence of Crito; and he then dismissed them and returned to us.

Now the hour of sunset was near, for a good deal of time had passed while he was within. When he came out, he sat down with us again after his bath, but not much was said. Soon the jailer, who was the servant of the Eleven, entered and stood by him, saying: To you, Socrates, whom I know to be the noblest and gentlest and best of all who ever came to this place, I will not impute the angry feelings of other men, who rage and swear at me when, in obedience to the authorities, I bid them drink the poison—indeed I am sure that you will not be angry with me; for others, as you are aware, and not I, are the guilty cause. And so fare you well, and try to bear lightly what must needs be; you know my errand. Then bursting into tears he turned away and went out.

Socrates looked at him and said: I return your good wishes, and will do as you bid. Then, turning to us, he said, How charming the man is: since I have been in prison he has always been coming to see me, and at times he would talk to me, and was as good as could be to me, and now see how generously he sorrows for me. But we must do as he says, Crito; let the cup be brought, if the poison is prepared: if not, let the attendant prepare some.

Yet, said Crito, the sun is still upon the hilltops, and many a one has taken the draught late, and after the announcement has been made to him, he has eaten and drunk, and indulged in sensual delights; do not hasten, then, there is still time.

Socrates said: Yes, Crito, and they of whom you speak are right in doing thus, for they think that they will gain by the delay; but I am right in not doing thus, for I do not think that I should gain anything by drinking the poison a little later; I should be sparing and saving a life which is already gone: I could only laugh at myself for this. Please then to do as I say, and not to refuse me.

Crito, when he heard this, made a sign to the servant; and the servant went in, and remained for some time, and then returned with the jailer carrying the cup of poison. Socrates said: You, my good friend, who are experienced in these matters, shall give me directions how I am to proceed. The man answered: You have only to walk about until your legs are heavy, and then to lie down, and the poison will act. At the same time he handed the cup to Socrates, who in the easiest and gentlest manner, without the least fear or change of color or feature, looking at the man with all his eyes, Echecrates, as his manner was, took the cup and said: What do you say about making a libation out of this cup to any god? May I, or not? The man answered: We only prepare, Socrates, just so much as we deem enough. I understand, he said: yet I may and must pray to the gods to prosper my journey from this to that other world—may this, then, which is my prayer, be granted to me. Then holding the cup to his lips, quite readily and cheerfully he drank off the poison. And hitherto most of us had been able to control our sorrow; but now when we saw him drinking, and saw too that he had finished the draught, we could no longer forbear, and in spite of myself my own tears were flowing fast;

so that I covered my face and wept over myself, for certainly I was not weeping over him, but at the thought of my own calamity in having lost such a companion. Nor was I the first, for Crito, when he found himself unable to restrain his tears, had got up and moved away, and I followed;

and at that moment, Apollodorus, who had been weeping all the time, broke out into a loud cry which made cowards of us all. Socrates alone retained his calmness: What is this strange outcry? he said. I sent away the women mainly in order that they might not offend in this way, for I have heard that a man should die in peace. Be quiet, then, and have patience.

When we heard that, we were ashamed, and refrained our tears; and he walked about until, as he said, his legs began to fail, and then he lay on his back, according to the directions, and the man who gave him the poison now and then looked at his feet and legs; and after a while he pressed his foot hard and asked him if he could feel; and he said, no; and then his leg, and so upwards and upwards, and showed us that he was cold and stiff. And he felt them himself, and said: When the poison reaches the heart, that will be the end. He was beginning to grow cold about the groin, when he uncovered his face, for he had covered himself up, and said (they were his last words)—he said: Crito, I owe a cock to Asclepius; will you remember to pay the debt? The debt shall be paid, said Crito; is there anything else? There was no answer to this question; but in a minute or two a movement was heard, and the attendants uncovered him; his eyes were set, and Crito closed his eyes and mouth.

Such was the end, Echecrates, of our friend, whom I may truly call the wisest, and justest, and best of all the men whom I have ever known.

# READING 4

## The Materialists

*The Materialists, while quite the opposite from the Idealists with the latters' belief in innate ideas, did not naively embrace knowledge derived from the senses as either accurate or complete. Rather, they reflect a generally skeptical view of man's capacity to apprehend truth. Still, they focused on the material world as the best way to learn what we can about reality. Their insistence that all things consist of atoms is strikingly modern. The fragments of Democritus (late 5th-early 4th cent. B.C.), a spokesman of this philosophy, are reproduced from Philip Wheelwright, ed.,* The Presocratics *(New York: The Odyssey Press, Inc" 1966), pp. 182–186.*

### Discussion Questions

1. How did the Materialists, as represented by the views of Democritus provided below, differ from modern thought concerning the nature of reality?
2. Would it be possible for a Materialist, such as Democritus, to believe in the existence of any kind of deity?

### FRAGMENTS FROM DEMOCRITUS

1. The truth is that what we meet with perceptually is nothing reliable, for it shifts its character according to the body's dispositions, influences, and confrontations.

2. By this criterion man must learn that he is divorced from reality.

3. It has been demonstrated more than once that we do not discover by direct perception what the nature of each thing is or is not.

4. My argument makes it evident that we know nothing authentically about anything, but each one's opinions are simply what flows into him [from the outside world].

7. By convention there is sweet, by convention there is bitter, by convention hot and cold, by convention color; but in reality there are only atoms and the void.

20. He who wishes to have children, it seems to me, would do better to adopt them from families with which he is on friendly terms. Thereby, being able to select, he can get the kind of child he wants. And the child whom he chooses as most suitable should be one who best follows the true bent of his nature. There is a great advantage to this procedure, whereby a man selects out of many the child whom he prefers; for if he begets a child of his own, the risks are many and he is bound to accept whatever comes.

21. It is well to realize that human life is fragile, short, and mixed with many cares and difficulties; thereby one learns to possess in moderation and to measure hardship by real need.

22. It is needful either to be good or else to imitate the good.

23. Magnanimity consists in enduring tactlessness with composure.

24. The envious man torments himself like an enemy.

25. The man who is enslaved by wealth can never be honest.

26. Virtue consists not in avoiding wrong-doing, but in being without any wish for it.

28. Immoderate desire marks the child, not the man.

29. Untimely pleasures result in displeasure.

30. Old age is scattered mutilation: it still has all its parts, but each of them is somehow lacking.

31. Some men, with no understanding of how our mortal nature dissolves [at death] but keenly aware of the ills of this life, afflict life still more with anxieties and fears by making up false tales about the time that comes after the end.

# LECTURE TOPIC 11

## The Coming of the Hellenistic World

I. The Pelopon nesian War: 431–404 B.C.: Athens vs. Sparta
  A. Thucydides (471–400 B.C.): Our Chief Source
  B. Causes of the War
    1. The Delian League
    2. Athenian Imperialism
  C. War Strategies
    1. Athenian Domination at Sea
    2. Spartan Invasion of Attica
      a) Pericles' Funeral Oration: 429 B.C.
      b) The Plague in Athens
  D. Peace and the Resumption of War
    1. The Peace of Nicias: 421 B.C.
    2. Syracusan Expedition: 415 B.C.
      a) Alcibiades
      b) Persian/Spartan Alliance
    3. The Melian Disaster
  E. The Defeat of Athens
    1. Delian League Desertions
    2. Battle of Aegospotami: 405 B.C.
    3. Athenian Surrender: 404 B.C.

II. What Was the Significance of the Peloponnesian War?
  A. Contrasting Military Styles
  B. Contrasting Political Systems
  C. Did Athens Really Lose?

III. Triumph of Greek Culture in the Hellenistic Age: 323–30 B.C.
  A. The Emergence of Philip of Macedon (r. 359–336 B.C.)
    1. Military Innovations
    2. Expansion
  B. Athenian Opposition to Philip II
    1. Isocrates (436–338 B.C.) and the Pan-Hellenic Argument
    2. Demosthenes (384–322 B.C.) and the "Phillipics"
    3. Battle of Chaeronea: 338 B.C.
  C. Alexander the Great (356–323 B.C.)
    1. His Character
    2. His Conquests
    3. The Diadochi
  D. What Were the Consequences of Alexander's Campaigns?
    1. Hellenization of the Ancient World
      a) Political Organization under the Diadochi
      b) Spread of Greek *Koinè* and Greek Art
    2. Aristotle (384–322 B.C.)

a) His Philosophy and Works
b) The Lyceum
c) University and Library at Alexandria

E. Hellenistic Philosophy: How Was It Different?
1. Philosophies of Retreat
a) Cynicism: Diogenes (412–323 B.C.)
b) Epicureanism: Epicurus (340–270 B.C.)
c) Hedonism: Aristippus (435–356 B.C.)
2. Stoicism: A Philosophy of Duty and Law
a) Zeno (335–262 B.C.)
b) The Most Popular Philosophy of Rome

F. General Attitude and Mood of the People
1. Skepticism
2. *Tyche* = Chance

IV. Conclusion
A. Rise of Rome Simultaneous With Hellenistic Period
B. Hellenistic Philosophy and Culture Will Profoundly Affect Romans

# READING 1

## The Plague in Athens

*This account from Thucydides is one of the most often cited as an example of the excellence of his historical record. This is owing not only to the dramatic nature of the subject matter but to the care and precision with which Thucydides describes it. It was one of a series of misfortunes that would tell against Athens in its great struggle with Sparta. What is quoted here is from the translation by R. Crawley, published as* The Complete Writings of Thucydides: The Peloponnesian War *(New York: Modern Library, 1934), pp. 109–114.*

---

### Discussion Questions

1. Is the despair and abandon brought by the plague in Athens, in your opinion, characteristic of people generally, regardless of religion or time period?
2. Given Thucydides' description of the symptoms of the malady that swept through Athens, can you identify the precise disease involved?

### THUCYDIDES

. . . In the first days of summer the Lacedaemonians [Spartans] and their allies, with two-thirds of their forces as before, invaded Attica, under the command of Archidamus . . . and sat down and laid waste the country. Not many days after their arrival in Attica the plague first began to show itself among the Athenians. It was said that it had broken out in many places previously in the neighbourhood of Lemnos and elsewhere; but a pestilence of such extent and mortality was nowhere remembered. Neither were the physicians at first of any service, ignorant as they were of the proper way to treat it, but they died themselves the most thickly, as they visited the sick most often; nor did nay human art succeed any better. Supplications in the temples, divinations, and so forth were found equally futile, till the overwhelming nature of the disaster at last put a stop to them altogether.

It first began, it is said, in the parts of Ethiopia above Egypt, and thence descended into Egypt and Libya nd into most of the king's country. Suddenly falling upon Athens, it first attacked the population in Piraeus,—which was the occasion of their saying that Peloponnesians had poisoned the reservoirs, there being as yet no wells there—and afterwards appeared in the upper city, when the deaths became much more frequent. All speculation as to its origin and its causes, if causes can be found adequate to produce so great a disturbance, I leave to other writers, whether lay or professional; for myself, I shall simply set down its nature, and explain the symptoms by which perhaps it may be recognized by the student, if it should ever break out again. This I can the better do, as I had the disease myself, and watched its operation in the case of others.

That year then is admitted to have been otherwise unprecedentedly free from sickness; and such few cases as occurred, all determined in this. As a rule, however, there was no ostensible cause; but people in good health were all of a sudden attacked by violent heats in the head, and redness and inflammation in the eyes, the inward parts, such as the throat or tongue, becoming bloody and emitting an unnatural and fetid breath. These symptoms were followed by sneezing and hoarseness, after which the pain soon reached the chest, and produced a hard cough. When it fixed in the stomach, it upset it; and discharges of bile of every kind named by physicians ensued, accompanied by very great distress. In most cases also an ineffectual retching followed, producing violent spasms, which in some cases ceased soon after, in others much later. Externally the body was not very hot to the touch, nor pale in its appearance, but reddish, livid, and breaking out into small pustules and ulcers. But internally it burned so that the patient could not bear to have on him clothing or linen even of the very lightest description; or indeed to be otherwise than stark naked. What they would have liked best would have been to throw themselves into cold water, as indeed was done by some of the neglected sick, who plunged into the rain-tanks in their agonies of unquenchable thirst; though it made no difference whether they drank little or much. Besides this, the miserable feeling of not being able to rest or sleep never ceased to torment them. The body meanwhile did not waste away so long as the distemper was at its height, but held out to a marvel against its ravages; so that when they succumbed, as in most cases, on the seventh or eighth day to the internal inflammation, they had still some strength in them. But if they passed this stage, and the disease descended further into the bowels, inducing a violent ulceration there accompanied by severe diarrhea, this brought on a weakness which was generally fatal. For the disorder first settled in the head, ran its course from thence through the whole of the body, and even where it did not prove mortal, it still left its mark on the extremities; for it settled in the privy parts, the fingers and the toes, and many escaped with the loss of these, some too with that of their eyes. Others again were seized with an entire loss of memory on their first recovery, and did not know either themselves or their friends . . .

Such then, if we pass over the varieties of particular cases, which were many and peculiar, were the general features of the distemper. Meanwhile the town enjoyed an immunity from all the ordinary disorders; of if any case occurred, it ended in this. Some died in neglect, others in the midst of every attention. No remedy was found that could be used as a specific; for what did good in one case, did harm in another. Strong and weak constitutions proved equally incapable of resistance, all alike being swept away, although dieted with the utmost precaution. By far the most terrible feature in the malady was the dejection which ensued when any one felt himself sickening, for the despair into which they instantly fell took away their power of resistance, and left them a much easier prey to the disorder; besides which, there was the awful spectacle of men dying like sheep, through having caught the infection in nursing each other. This cause the greatest mortality. On the one hand, if they were afraid to visit each other, they perished from neglect; indeed many houses were emptied of their inmates for want of a nurse; on the other, if they ventured to do so, death was the consequence. This was especially the case with such as made any pretensions to goodness: honour made them unsparing of themselves in their attendance in their friends' houses, where even the members of the family were at least worn out by the moans of the dying, and succumbed to the force of the disaster. Yet it was with those who had recovered from the disease that the sick and the dying found most compassion. These knew what it was from experience, and had now no fear for themselves; for the same man was never attacked twice—never at least fatally. And such persons not only received the congratulations of others, but themselves also, in the elation of the moment, half entertained the vain hope that they were for the future safe from any disease whatsoever.

An aggravation of the existing calamity was the influx from the country into the city, and this was especially felt by the new arrivals. As there were no houses to receive them, they had to be lodged at the hot season of the year in stifling cabins, where the mortality raged without restraint. The bodies of dying men lay one upon another, and half-dead creatures reeled about the streets and gathered round all the fountains in their longing for water. The sacred places also in which they had quartered themselves were full of corpses of persons that had died there, just as they were; for as the disaster passed all bounds, men, not knowing what was to become of them, became utterly careless of everything, whether sacred or profane. All the burial rites before in use were entirely upset, and they buried the bodies as best they could. Many from want of the proper appliances, through so many of their friends having died already, had recourse to the most shameless sepultures: sometimes getting the start of those who had raised a pile, they threw their own dead body upon the stranger's pyre and ignited it; sometimes they tossed the corpse which they were carrying on the top of another that was burning, and so went off.

Nor was this the only form of lawless extravagance which owed its origin to the plague. Men now coolly ventured on what they had formerly done in a corner, and not just as they pleased, seeing the rapid transitions produced by persons in prosperity suddenly dying and those who before had nothing succeeding to their property. So they resolved to spend quickly and enjoy themselves, regarding their lives and riches as alike things of a day. Perseverance in what men called honour was popular with none, it was so uncertain whether they would be spared to attain the object; but it was settled that present enjoyment, and all that contributed to it, was both honourable and useful. Fear of gods or law of man there was none to restrain them. As for the first, they judged it to be just the same whether they worshipped them or not, as they saw all alike perishing; and for the last, no one expected to live to be brought to trial for his offences, but each felt that a far severer sentence had been already passed upon them all and hung ever over their heads, and before this fell it was only reasonable to enjoy life a little.

Such was the nature of the calamity, and heavily did it weigh on the Athenians; death raging within the city and devastation without. Among other things which they remembered in their distress was, very naturally, the following verse which the old men said had long ago been uttered:

"A Dorian [Spartan] war shall come and with it death."

# READING 2

## *Alexander the Great* (356–323 B.C.)

*The military campaigns of Alexander the Great led to the spread of Greek thought and culture everywhere he conquered. More than anything, he was remembered for being invincible on the battlefield. Perhaps his most important encounter was with the Persian king Darius III, at Gaugamela. This opened the door for his advance into India. The following account comes from Plutarch. See John Dryden, trans., rev. by Arthur Hugh Clough,* Plutarch: The Lives of the Noble Grecians and Romans *(New York: Modern Library, n.d.), pp. 822–826.*

---

### Discussion Questions

1. Do you think it extraordinary that Alexander and his associates were so attentive to omens, signs and gods?
2. What can you tell from this reading about Alexander's personality and values?

### PLUTARCH'S "ALEXANDER"

But the great battle of all that was fought with Darius was not, as most writers tell us, at Arbela, but at Gaugamela, which, in their language, signifies the camel's house . . . Darius kept his men in arms, and by torchlight took a general review of them. But Alexander, while his soldiers slept, spent the night before his tent with his diviner, Aristander, performing certain mysterious ceremonies, and sacrificing to the god Fear. In the meanwhile the oldest of his commanders, and chiefly Parmenio, when they beheld all the plain between Niphates and the Gordycean mountains shining with the lights and fires which were made by the barbarians, and heard the uncertain and confused sounds of voices out of their camp, like the distant roaring of a vast ocean, were so amazed at the thoughts of such a multitude, that after some conference among themselves, they concluded it an enterprise *too* difficult and hazardous for them to engage so numerous an enemy in the day, and therefore meeting the king as he came *from* sacrificing, besought him to attack Darius by night, that the darkness might conceal the danger of the ensuing battle. To this he gave them the celebrated answer, "I will not steal a victory," which though some at the time thought a boyish and inconsiderate speech, as if he played with danger, others, however, regarded as an evidence that he confided in his present condition, and acted on a true judgment of the future, not wishing to leave Darius, in case he were worsted, the pretext of trying his fortune again, which he might suppose himself to have, if he could impute his overthrow to the disadvantage of the night, as he did before to the mountains, the narrow passages, and the sea. For while he had such numerous forces and large dominions still remaining, it was not any want of men or arms that could induce him to give up the war, but only the loss of all courage and hope upon the conviction of an undeniable and manifest defeat.

After they were gone from him with this answer, he laid himself down in his tent and slept the rest of the night more soundly than was usual with him, to the astonishment of the commanders, who came to him early in the morning, and were fain themselves to give order that the soldiers should breakfast. But at last, time not giving them leave to wait any longer, Parmenio went to his bedside, and called him twice or thrice by his name, till he waked him, and then asked him how it was possible, when he was to fight the most important battle of all, he could sleep as soundly as if he were already victorious. "And are we not so, indeed," replied Alexander, smiling, "since we are at last relieved from the trouble of wandering in pursuit of Darius through a wide and wasted country, hoping in vain that he would fight us?" And not only before the battle, but in the height of the danger, he showed himself great, and manifested the selfpossession of a just foresight and confidence. For the battle for some time fluctuated and was dubious. The left wing, where Parmenio commanded, was so impetuously charged by the Bactrian horse that it was disordered and forced to give ground, at the same time that Mazreus had sent a detachment round about to fall upon those who guarded the baggage, which so disturbed Parmenio that he sent messengers to acquaint Alexander that the camp and baggage would be all lost unless he immediately relieved the rear by a considerable reinforcement drawn out of the front. This message being brought him just as he was giving the signal to those about him for the onset, he bade them tell Parmenio that he must have surely lost the use of his reason, and had forgotten, in his alarm, that soldiers, if victorious, became masters of their enemies' baggage; and if defeated, instead of taking care of their wealth or their slaves, have nothing more to do but to fight gallantly and die with honour. When he had said this, he put on his helmet, having the rest of his arms on before he came out of his tent, which were a coat of the Sicilian make, girt close about him, and over that a breast-piece of thickly quilted linen, which was taken among other booty at the battle of Issus. The helmet, which was made by Theophilus, though of iron, was so well wrought and polished that it was as bright as the most refined silver. To this was fitted a gorget of the same metal, set with precious stones. His sword, which was the weapon he most used in fight, was given him by the King of the Citieans, and was of an admirable temper and lightness. The belt which he also wore in all engagements was of much richer workmanship than the rest of his armour. It was a work of the ancient Helicon, and had been presented to him by the Rhodians, as a mark of their respect to him. So long as he was engaged in drawing up his men, or riding about to give orders or directions, or to view them, he spared Bucephalus, who was now growing old, and made use of another horse; but when he was actually to fight, he sent for him again, and as soon as he was mounted, commenced the attack.

He made the longest address that day to the Thessalians and other Greeks, who answered him with loud shouts, desiring him to lead them on against the barbarians, upon which he shifted his javelin into his left hand, and with his right lifted up towards heaven, besought the gods, as Callisthenes tells us, that if he was of a truth the son of Jupiter, they would be pleased to assist and strengthen the Grecians. At the same time the augur Aristander, who had a white mantle about him, and a crown of gold on his head, rode by and showed them an eagle that soared just over Alexander, and directed his flight towards the enemy; which so animated the beholders, that after mutual encouragements and exhortations, the horse charged at full speed, and were followed in a mass by the whole phalanx of the foot. But before they could well come to blows with the first ranks, the barbarians shrunk back, and were hotly pursued by Alexander, who drove those that fled before him into the middle of the battle, where Darius himself was in person, whom he saw from a distance over the foremost ranks, conspicuous in the midst of his life-guard, a tall and fine-looking man, drawn in a lofty chariot, defended by an abundance of the best horse, who stood close in order about it ready to receive the enemy. But Alexander's approach was so terrible, forcing those who gave back upon those who yet maintained their ground, that he beat down and dispersed them almost all. Only a few of the bravest and valiantest opposed the pursuit, who were slain in their king's presence, falling in heaps upon one another, and in the very pangs of death striving to catch hold of the horses. Darius now seeing all was lost, that those who were placed in front to defend him were broken and beat back upon him, that he could not turn or disengage his chariot without great difficulty, the wheels being clogged and entangled among the dead bodies, which lay in such heaps as not only stopped, but almost covered the horses, and made them rear and grow so unruly that the frightened charioteer could govern them no longer, in this extremity was glad to quit his chariot and his arms, and mounting, it is said, upon a mare that had been taken from her foal, betook himself to flight. But he had not escaped so either, if Parmenio had not sent fresh messengers to Alexander, to desire him to return and assist him against a considerable body of the enemy which yet stood together, and would not give ground. For, indeed, Parmenio is on all hands accused of having been sluggish and unserviceable in this battle, whether age had impaired his courage, or that, as Callisthenes says, he secretly disliked and envied Alexander's growing greatness. Alexander, though he was not a little vexed to be so recalled and hindered from pursuing his victory, yet concealed the true reason from his men, and causing a retreat to be sounded, as if it were too late to continue the execution any longer, marched back towards the place of danger, and by the way met the news of the enemy's total overthrow and flight.

This battle being thus over, seemed to put a period to the Persian empire; and Alexander, who was now proclaimed King of Asia, returned thanks to the gods in magnificent sacrifices, and rewarded his friends and followers with great sums of money, and places, and governments of provinces. Eager to gain honour with the Grecians, he wrote to them that he would have all tyrannies abolished, that they might live free according to their own laws . . . He sent also part of the spoils into Italy, to the Crotoniats, to honour the zeal and courage of their citizen Phayllus, the wrestler, who, in the Median war, when the other Grecian colonies in Italy disowned Greece, that he might have a share in the danger, joined the fleet at Salamis, with a vessel set forth at his own charge. So affectionate was Alexander to all kind of virtue, and so desirous to preserve the memory of laudable actions.

# READING 3

## *Aristotle* (384–322 B.C.)

*One of the reasons Alexander the Great was so superbly educated was that he counted Aristotle among his tutors. If any in antiquity could rival Plato and Socrates in the breadth and influence of ideas, it was surely Aristotle. The following selection from his Ethics first sets forth his views on the importance of moderation, "the golden mean." Of even greater importance are his statements on and praise for man's contemplative inclinations. This, he suggests, gives man his extraordinary nature and capacities. It is the premise on which all humanistic philosophy is built. These passages are reprinted from* The Ancient Legacy to the Modem World, *ed. by the Interdisciplinary Studies Staff, Valencia Community College (New York: American Heritage Custom Publishing Group, 1993), pp. 129–132.*

---

### Discussion Questions

1. Can you think of exceptions to Aristotle's rule of the golden mean?
2. Do you agree with Aristotle that intelligence and contemplation are not only humankind's most distinguishing gifts but the ones that also bring greatest happiness?

### THE GOLDEN MEAN

Let's begin with the following observations: It is the nature of moral qualities that they can be destroyed by deficiency on the one hand and by excess on the other. We can see this in an example—physical health. Physical health is ruined by eating and drinking either too much or too little, while it is produced, increased, and preserved by taking the right quantity of food and drink.

Well, it is the same with temperance, courage and the other virtues. The man who shuns and fears everything and can stand up to nothing becomes a coward. The man who is afraid of nothing at all, but marches up to every danger, becomes foolhardy. In the same way, the man who indulges in every pleasure without refraining from a single one becomes incontinent. If, on the other hand, a man behaves like a prude and turns his back on every pleasure, he will find his sensibilities becoming blunted. So moral qualities are destroyed both by excess and deficiency, and they are kept alive by observance of the Mean.

. . . But, of course, difficulties spring up, especially when we are confronted with an exceptional case. For example: it is not easy to say precisely what is the right way to be angry and with whom and on what grounds and for how long. In fact, we are inconsistent on this point, sometimes praising people who lack the capacity for anger and calling them "gentle," sometimes praising the easily angered and calling them "forceful" We are not hard on the man who strays from the path a little too much or not quite enough; we reserve our censure for the man who swerves widely from the path. . .

Yet, it is not easy to find a formula by which we may determine how far and up to what point a man may go wrong before he incurs blame. But this difficulty of definition is inherent in everything we perceive; such questions of degree are bound up with the circumstances of the individual case where our only criterion is our own perception.

I hope that I have made this point clear. In all our conduct it is the Mean that is to be praised. But one must sometimes lean in the direction of the more and sometimes in that of the less in order to attain goodness and to honor the principle of the Golden Mean.

## Man's Tendency to Reflection

Since intelligence is the highest faculty within us and the objects of intelligence are the highest things we can know, contemplation is the highest form of human activity. It is also the longest-lasting activity because we can think about intellectual issues longer than we can sustain any physical activity. And since we know that pleasure is one of the ingredients of happiness, we must admit that philosophy, which is the pursuit of wisdom, has the purest and longest-lasting pleasures. We also know that wise men who possess knowledge spend their time more pleasantly than men who have not yet found knowledge. Therefore, wisdom brings the greatest happiness.

But there is another reason why the wise man is the happiest man. The exercise of intelligence provides a man with the greatest degree of independence. The wise man, as well as the just man and everyone else, must have the necessities of life. But given an adequate store of these, the just man must also have people with whom he can practice his justice; the same could be said of the brave man, the prudent man, etc. The wise man can do more. He can think independently and the wiser he is, the more independent he becomes. The mental activity of contemplation is the only activity that is praised for its own sake. Unlike other practical activities which are a means to an end, the goal of contemplation is the act of contemplation itself . . .

You should not listen to those people who say to you, "O man, think as man should," or "O mortal, remember your mortality," Rather we should, as much as possible, put on our immortality and stop at nothing in our effort to live in harmony with the highest faculty in us. Though it is small in size, yet in its value and its power, it transcends all the rest. We may in fact believe that the intelligence *is* the true self, since it is the ruler and better part of us . . .

# READING 4

## Lucretius (96?–55 B.C.)

*Identified as an Epicurian, Lucretius also was part of the Materialistic tradition of Leucippus and Democritus. As a Roman, in the first century B.C., he illustrates the widespread, continuing influence of Hellenistic thought. The following selections appear, in translation, in* The Ancient Legacy to the Modem World, *ed. by The Interdisciplinary Studies Staff, Valencia Community College (New York: American Heritage Custom Publishing Group, 1993), pp. 117–120.*

---

### Discussion Questions

1. Given Lucretius' description of reality below, do you think it likely that he believed in the Gods?
2. How close is the thought of a Materialist like Lucretius to that of modern scientists today?

## On the Nature of Things

. . . To resume my story, all nature consists of two things: matter and the space through which matter moves in different directions. The existence of matter is proved by all our senses; if we cannot agree to this we can agree on nothing. If there were no place or space which we call a vacuum these bodies could not exist or move in any way. Therefore we have proved that matter and space exist and also that there could be no other substance in the universe because if something else exists then it must be something or nothing, in which case it is either matter or space. . .

. . . for this reason, time by itself does not exist; rather, things themselves show us what has happened, what is going on, and what will follow. No one can perceive time itself apart from the movement of things or apart from immobility. . . Whatever takes place is an accident of a particular place on earth or of the space which its things occupied. It is clear that events cannot BE by themselves, in the way that matter exists or that space exists. Events must be described as accidents of matter or of the place in which things happen.

. . . Anaxagoras the Greek believed that the atoms composing matter were the same as the matter itself; that is, bones were made from tiny, tiny little bones, flesh made from minute morsels of flesh, blood the result of countless drops of blood, the earth itself a conglomeration of little earths, and so on. He says that all is formed in this way and there is no vacuum in anything and there is no limit to the splitting of matter, no morsel too small for breaking apart. This is why I think him wrong; he makes the elements too frail. Nothing can remain where all is as perishable as that matter we see vanishing under our eyes from some force for example—fire. For how can growth occur from nothing? . . .

. . . We know that food nourishes our bodies, therefore our blood and bones and sinews are composed of things unlike themselves. If we say that food is a mixture of little drops of blood and tiny bones and bits of sinew, then we admit that food is composed of substance unlike itself, namely bones and sinews, pus and blood. Also, if all that grows from the earth comes from similar material in the earth then the earth consists of matter unlike that which rises from it. If flame, smoke and ash are hidden within wood, then wood contains that which is unlike it. . . .

. . . Anaxagoras defends his view by saying that there is a mixture of everything in everything, but all ingredients are invisible except the one whose particles are most numerous and lie nearest the surface. This is not true, because if it were, then corn, crushed by the grindstone, would show some signs of blood, and all the food which nourished our body would, when crushed, show bits of bone and blood and sinew. . . Likewise, grass and water would yield sweet drops of milk as our ewes do, and when soil is crumbled, tiny plants and grain would appear, and when a twig is snapped a little fire would glow. But we know this is not so. It is therefore clear that one thing is not mixed with another this way, but there must be in things a mixture of invisible seeds that are very different from the matter itself and common to many other things.

"But it is obvious," you may say, "that the tops of the tall trees rubbed together in a gale suddenly burst into flame. Surely there is fire in the wood." What is contained in the wood is a multitude of seeds of heat which start a fire when they have been concentrated by rubbing. If there was flame in the wood it could not be concealed but would consume the forest. Now you can understand what I mean when I say that it makes a great difference in what combinations and positions the elements occur, and what motions they pass on and take over, for you see that a little reshuffling may produce both forests and fires. This is how the words themselves are formed. By a little reshuffling of letters "forests" and "fires" are two different things. . . . If you cannot conceive of matter as made up of particles very different from itself, then you must imagine atoms which hold their sides in uproarious laughter, or weep sad and salty tears, as we do.

. . . The universe is not bounded in any direction. If it were it would have a limit, but there can be no limits without something on the other side. But the universe contains all the matter and space that there is, and there is no other thing. There can be nothing outside it. Whatever spot you stand in, the universe stretches away in all directions without limit. . .

. . . If all the space in the universe were confined by definite boundaries, matter would have accumulated at the bottom because of its weight. There would be no sky or sun, since everything would have accumulated in a heap at the bottom. Since there is no bottom, the atoms cannot come to rest. Things happen continuously because of the ceaseless movement in all directions. Atoms bouncing about are from the infinite reaches of space. Dazzling lightning cannot cover the universe even in an interminable tract of time, not even in traveling as fast as it does can it even shorten the distance yet to be covered.

. . . Atoms travel straight down through space by their own weight but now and then for some unknown reason, they swerve a little from their course. If it were not for this swerve, everything would fall like raindrops through the abyss of space. No collision could take place, there would be no impact of atom on atom. Thus nature could have created nothing. . .

If you suppose that heavier atoms fall faster than light ones through empty space, then you are wrong. The reason objects falling through water or air vary in speed according to their weight is simply that water and air do not obstruct equally, but are forced to give way more quickly to heavier objects. But empty space can offer no resistance to any object: therefore through a vacuum all bodies must travel at equal speed although they are at unequal weight. The heavier will never be able to fall on the lighter from above or to generate impacts of themselves which nature can use to produce things. Thus we are forced to conclude that atoms swerve a little—but only a very little, for otherwise we will have to postulate diagonal movements, and facts will prove us wrong. We see plainly that weights when they come tumbling down have no power to move diagonally. But who can possibly say they do not diverge the tiniest bit from their vertical course?

. . . There was never more matter or less matter in the universe than there is now. Nothing is ever added or taken away from it. The movements of the atoms in space are no different today than they were in the past or ever will be in the future. Things that have come into being will continue to do so and continue to flourish according to the laws of Nature. The sum of things cannot be changed by any force. There is no place into which matter might escape out of the universe or where new matter could break into the universe. For such would transform the whole nature of things and reverse their movements.

# LECTURE TOPIC 12

## "*An Old and Sturdy Race*": *The Rise of Rome*

I. Italian Geography: The Boot of Italy
II. Those First in the Land: Etruscans, fl. 800–500 B.C.
  A. Life and Society
    1. City States
    2. Engineering and Commerce
    3. Militaristic
    4. Festive and Hedonistic: Music
    5. Religion and Language
  B. Etruscan Archeology
III. Who Were The Romans?
  A. The City of Rome
    1. Mythic Origins
      a) Paris the Trojan
      b) Romulus and Remus
    2. Expulsion of the Tarquins: 509 B.C.
  B. Early Roman Society
    1. The Family
      a) *Patria Potestas*
      b) Status of Women
      c) Slavery
    2. "Conflict of the Orders"
      a) Patricians
      b) Plebians
  C. Early Roman Government
    1. Consuls
    2. Censors
    3. Senate
IV. How Did Rome Become Master of The Ancient World?
  A. Military Conquests of the Republic
    1. Pyrrhic War: 280–275 B.C.
    2. The Three Punic Wars: 264–146 B.C.
      a) Scipio Africanus (237–183 B.C.)
      b) Hannibal (247–183 B.C.)
    3. Macedonian and Syrian Wars: 215–148 B.C.
      a) Greece Becomes a Roman Province: 146 B.C.
      b) The Mediterranean Becomes a Roman Lake
  B. The Roman Army
    1. Gravitas and Discipline

2. Illustration of MaCaulay's "Horatius"

V. Why Did the Roman Republic Decline?
   A. Diminishing Regard for Law: Gracchan Crisis: 133 B.C.
   B. Increasing Authoritarianism
      1. Marius (155–86 B.C.)
      2. Sulla (138–79 B.C.)
      3. Personal Loyalty of the Army
   C. The First Triumverate
      1. Julius Caesar (101–44 B.C.)
      2. Pompey (106–48 B.C.)
      3. Crassus (115–53B.C.)
   D. The Role of Cleopatra and Egypt
      1. Caesar vs. Pompey
      2. Death of Caesar: 44 B.C.
   E. The Second Triumverate
      1. Mark Antony (82–30 B.C.)
      2. Gaius Octavius (63 B.C.–14 A.D.)
      3. Marcus Aemilius Lepidus (d. 13 B.C.)

VI. End of the Republic:
   A. "The Roman Revolution"
   B. The Question of Parallels Between the Republic and Modern States

# READING 1

## *Marcus Cato* (234–149 B.C.)

*A contemporary of Scipio Africanus, the image of Marcus Porcius Cato has survived through the centuries as a model of Roman probity and conservatism. Plutarch's description gives us insight into Roman social life during the period of the Republic. This sketch is excerpted from the John Dryden translation, revised by Arthur Hugh Clough,* Plutarch: The Lives of the Noble Grecians and Romans *(New York: Modern Library, n.d.), pp. 414–419, 422–423, 425–426.*

---

### Discussion Questions

1. What do you think of Cato's attitudes toward slaves compared to his comments about the treatment of wives?
2. Why is Cato described as possessing "republican" virtues?

## PLUTARCH

Cato grew more and more powerful by his eloquence, so that he was commonly called the Roman Demosthenes; but his manner of life was yet more famous and talked of. For oratorical skill was, as an accomplishment, commonly studied and sought after by all young men; but he was very rare who would cultivate the old habits of bodily labour, or prefer a light supper, and a breakfast which never saw the fire, or be in love with poor clothes and a homely lodging, or could set his ambition rather on doing without luxuries than on possessing them. For now the state, unable to keep its purity by reason of its greatness, and having so many affairs, and people from all parts under its government, was fain to admit many mixed customs and new examples of living. With reason, therefore, everybody admired Cato, when they saw others sink under labours and grow effeminate by pleasures; and yet beheld him unconquered by either, and that not only when he was young and desirous of honour, but also when old and grey-headed, after a consulship and triumph; like some famous victor in the games, persevering in his exercise and maintaining his character to the very last. He himself says that he never wore a suit of clothes which cost more than a hundred drachmas; and that, when he was general and consul, he drank the same wine which his workmen did; and that the meat or fish which was bought in the meat-market for his dinner did not cost above thirty *asses.* All which was for the sake of the commonwealth, that so his body might be the hardier for the war. Having a piece of embroidered Babylonian tapestry left him, he sold it; because none of his farmhouses were so much as plastered. Nor did he ever buy a slave for above fifteen hundred drachmas; as he did not seek for effeminate and handsome ones, but able sturdy workmen, horse-keepers and cow-herds: and these he thought ought to be sold again, when they grew old, and no useless servants fed in the house. In short, he reckoned nothing a good bargain which was superfluous; but whatever it was, though sold for a farthing, he would think it a great price, if you had no need of it; and was for the purchase of lands for sowing and feeding, rather than grounds for sweeping and watering . . .

His very manner of speaking seemed to have such a kind of idea with it; for it was courteous, and yet forcible; pleasant, yet overwhelming; facetious, yet austere; sententious, and yet vehement; like Socrates, in the description of Plato, who seemed outwardly to those about him to be but a simple, talkative, blunt fellow; whilst at the bottom he was full of such gravity and matter, as would even move tears and touch the very hearts of his auditors . . .

He was also a good father, an excellent husband to his wife, and an extraordinary economist; and as he did not manage his affairs of this kind carelessly, and as things of little moment, I think I ought to record a little further whatever was commendable in him in these points. He married a wife more noble than rich; being of opinion that the rich and the high-born are equally haughty and proud; but that those of noble blood would be more ashamed of base things, and consequently more obedient to their husbands in all that was fit and right. A man who beat his wife or child laid violent hands, he said, on what was most sacred; and a good husband he reckoned worthy of more praise than a great senator; and he admired the ancient Socrates for nothing so much as for having lived a temperate and contented life with a wife who was a scold, and children who were half-witted.

# READING 2

## "This Female Madness"

*The following passage, written by the famous Roman historian Titus Livius (59 B.C.–17 A.D.), describes an uprising by Roman women against a conservative law restricting female dress and behavior during the Second Punic War. The selection is taken from* Livy, *trans. Evan T. Sage, 14 vols.(Cambridge, Mass: Harvard Univ. Press; London: William Heinemann Ltd., 1953), vol. 9, bk. XXXIV, secs. 1–2, 4, 8.*

### Discussion Questions

1. Apart from arguments advanced by Cato, can you think of any reasons to justify the Oppian law?
2. What parallels can be drawn between restrictions placed by the Oppian law on women in republican Rome and those existing in the nineteenth and early twentieth-century United States?

## LIVY

Amid the anxieties of great wars, either scarce finished or soon to come, an incident occurred, trivial to relate, but which, by reason of the passions it aroused, developed into a violent contention. Marcus Fudanius and Lucius Valerius, tribunes of the people, proposed . . . the abrogation of the Oppian law. The tribune Gaius Oppius had carried this law in the heat of the Punic War . . . that no woman should possess more than half an ounce of gold or wear a parti-coloured garment or ride in a carriage in the City or in a town within a mile thereof, except on the occasion of a religious festival . . . many distinguished men came forward to speak for and against . . . [the law]; the Capitoline was filled with crowds of supporters and opponents . . . The matrons could not be kept at home by advice or modesty or their husbands' orders, but blocked all the streets and approaches to the Forum, begging the men as they came down in the Forum that, in the prosperous condition of the state, when the private fortunes of all men were daily increasing, they should allow the women too to have their former distinctions restored. The crowd of women grew larger day by day; for they were now coming from the towns and rural districts. Soon they dared even to approach and appeal to the consuls, the praetors, and the other officials, but one consul, at least, they found adamant, Marcus Porcius Cato, who spoke thus in favour of the law whose repeal was being urged.

"If each of us, citizens, had determined to assert his rights and dignity as a husband with respect to his own spouse, we should have less trouble with the sex as a whole; as it is, our liberty, destroyed at home by female violence, even here in the Forum is crushed and trodden underfoot, and because we have not kept them individually under control, we dread them collectively. For my part, I thought it a fairy-tale and a piece of fiction that on a certain island all the men were destroyed, root and branch, by a conspiracy of women; . . . And I can scarcely decide in my own mind whether the act [to repeal the Oppian law] or the precedent it sets is worse; the act concerns us consuls and other magistrates; the example, citizens, rather concerns you. For whether the proposal which is laid before you is in the public interest or not is a question for you who are soon to cast your votes; but this female madness, whether it is spontaneous or due to your instigation . . . I do not know . . . For myself, I could not conceal my blushes a while ago, when I had to make my way to the Forum through a crowd of women. Had not respect for the dignity and modesty of some individuals among them rather than of the sex as a whole kept me silent, lest they should seem to have been rebuked by a consul, I should have said, 'What sort of practice is this, of running out into the streets and blocking the roads and speaking to other women's husbands? Could you not have made the same requests, each of your own husband, at home? Or are you more attractive outside and to other women's husbands? Than to your own? And yet, not even at home, if modesty would keep matrons within the limits of their proper rights, did it become you to concern yourselves with the question of what laws should be adopted in this place or repealed.' Our ancestors permitted no woman to conduct even personal business without a guardian to intervene in her behalf; they wished them to be under the control of fathers, brothers, husbands; we (Heaven help us!) allow them now even to interfere in public affairs, yes, and to visit the Forum and our informal and formal sessions. What else are they doing now on the streets and at the corners except urging the bill of the tribunes and voting for the repeal of the law? Give loose rein to their uncontrollable nature and to this untamed creature and expect that they will themselves set bounds to their licence; unless you act, this is the least of the things enjoined upon women by custom or law and to which they submit with a feeling of injustice. It is complete liberty or, rather, if we wish to speak the truth, complete licence that they desire . . .

"You have often heard me complaining of the extravagance of the women and often of the men, both private citizens and magistrates even, and lamenting that the state is suffering from those two opposing evils, avarice and luxury, which have been the destruction of every great empire. The better and the happier becomes the fortune of our commonwealth day by day and the greater the empire grows—and already we have crossed into Greece and Asia, places filled with all the allurements of vice, and we are handling the treasures of kings—the more I fear that these things will capture us rather than we them. Tokens of danger, believe me, were those statues which were brought to this city from Syracuse. Altogether too many people do I hear praising the baubles of Corinth and Athens and laughing at . . . our Roman gods . . . "

When . . . [all]speeches against and for the bill had been delivered, the next day an even greater crowd of women appeared in public, and all of them in a body beset the doors of . . . [those opposing repeal of the law], and they did not desist until the threat . . . was withdrawn by the tribunes . . . After that there was no question that . . . [everyone] would vote to repeal the law. The law was repealed twenty years after it was passed.

# READING 3

## The Murder of Tiberius Gracchus

*After the final defeat of Carthage in 146 B.C. the stress of class warfare in Rome between landless farmers and the aristocracy increased. When Tiberius Gracchus, as Tribune, sponsored a law limiting landholdings, a conspiracy of wealthy landowners followed. Before the law could be implemented, Tiberius' term as tribune expired. In violation of rules prohibiting a second term, Tiberius stood for reelection, thus giving the aristocrats an excuse for violence. During the ensuing election riots, opponents of the land reform assassinated Tiberius and slaughtered many of his followers. The so-called Gracchan Crisis in 133 B.C. constitutes the beginning of the decline of the Roman Republic because it set a dangerous precedent for disregard of the law. The following account of the murder of Tiberius Gracchus is excerpted from the John Dryden translation, revised by Arthus Hugh Clough,* Plutarch: The Lives of the Noble Grecians and Romans *(New York: Modern Library, n.d.), pp. 1004–1006.*

---

### Discussion Questions

1. Do you believe it was right to assassinate Tiberius Gracchus inasmuch as he had broken the law by continuing in the office of Consul beyond what was prescribed by law?
2. Do you find it curious that Romans were, at this late date, yet observant of the behavior of birds as communicating warnings to men?

### PLUTARCH

Tiberius then went down into the market-place amongst the people, and made his addresses to them humbly and with tears in his eyes; and told them he had just reason to suspect that his adversaries would attempt in the night-time to break open his house and murder him. This worked so strongly with the multitude, that several of them pitched tents round about his house, and kept guard all night for the security of his person. . . . [The next day] he went towards the capitol as soon as he understood that the people were assembled there; . . . He was not gone very far before he saw two ravens fighting on the top of a house which stood on his left hand as he passed along; and though he was surrounded with a number of people, a stone struck from its place by one of the ravens, fell just at his foot. This even the boldest men about him felt as a check. But Blossius of Cuma, who was present, told him that it would be a shame and an ignominious thing for Tiberius, who was a son of Gracchus, the grandson of Scipio Africanus, and the protector of the Roman people to refuse, for fear of a silly bird, to answer when his countrymen called to him; . . . At the same time several messengers came also from his friends, to desire his presence at the capitol, saying that all things went there according to expectation. And indeed Tiberius's first entrance there was in every way successful; as soon as ever he appeared, the people welcomed him with loud acclamations, and as he went up to his place, they repeated their expressions of joy, and gathered in a body around him, so that no one who was not well known to be his friend might approach. . . .

Whilst things were in this confusion, Flavius Flaccus, a senator, standing in a place where he could be seen, but at such a distance from Tiberius that he could not make him hear, signified to him by motions of his hand, that he wished to impart something of consequence to him in private. Tiberius ordered the multitude to make way for him, by which means, though not without some difficulty, Flavius got to him, and informed him that the rich men, in a sitting of the senate, seeing they could not prevail upon the consul to espouse their quarrel, had come to a final determination amongst themselves that he should be assassinated, and to that purpose had a great number of their friends and servants ready armed to accomplish it. Tiberius no sooner communicated this confederacy to those about him, but they immediately tucked up their gowns, broke the halberts which the officers used to keep the crowd off into pieces, and distributed them among themselves, resolving to resist the attack with these. Those who stood at a distance wondered, and asked what was the occasion; Tiberius, knowing that they could not hear him at that distance, lifted his hand to his head wishing to intimate the great danger which he apprehended himself to be in. His adversaries, taking notice of that action, ran off at once to the senate-house, and declared that Tiberius desired the people to bestow a crown upon him, as if this were the meaning of his touching his head. This news created general confusion in the senators, and Nasica at once called upon the consul to punish this tyrant, and defend the government. The consul mildly replied, that he would not be the first to do any violence; and as he would not suffer any freeman to be put to death, before sentence had lawfully passed upon him, so neither would he allow any measure to be carried into effect, if by persuasion or compulsion on the part of Tiberius the people had been induced to pass an unlawful vote. But Nasica, rising from his seat, "Since the consul," said he, "regards not the safety of the commonwealth, let every one who will defend the laws, follow me." He then, casting the skirt of his gown over his head, hastened to the capitol; those who bore him company, wrapped their gowns also about their arms, and forced their way after him. And as they were persons of the greatest authority in the city, the common people did not venture to obstruct their passing, but were rather so eager to clear the way for them, that they tumbled over one another in haste.

The attendants they brought with them had furnished themselves with clubs and staves from their houses, and they themselves picked up the feet and other fragments of stools and chairs, which were broken by the hasty flight of the common people. Thus armed, they made towards Tiberius, knocking down those whom they found in front of him, and those were soon wholly dispersed and many of them slain. Tiberius tried to save himself by flight. As he was running, he was stopped by one who caught hold of him by the gown; but he threw it off, and fled in his under-garment only. And stumbling over those who before had been knocked down, as he was endeavouring to get up again, Publius Satureius, a tribune, one of his colleagues, was observed to give him the first fatal stroke, by hitting him upon the head with the foot of a stool. The second blow was claimed, as though it had been a deed to be proud of, by Lucius Rufus. And of the rest there fell above three hundred killed by clubs and staves only, none by an iron weapon.

This, we are told, was the first sedition amongst the Romans, since the abrogation of kingly government, that ended in the effusion of blood. All former quarrels which were neither small nor about trivial matters, were always amicably composed, by mutual concessions on either side, the senate yielding for fear of the commons, and the commons out of respect to the senate. And it is probable indeed that Tiberius himself might then have been easily induced, by mere persuasion, to give way, and certainly, if attacked at all, must have yielded without any recourse to violence and bloodshed, as he had not at that time above three thousand men to support him. But it is evident, that this conspiracy was fomented against him, more out of the hatred and malice which the rich men had to his person, than for the reasons which they commonly pretended against him. In testimony of which we may adduce the cruelty and unnatural insults which they used to his dead body. For they would not suffer his own brother, though he earnestly begged the favour, to bury him in the night, but threw him, together with the other corpses, into the river.

# LECTURE TOPIC 13

## The Roman Empire

I. Early Experience with Dictatorship
   A. Gaius Julius Caesar Octavianus
   B. Augustus (Emperor 29 B.C.–14 A.D.)
      1. Enlargement of the Senate
      2. "Puritanical" Reforms
      3. Support for Culture
      4. Colonization of the Poor
      5. Praetorian Guard: Consequences
II. Selected Emperors, Bad and Good
   A. Nero (r. 54–68 A.D.)
      1. Tutored by Seneca (54 B.C.–39 A.D.)
      2. Profligate Activities
      3. Paranoia and Suicide
   B. Vespasian (r. 69–79 A.D.)
      1. Restored Order and Solvency
      2. Constructed the Coliseum
   C. Who Were the "Five Good Emperors"?
      1. Nerva (r. 96–98 A.D.)
      2. Trajan (r. 98–117 A.D.)
      3. Hadrian (r. 117–138 A.D.)
      4. Antoninus Pius (r. 138–161 A.D.)
      5. Marcus Aurelius (r. 161–180 A.D.)
   D. Collapse under the Severids: 193–284 A.D.
III. How Did the Empire Recover?
   A. Diocletian (r. 284–305 A.D.)
      1. Increased Authoritarianism
         a) Control of the Economy
         b) Severity of the Criminal Law
      2. Division of the Empire
   B. Constantine (r. 306–337 A.D.)
      1. Moved Capital to Byzantium
      2. Renamed City Constantinople
      3. Edict of Milan: 313 A.D.
         a) Toleration of Christianity
         b) Christians No Longer Persecuted
      4. The Council of Nicea: 325 A.D.
         a) Theological Debate
         b) Defined Nature of God
IV. The Empire In Old Age
   A. Military Failures and the Triumph of Christianity
      1. Battle of Adrianople: 378 A.D.

2. Theodosius I (r. 379–395 A.D.)
    a) Christianity Made Official Religion of Empire
    b) Christians Begin Persecution of Other Religions
3. Rome Sacked by Visigoths: 410 A.D.
4. Rome Sacked Again by Vandals: 455 A.D.

B. Italy and Rome Governed by Germanic Rulers after 476 A.D.

V. A Roman Imperial Revival
  A. An Indian Summer under Justinian (r. 527–565 A.D.)
  B. Codification of Roman Law
  C. Role of Empress Theodora

VI. Why Did Rome "Fall"?
  A. Edward Gibbon's *Decline and Fall of the Roman Empire* (1776)
    1. Christians Weakened Rome from Within
    2. Barbarians Broke It from Without
  B. Other Theories
    1. The Loss of *Gravitas*
    2. Decline of the Patrician Class
  C. The Debate Continues

# READING 1

## *Imperial Instability After Nero*

*A major difficulty afflicting dictatorships, in every time and society, is that of managing transitions of power. After Nero's suicide, the violence and upheaval that befell Roman society was repeated over and again. Tacitus (55?–117 AD.), critical of the decline of old Roman virtues, describes the uncertainties that followed Nero's death. This excerpt appears in his* Histories, *published as The Works of Tacitus, Oxford revised translation (London: George Bell and Sons, 1889), Vol. II: pp. 2–5.*

---

### Discussion Questions

1. What was the "secret empire" Tacitus referred to when discussing the Praetorian Guard?
2. Do you think civilizations have life cycles comparable to those of living organisms, such as youth, adolescence and old age?

## THE HISTORIES

*Cornelius Tacitus*

2. The period now before me is fertile in vicissitudes, pregnant with sanguinary encounters, embroiled with intestine dissensions, and, even in the intervals of peace, deformed with horrors: four princes put to death; three civil wars; with foreign enemies more; and, in some conjunctures, both at once: prosperity in the East, disasters in the West; Illyricum convulsed; both the Gauls on the eve of revolt; Britain conquered, and, in the moment of conquest, lost again; the Sarmatians and the Suevians rising up at once against us; the Oacians renowned for defeats given and sustained; and even the Parthians well nigh induced to take up arms by the trick of a pretended Nero. Italy afflicted moreover with calamities, unheard of, or occurring again after a long series of ages; cities overwhelmed or swallowed up by earthquakes in the fertile country of Campania; Rome laid waste by fire; her most ancient temples destroyed; the Capitol itself wrapped in flames by the hands of citizens; the ceremonies of religion violated; enormous adulteries; the sea crowded with exiles; rocks stained with blood of murdered citizens; Rome itself a theatre of still greater horrors: there nobility and wealth, dignities borne and declined, were alike treated as crimes: there virtue was a source of certain ruin; the guilty acts of informers, and their wages, were alike detestable; for some of them having obtained priesthoods and consulates, which they regarded as spoils; others, imperial procuratorships, and posts of greater influence with the prince, they carried rapine and plunder in every direction, impelled by personal hate, and armed with terror. Slaves were practised upon against their masters; freedmen betrayed their patrons; and he who had no enemy, died by the treachery of friends.

3. And yet this period, barren as it was of virtue, produced some honourable examples. Mothers went with their sons into voluntary exile; wives followed their husbands in banishment; relations stood boldly forth in the cause of their kindred; sons-in-law shrunk not; slaves, even on the rack, scorned to renounce their fidelity; eminent citizens, doomed to die, bore their lot with fortitude, and their deaths were nothing inferior to those of the applauded characters of antiquity. In addition to the misfortunes incident to humanity, the earth and skies teemed with prodigies, terrific warnings by thunder and lightning, and prognostics, auspi-

cious or disastrous, ambiguous or plain. Indeed never was it established by more terrible calamities on the Roman people, or by more decisive indications, that the gods are not concerned about the protection of the innocent, but the punishment of the guilty.

4. Before, however, I proceed in the execution of my plan, it will be proper, I think, to inquire what was the date of affairs at Rome, what the feeling in her armies: how the provinces stood affected, wherein consisted the strength or weakness of the empire, that we may not only have a recital of events, and the issues of things which are often ascribable to change, but may learn the plans pursued, and the causes of events. As the death of Nero, in the first burst of joy, was hailed with exultation, so the senate, the people of Rome, the prretorian guards, and the legions, wherever stationed, were variously affected by that event. A secret of empire was then let out, namely, that elsewhere than at Rome an emperor might be created. The fathers were highly pleased, as they were at once restored to their legislative independence, which they exercised freely, considering that the prince was new to his office, and absent. The principal Roman knights were next to them the most justified. Honest men among the peoples such as were connected with families of credit; and the clients and freedmen of condemned and exiled men, were animated with hope. The inferior populace, who loitered in the theatre and circus; the slaves of abandoned character, and those who, having wasted their substance, were supported by the vices of Nero, were plunged in grief, and eager to learn the floating rumour.

# READING 2

## Free Public Entertainment

*The problem of keeping large city crowds happy grew larger during the period of the empire than in the late republic. The following description of entertainments provided by one of the Flavian emperors ( 69–96 A.D.) is especially notable inasmuch as they are generally thought to have been less extravagant than either their predecessors or successors. The following description provided by Gaius Suetonius Tranquillus (69–122 A.D.) is taken from Dana Carleton Munro,* A Source Book of Roman History *(Boston: D.C. Heath & Co., 1904), 212–13.*

---

### Discussion Questions

1. Do you find it contradictory that the Romans were entertained by elocution and musical concerts as well as bloody duels between male and female gladiators? Do we have anything comparable in modern society?
2. Is the modern American practice of welfare payments to the poor by our government comparable to entertainments provided by Roman emperors?

## GAIUS SUETONIUS TRANQUILLUS

He frequently entertained the people with most magnificent and costly shows, both in the amphitheatre, and in the circus; where, besides the usual races with chariots drawn by two or four horses abreast, he exhibited the representation of an engagement between both horse and foot, and a sea-fight in the amphitheatre. The people were also entertained with the chase of wild beasts and the combat of gladiators, even in the night-time, by torch-light. Nor did men only fight in these spectacles, but women also. He constantly attended at the games given by the quaestors, which had been disused for some time, but were revived by him; and upon these occasions always gave the people the liberty of demanding two pair of gladiators out of his own school, who appeared last in court uniforms . . . He instituted, in honor of [the god] Jupiter Capitolinus, a solemn contest in music to be performed every five years; besides horse-racing and gymnastic exercises, with more prizes than are at present allowed. There was also a public performance in elocution, both Greek and Latin; and besides the musicians who sung to the harp, there were others who played concerted pieces or solos, without vocal accompaniment. Young girls also ran races in the Stadium, at which he presided in his sandals, dressed in a purple robe, made after the Grecian fashion, and wearing upon his head a golden crown bearing the effigies of Jupiter, Juno, and Minerva . . . He thrice bestowed upon the people a largess of three hundred sesterces for each man; and, at a public show of gladiators, a very plentiful feast. At the festival of the Seven Hills he distributed large hampers of provisions to the senatorial and equestrian orders, and small baskets to the common people, and encouraged them to eat by setting them the example. The day after, he scattered among the people a variety of cakes and other delicacies to be scrambled for; and on the greater part of them falling amidst the seats of the crowd, he ordered five hundred tickets to be thrown into each range of benches belonging to the senatorial and equestrian orders.

# READING 3

## Stoic Philosophy in Rome

*Despite its difficulties, the Roman Empire also had glories and heroes. In the area of philosophy, Stoicism seemed especially suited to the Roman temper and to Roman administrative needs. Seneca (4 B.C–65 AD.), a Spaniard, was a tutor of the emperor Nero who, in an act of heinous ingratitude, ordered his old teacher to take his life. Two brief examples of Seneca's teachings are provided here.*

*Epictetus (1st Cent. AD.) was a Greek slave and Stoic philosopher as well. His teachings are known to us chiefly from his student Flavius Arrian. Notice how similar his admonitions are to those of Buddhism. He was banished from Rome by the Emperor Domitian.*

*Marcus Aurelius (121–180 AD.), whom some consider history's single example of a philosopher prince, was also a Stoic. In his Meditations he described Stoicism in the course of acknowledging what he had received from others. All these excerpts are taken from* The Ancient Legacy to the Modem World, *ed. by The Interdisciplinary Studies Staff, Valencia Community College (New York: American Heritage Custom Publishing Group, 1993), pp. 77–86.*

---

### Discussion Questions

1. Does Seneca persuade you that suicide and euthanasia can be honorable?
2. In the selection "On Providence", how does Seneca's advice differ from the Christian work ethic?
3. Do you think Epictetus and his views are noble? Or, do you see them as excessively puritan?
4. In the essay by Marcus Aurelius, what can be described as specifically "Stoic"?

## ON SUICIDE

*Seneca*

After a long span of time, Lucilius, I have seen your beloved Pompeii and it brought back memories of my youthful days. It seemed that all of the things which I did as a young man were such a short time ago. We have sailed past life as if we were on a voyage, and, like putting to sea, I am reminded of the poet Virgil who says, "Lands and towns are left astern." In the journey of life, time flies with the greatest of speed. From boyhood and youth to young manhood, we proceed to middle age and, finally, to the best years of old age itself. It is only here that we begin to sight that terminal point of the race of man. Most men see this point as a dangerous reef but it is really the harbour which we cannot refuse to enter. Some men reach the harbour quickly and early in life while for others the voyage is fretful and filled with all sorts of harassment. But though they still cling to the voyage, they are all bound to reach the harbour.

One should not always cling to the life of harassment, for it is living well that is good, not merely living. The wise man will live as long as he ought, not as long as he can and he will select what place, with whom, and how to live his life. He always reflects on the quality and not the quantity of his life. When many events in life give him trouble and disturb his peace of mind, he sets himself free. This privilege is his. It makes no difference if his passing is natural or self-inflicted or whether it comes later or earlier. He does not regard it with fear or as a great loss, for there is little to lose when only a drop remains. It is not a question of dying earlier or later but of dying well or ill, and dying well means escape from the danger of living ill.

There was a well-known man whose words I regard as most unvirtuous. He was thrown into a cage by a tyrant and fed like some wild animal. When he was advised to end his life by fasting, he replied, "A man may hope for anything while he has life." Though this be true, life is not to be purchased at any priceespecially if the price is a shameful confession of weakness...

When a power beyond our control threatens us with death, should we anticipate death or await it? There are arguments for either side and if one death is accompanied by torture and the other is simple and easy, why not take the latter? Just as I select my ship for a voyage, so I shall choose my death when I am about to part from this life. A long-drawn-out life does not necessarily mean a better one, but a long-drawn-out death necessarily means a worse one. There is no occasion upon which the soul should be honored more than at the moment of death. Every man should strive to make his life acceptable to others besides himself, but his death is to himself alone. The best form of death is the one you like, and it is foolish to reflect on what others might say about your action.

There are those who profess wisdom who maintain that no one should end their own life and that one should wait for nature's decree. However, the finest thing which the eternal law ever ordained is that we are allowed only one entrance into life, but many exits. This is one reason why we cannot complain. Life keeps no one against his will and no man is unhappy except through his own choice. Live, if you desire, and if not, return to the place from which you came...

Do not think that it is only the great man who has the courage to break the bond of human servitude. Many men, some of them of the meanest lot in life, by an act of sheer will, have snatched up objects which are seemingly harmless and used them as weapons to end their life. There was a German gladiator making preparations for the morning exhibitions who was excused to relieve himself (the only thing which was allowed to do without the presence of a guard). He took this opportunity to take a stick of wood tipped with a sponge, which was devoted to the vilest uses, and stuffed it down his throat and choked the breath from his body. It was not an elegant way to die. But what is more foolish than to be over-nice about dying? What a brave fellow! He deserved to be allowed to choose his fate. However, cut off from all resources, he found a weapon suitable to end his life. I think that you will see that nothing but the will need postpone death, and the foulest death is preferable to the cleanest slavery...

If such a spirit is possessed by slaves and gladiators, cannot this same spirit be possessed by those who have trained themselves through reason? Reason teaches us that fate has many approaches but the same end. Reason advises us to die according to our own taste and, if this is not possible, to die according to our ability. Farewell.

## On Providence

*Seneca*

"Why does so much bad luck come to good men?" It is impossible for any evil to happen to a good man. Opposites do not combine. Just as the influx of many streams and mineral springs do not change the saltiness of the sea or dilute it, just so the assaults of adversity do not affect the spirit of a righteous man. He maintains his poise and takes into his being all the things that happen to him, for he is more powerful than the external world.

I do not mean that he is insensitive to external things, but that he has conquered them; calm and composed, he rises to meet every attack. He considers all bad fortune as a test.... What energetic man does not consider idleness a punishment? For example, take the case of boxers. They use the strongest possible sparring partners.... They submit to battering and bruises. Without a strong opponent, their strength shrivels away.... This same behavior is required of good men. They should not shun hardship and difficulty or complain about their fate; whatever happens they should take it and turn it to their advantage. The thing that matters is not what you bear, but how you bear it . . .

God's attitude toward man is a fatherly one. . . "Let them be afflicted by toil, sorrow and loss," he says, "so that they may acquire true strength." Bodies grow fat through inactivity and are weak; they are exhausted not only by work but by their own weight. A charmed life that has never known adversity cannot endure a single blow, but a man who has been at constant war with adversity develops a thick skin from his suffering; he does not give in to evil, and even when he's down, he fights on his knees.

Do not, I beg you, be afraid of the tests that the gods apply to our souls. Avoid luxury, avoid the weakening effects of prosperity, which cause men's minds to become soggy and, unless something intervenes to remind them of their human condition, remain comatose-in perpetual drunkenness. All excesses are harmful, but unlimited prosperity is the most dangerous of all. It affects the mind, it conjures up empty fantasies, and it obscures the distinction between right and wrong.

In the case of good men, the gods adopt the same plan that teachers use with their pupils. They demand the greatest effort from those in whom they have the most confidence. . . . Why are we amazed, then, if the gods test noble spirits with sternness? The test of courage is never gentle. Fortune whips and tears at us; we must endure it. It is not cruelty, but a contest; and the more often we take part in it, the stronger we become.

What is the duty of a good man? To offer himself to fate. . . His way will not be even; it will have its ups and downs. He will be storm-tossed and must steer his ship through troubled waters, but he must hold his course. . . Much that is harsh and rough will test him, but he will soften and smooth it. The purity of gold is tested by heating it, brave men are tested by misfortune . . .

## On Stoic Behavior

*Epictetus*

Remember, you ought to live your life as if it is a banquet. If a dish is offered to you, extend your hand and take a modest portion. What if the server skips you? Don't stop him. What if the dish hasn't yet gotten to you? Don't send your desire out to meet it—wait until it comes to you. Act the same way with your children, your wife, your official duties and your wealth, and you will be a worthy guest at the banquet of the gods. But if you do not take any of the dishes that are set before you, and you even refuse to want them, you will not only be a guest of the gods, but will also share their power.

Whoever wishes to be free, neither wishes for things nor makes himself dependent on others.

Remember, you are an actor in a play, the nature of which the author is chosen. If it's a short play, then a short part. If it's a long play, then a long part. If he wishes you to act the part of a poor man, see that you act that part naturally; if the part is for a lame man, or a judge, or a private citizen, do likewise. This is your duty—to act well the part that is given to you. The selection of the part belongs to someone else.

Don't make a habit of frequenting the theater, but if there is ever a proper occasion for going, do not favor any actor except yourself. In other words, desire only that what will be done will be done, and that the actor who wins the prize wins it. Refrain from shouting or laughing at anything or anybody. Show no violent emotions. After you leave, don't talk much about what happened on stage unless it will help you improve yourself. It is obvious that if you talk a lot about it, people will think you liked it.

Remember, it is not the person who hates you or strikes you who hurts you, but it is your idea about these people which hurts you. When a person irritates you, know that it is your own idea about him that irritates you. Therefore, try not to be carried away by the appearance of things. If you can stop and think, you will easily master yourself.

Let silence be your general rule. Say only what is necessary in the fewest possible words. When the occasion commands, you might say something, but not about common subjects, not about gladiators, or horse races, or athletes, or eating or drinking—the usual subjects—and especially not about other people, either praising, blaming them or comparing them. If you can, direct your conversation and that of your friends to proper topics; but if you are among strangers, be silent.

Avoid banquets given by strangers and ignorant people. But if you must dine with them, watch yourself carefully and don't slip into vulgar mannerisms. Certainly you know that a man becomes like the company he keeps.

Take only the barest necessities of life: food, drink, clothing, housing, and slaves; exclude all show and luxury.

As for sexual intercourse, abstain as much as you can before you are married. If you do indulge, do it in a way which conforms to custom. Do not make an issue of it with those who do. Do not chastise them, and do not boast about your abstinence.

Among friends, be careful not to talk too much about your own deeds or difficulties you have encountered; because, while it is pleasant to talk about your problems, it is not pleasant to listen to other people's. Also, be careful not to make people laugh; because this is an easy way to slip into vulgar manners, and you will lose respect among your neighbors. It is also dangerous to use obscene language. Whenever this happens, if the opportunity arises, scold the man who has spoken thus, or—if the opportunity does not arise—show by your silence, your blushing and your expression, that you are clearly offended by such talk.

If you want to be a philosopher, be prepared to be ridiculed from the start. Many will laugh at you and say, "All at once, he has become a philosopher. Now he thinks he is better than we are." Do not be self-righteous, but keep in mind what you think is right and what is sent by God to be your lot in life. And remember, if you are true to your principles, the same men who first ridiculed you will later admire you. But if you give in to them, you will bring on yourself double the ridicule.

## On Stoicism and His Debts to Others

### *Marcus Aurelius*

*From the gods:* [I am thankful]to have had good grandparents, good parents, a good sister, good teachers, a good household, good relations and friends, and almost everything; that I did not happen to give offense to anyone of them although I had a disposition that might have led me to do so, and I owe it to the beneficence of the gods that no combination of circumstances was to test me in this respect; . . . that I preserved my adolescence and did not become a man before the proper time but even took a little longer; that I was subjected to the rule of a father who rid me of vanity and made me realize that it was possible to live in a palace without feeling the need of bodyguards or striking clothes or chandeliers or statues or other such vanities, but to live very nearly like private citizen without abasing oneself or neglecting the duties of leadership for the common good.

That I had a brother whose moral character taught me to care for my own, and whose affection and respect brought me joy; . . . that I had a clear picture in mind of what it means to live in accord with nature, so that, insofar as it lay with the gods, nothing stops me from living in accord with nature, and if I still fall short of this it is through my own fault, and because I have not paid attention to the reminders and the teachings of the gods; that my health has been adequate for my kind of life; that I had no sexual relations with Benedicta or Theodotus, and that even later when erotic passion came to me, I retained my health; . . . that, although my mother was fated to die young, she lived her last years with me; that whenever I wished to help someone in poverty or need, I was never told that I did not have the means to do so, and that I myself never fell into similar need and had to accept help from another; that my wife was obedient, affectionate and artless; . . . that I was granted help through dreams, especially on how to avoid spitting blood or feeling dizzy, and by the oracle at Caieta: "as you will treat yourself"; that, though I longed for philosophy, I did not fall in with any Sophist or withdraw from active life to analyze literary compositions or syllogisms, or busy myself with questions of natural science, for all these things need the help of the gods and of Fortune . . .

.Acquire the contemplative view of how all things change into one another. Constantly apply and train your thoughts to this aspect of the universe. The man who accomplishes this has put off the restraints of the body and realizes that he will soon leave the company of men and all things behind. He then devotes himself to the righteousness of his own actions in accordance with *Nature.* When dealing with external events, he never thinks of what others might say about him or do against him. He contents himself with only two things: to act justly in what he does and to be satisfied with what has been assigned to him by *Nature.* He desires to accomplish the straight course according to law and by accomplishing this course to follow the god. . .

To *Nature* who gives all things and takes them away, the truly educated and reverent man says: "Give what you wish; take away what you wish," and he says this not in a spirit of recklessness but of obedience and good will toward her.

Do not discuss in general terms the question of what is a good man. Be one.

# READING 4

## Devastation By the Barbarians

*The destruction of classical civilization by barbarians in the fifth and sixth centuries A.D. was startling. The great church father Jerome (340–420 A.D.), though in Palestine at the time of the events about which he writes, leaves us with a good sense of the disillusionment brought by invasion, displacement and pillage. The passage provided here was translated by James H. Hanscom from Jerome's "Epistolae," and is found in James Hanscom, Leon Hellerman, and Ronald Posner, eds.* Voices of the Past: Readings in Ancient History *(New York: The Macmillan Co; and London: Collier-Macmillan, Ltd.,1967), 172–73.*

---

### Discussion Questions

1. Is there anything in modern times of which you are aware that compares with losses brought by the barbarian invasions of ancient Rome?
2. Was this an unpreventable event? What could Rome have done to avoid the disaster?

### HIERONYMUS EUSEBIUS JEROME

---

[When I was told of the sack of Rome,] my voice failed, and I could not speak through weeping. The city that once conquered the whole world is herself a prisoner. What can I say? She died from hunger before perishing by the sword . . .

[I am told that] that famous city, head of the Roman Empire, is laid waste by fire. There is no spot that is not receiving fugitives from Rome. Today I tried to set to work to study the prophet Ezekiel, but at the very moment when I began to dictate I felt such pain in thinking of the catastrophe in the West that the words failed me. I could only be silent, thinking that this indeed is a time for weeping.

* * *

Countless nations of the most savage kind have invaded all Gaul. The whole region between Switzerland and Spain, the Rhine River and the Ocean, has been devastated by the Quadi, the Vandals, the Sarmatians, the Alani, the Heruli, the Saxons, the Burgundians, the Alemanni, and the Pannonians. O unfortunate empire! Mainz, which was once so noble a city, has been captured and devastated, and even in the churches thousands have been slaughtered. Worms has been destroyed after a long siege. Rheims, that mighty city, Amiens, Arras, Speyer, Strasbourg—all have seen their citizens led as captives into Germany. In Aquitaine, Lyons, and Narbonne, all but a few towns have been depopulated, and the remaining ones are threatened by the sword on the outside while famine rages within.

. . . Spain is in daily terror lest it perish, because it remembers the invasion of the Cimbri . . . I will keep silent about the rest, lest I seem to despair of the mercy of God. It has been a long time now that from the Black Sea to the Julian Alps our property has not been our own; and for thirty years, since the Danube boundary was broken through, war has been waged in the very heart of the Roman Empire . . . Except for a few old men, everyone in that region has been born in captivity and war; they do not desire liberty, because they have never known it . . .

# LECTURE TOPIC 14

## Christianity: The Rise of a New World Religion

I. Who was Jesus?
   A. His Historicity
   B. Teachings
      1. Judaic Influences: An Essene?
      2. Emphasis on Love
II. What Contributed to the Extraordinary Growth of Christianity?
   A. Reasons:
      1. Socio-Political Milieu: Instability
      2. Egalitarian Appeal
      3. Theological Simplicity
      4. Vigor of Early Missionaries: St. Paul (d. 67 AD.)
III. Why were the Christians Persecuted?
   A. Reasons
      1. Misunderstanding of Christian Ritual
      2. Charge of Christian Atheism
      3. Civil Disobedience
      4. Millennialism/Intolerance
      5. Christians as Scapegoats
IV. Medieval Foundations
   A. Augustine (354–430 AD.): Civitas Dei
   B. Jerome (340–420 AD.): the Bible
   C. Benedict (480–543 AD.): Monasticism/Monte Cassino
      1. Poverty; chastity; obedience
V. What Impact did Christianity have on Europe and the World?
   A. The Christian Community: A New Roman Empire
   B. Withdrawal and the Middle Ages

# READING 1

## The Teachings of Jesus

*That Christianity was an outgrowth of Judaism has never been disputed. But Jesus took parts of Jewish thought and fashioned them into an entirely new religious tradition. He gave particular emphasis to love, charity and forgiveness.*

*The following two selections are from the Bible. The first, from the book of Matthew, reports Jesus' famous Sermon on the Mount, some of the miracles he performed, and his interaction with the people. The second reading is from the book of Acts, telling of missionary work by St. Paul in Athens and elsewhere.*

---

### Discussion Questions

1. According to the teachings of Jesus, what behavior would God deem righteous? Do you think his teachings set an easier path to follow than the old Judaic traditions?
2. How does the God portrayed by Jesus differ from the God portrayed in the Old Testament? (See excerpts from Ancient Israel)
3. Consider the second reading from the book of Acts. What Hellenistic philosophies did St. Paul encounter in Greece? How was St. Paul received in general and why?

## The Book of Matthew: Sermon On the Mount and Other Activities By Jesus

5Seeing the crowds, he (Jesus) went up on the mountain, and when he sat down his disciples came to him. [2]And he opened his mouth and taught them, saying: [3]"Blessed are the poor in spirit, for theirs is the kingdom of heaven. [4]"Blessed are those who mourn, for they shall be comforted. [5]"Blessed are the meek, for they shall inherit the earth. [6]"Blessed are those who hunger and thirst for righteousness, for they shall be satisfied. [7]"Blessed are the merciful, for they shall obtain mercy. [8]"Blessed are the pure in heart, for they shall see God. [9]"Blessed are the peacemakers, for they shall be called sons of God. [10] "Blessed are those who are persecuted for righteousness' sake, for theirs is the kingdom of heaven. [11] "Blessed are you when men revile you and persecute you and utter all kinds of evil against you falsely on my account. [12]Rejoice and be glad, for your reward is great in heaven, for so men persecuted the prophets who were before you . . .

[19]Whoever then relaxes one of the least of these commandments and teaches men so, shall be called least in the kingdom of heaven; but he who does them and teaches them shall be called great in the kingdom of heaven. [20]For I tell you, unless your righteousness exceeds that of the scribes and Pharisees, you will never enter the kingdom of heaven.

[21]"You have heard that it was said to the men of old, 'You shall not kill; and whoever kills shall be liable to judgment.' [22]But I say to you that everyone who is angry with his brother shall be liable to judgment: whoever insults his brother shall be liable to the council, and whoever says, 'You fool!' shall be liable to the hell of fire. [23]So if you are offering your gift at the altar, and there remember that your brother has something against you, [24]leave your gift there before the altar and go; first be reconciled to your brother, and then come and offer your gift . . .

[27]"You have heard that it was said, 'You shall not commit adultery.' [28]But I say to you that everyone who looks at a woman lustfully has already committed adultery with her in his heart. [29]If your right eye causes you to sin, pluck it out and throw it away; it is better that you

lose one of your members than that your whole body be thrown into hell. [30]And if your right hand causes you to sin, cut it off and throw it away; it is better that you lose one of your members than that your whole body go into hell.

[31]"It was also said, 'Whoever divorces his wife, let him give her a certificate of divorce.' [32]But I say to you that everyone who divorces his wife, except on the ground of unchastity, makes her an adulteress; and whoever marries a divorced woman commits adultery.

[33]"Again you have heard that it was said to men of old, 'You shall not swear falsely, but shall perform to the Lord what you have sworn.' [34]But I say to you, Do not swear at all, either by heaven, for it is the throne of God, [35]Or by the earth, for it is his footstool, or by Jerusalem, for it is the city of the great King. [36] And do not swear by your head, for you cannot make one hair white or black. [37]Let what you say be simply 'Yes' or 'No'; anything more than this comes from evil.

[38]"You have heard that it was said, 'An eye for an eye and a tooth for a tooth.' [39]But I say to you, Do not resist one who is evil. But if anyone strikes you on the right cheek, turn to him the other also; [40]and if anyone would sue you and take your coat, let him have your cloak as well; [41]and if anyone forces you to go one mile, go with him two miles. [42]Give to him who begs from you, and do not refuse him who would borrow from you.

[43]"You have heard that it was said, 'You shall love your neighbor and hate your enemy.' [44]But I say to you, Love your enemies and pray for those who persecute you, [45]so that you may be sons of your Father who is in heaven; for he makes his sun rise on the evil and on the good, and sends rain on the just and on the unjust. [46]For if you love those who love you, what reward have you? Do not even the tax collectors do the same? [47]And if you salute only your brethren, what more are you doing than others? Do not even the Gentiles do the same? [48]you, therefore, must be perfect, as your heavenly Father is perfect.

6[2]"Thus, when you give alms, sound no trumpet before you, as the hypocrites do in the synagogues and in the streets, that they may be praised by men. Truly, I say to you, they have received their reward. [3]But when you give alms, do not let your left hand know what you right hand is doing, [4]so that your alms may be in secret; and your Father who sees in secret will reward you.

[5]"And when you pray, you must not be like the hypocrites; for they love to stand and pray in the synagogues and at the street corners, that they may be seen by men. Truly, I say to you, they have received their reward. [6]But when you pray, go into your room and shut the door and pray to you father who is in secret; and your Father who sees in secret will reward you.

[7]"And in praying do not heap up empty phrases as the Gentiles do; for they think that they will be heard for their many words. [8] Do not be like them, for your Father knows what you need before you ask him. [9]Pray then like this: Our Father who are in heaven, Hallowed be thy name. [10] Thy kingdom come. Thy will be done, On earth as it is in heaven. [11] Give us this day our daily bread; [12]And forgive us our debts, As we also have forgiven our debtors; [13] And lead us not into temptation, But deliver us from evil.

[14] For if you forgive men their trespasses, your heavenly Father also will forgive you; [15] but if you do not forgive men their trespasses, neither will your Father forgive you trespasses . . .

[19]"Do not lay up for yourselves treasures on earth, where moth and rust consume and where thieves break in and steal, [20] but lay up for yourselves treasures in heaven, where neither moth nor rust consumes and where thieves do not break in and steal. [21] For where your treasure is, there will your heart be also . . .

[25]"Therefore I tell you, do not be anxious about your life, what you shall eat or what you shall drink, nor about your body, what you shall put on. Is not life more than food, and the body more than clothing? [26]Look at the birds of the air: they neither sow nor reap nor gather into barns, and yet your heavenly Father feeds them. Are you not of more value than they? [27] And which of you by being anxious can add one cubit to his span of life? [28] And why are you

anxious about clothing? Consider the lilies of the field, how they grow; they neither toil nor spin; [29] yet I tell you, even Solomon in all his glory was not arrayed like one of these. [30] But if God so clothes the grass of the field, which today is alive and tomorrow is thrown into the oven, will he not much more clothe you, O men of little faith? [31]Therefore do not be anxious, saying, 'What shall we eat?' or 'What should we drink?' or 'What shall we wear?' [32] For the Gentiles seek all these things; and your heavenly Father knows that you need them all. [33] But seek first his kingdom and his righteousness, and all these things shall be yours as well. [34] "Therefore do not be anxious about tomorrow, for tomorrow will be anxious for itself. Let the day's own trouble be sufficient for the day. . ."

7"Judge not, that you be not judged. [2] For with the judgment you pronounce you will be judged, and the measure you give will be the measure you get. [3] Why do you see the speck that is in your brother's eye, but do not notice the log that is in your own eye? . . . [6]"Do not give dogs what is holy; and do not throw your pearls before swine, lest they trample them under foot and turn to attack you.

[7]"Ask, and it will be given you; seek, and you will find; knock, and it will be opened to you. [8]For everyone who asks receives, and he who seeks finds, and to him who knocks it will be opened. [9]Or what man of you, if his son asks him for bread, will give him a stone? [10]Or if he asks for a fish, will give him a serpent? [11]If you then, who are evil, know how to give good gifts to your children, how much more will your Father who is in heaven give good things to those who ask him! [12] So whatever you wish that men would do to you, do so to them; for this is the law and the prophets.

[13]"Enter by the narrow gate; for the gate is wide and the way is easy, that leads to destruction, and those who enter by it are many. [14]For the gate is narrow and the way is hard, that leads to life, and those who find it are few . . . [21] "Not everyone who says to me, 'Lord, Lord,' shall enter the kingdom of heaven, but he who does the will of my Father who is in heaven. [22]On that day many will say to me, 'Lord, Lord, did we not prophesy in your name, and cast out demons in your name, and do many mighty works in your name?' [23] And then will I declare to them, 'I never knew you; depart from me, you evildoers.'

[24]"Every one then who hears these words of mine and does them will be like a wise man who built his house upon the rock; [25]and the rain fell, and the floods came, and the winds blew and beat upon that house, but it did not fall, because it had been founded on the rock.[26] And everyone who hears these words of mine and does not do them will be like a foolish man who built his house upon the sand; [27] and the rain fell, and the floods came, and the winds blew and beat against that house, and it fell; and great was the fall of it."

[28] And when Jesus finished these sayings, the crowds were astonished at his teaching, [29]for he taught them as one who had authority, and not as their scribes.

8When he came down from the mountain, great crowds followed him; [2]and behold, a leper came to him and knelt before him, saying, "Lord, if you will, you can make me clean." [3] And he stretched out his hand and touched him, saying, "I will; be clean." And immediately his leprosy was cleansed. [4]And Jesus said to him, "See that you say nothing to anyone; but go, show yourself to the priest, and offer the gift that Moses commanded, for a proof to the people." . . . [14] And when Jesus entered Peter's house, he saw his mother-in-law lying sick with a fever; [15]he touched her hand, and the fever left her, and she rose and served him. [16]That evening they brought to him many who were possessed with demons; and he cast out the spirits with a word, and healed all who were sick. [17]This was to fulfill what was spoken by the prophet Isaiah, "He took our infirmities and bore our diseases." . . .

## The Book of Acts: St. Paul the Missionary

17Now when they had passed through Amphip'olis and Apollo'nia, they came to Thessaloni'ca, where there was a synagogue of the Jews. 2And Paul went in, as was his custom, and for three weeks he argued with them from the scriptures, 3explaining and proving that it was necessary for the Christ to suffer and to rise from the dead, and saying, "This Jesus, whom I proclaim to you, is the Christ." 4And some of them were persuaded, and joined Paul and Silas; as did a great many of the devout Greeks and not a few of the leading women. 5But the Jews were jealous, and taking some wicked fellows of the rabble, they gathered a crowd, set the city in an uproar, and attacked the house of Jason, seeking to bring them out to the people. 6 And when they could not find them, they dragged Jason and some of the brethren before the city authorities, crying, "These men who have turned the world upside down have come here also, 7 and Jason has received them; and they are all acting against the decrees of Caesar, saying that there is another king, Jesus." 8 And the people and the city authorities were disturbed when they heard this. 9 And when they had taken security from Jason and the rest, they let them go.

10The brethren immediately sent Paul and Silas away by night to Beroe'a; and when they arrived they went into the Jewish synagogue. 11Now these Jews were more noble than those in Thessaloni'ca, for they received the word with all eagerness, examining the scriptures daily to see if these things were so. 12Many of them therefore believed, with not a few Greek women of high standing as well as men. 13But when the Jews of Thessaloni'ca learned that the word of God was proclaimed by Paul at Beroe'a also, they came there too, stirring up and inciting the crowds. 14Then the brethren immediately sent Paul off on his way to the sea, but Silas and Timothy remained there. 15 Those who conducted Paul brought him as far as Athens; and receiving a command for Silas and Timothy to come to him as soon as possible, they departed.

16Now while Paul was waiting for them at Athens, his spirit was provoked within him as he saw that the city was full of idols. 17So he argued in the synagogue with the Jews and the devout persons, and in the market place every day with those who chanced to be there. 18Some also of the Epicurean and Stoic philosophers met him. And some said, "What would this babbler say?" Others said, "He seems to be a preacher of foreign divinities"—because he preached Jesus and the resurrection. 19 And they took hold of him and brought him to the Are-op'agus, saying, "May we know what this new teaching is which you present? For you bring some strange things to our ears; we wish to know therefore what these things mean." 21Now all the Athenians and the foreigners who lived there spent their time in nothing except telling or hearing something new.

22So Paul, standing in the middle of the Are-op'agus, said: "Men of Athens, I perceive that in every way you are very religious. 23 For as I passed along, and observed the objects of your worship, I found also an altar with this inscription, 'To an unknown god.' What therefore you worship as unknown, this I proclaim to you. 24The God who made the world and everything in it, being Lord of heaven and earth, does not live in shrines made by man, 25nor is he served by human hands, as though he needed anything, since he himself gives to all men life and breath and everything . . .

29Being then God's offspring, we ought not to think that the Deity is like gold, or silver, or stone, a representation by the art and imagination of man. 30The times of ignorance God overlooked, but now he commands all men everywhere to repent, 31because he has fixed a day on which he will judge the world in righteousness by a man whom he has appointed, and of this he has given assurance to all men by raising him from the dead."

32Now when they heard of the resurrection of the dead, some mocked; but others said, "We will hear you again about this." . . .

18After this he left Athens and went to Corinth . . . [4] And he argued in the synagogue every sabbath, and persuaded Jews and Greeks.

When Silas and Timothy arrived from Macedo'nia, Paul was occupied with preaching, testifying to the Jews that the Christ was Jesus. [6] And when they opposed and reviled him, he shook out his garments and said to them, "Your blood be upon your heads! I am innocent. From now on I will go to the Gentiles." [7] And he left there and went to the house of a man named Titius Justus, a worshiper of God; his house was next to a synagogue. [8]Crispus, the ruler of the synagogue, believed in the Lord, together with all his household; and many of the Corinthians hearing Paul believed and were baptized. [9] And the Lord said to Paul one night in a vision, "Do not be afraid, but speak and do not be silent; [10]for I am with you, and no man shall attack you to harm you; for I have many people in this city. [11] And he stayed a year and six months, teaching the word of God among them.

[12]But when Gallio was proconsul of Acha'ia, the Jews made a united attack upon Paul and brought him before the tribunal, [13]saying, "This man is persuading men to worship God contrary to the law." [14]But when Paul was about to open his mouth, Gallio said to the Jews, "If it were a matter of wrongdoing or vicious crime, I should have reason to bear with you, a Jews; [15]but since it is a matter of questions about words and names and your own law, see to it yourselves; I refuse to be a judge of these things." [16] And he drove them from the tribunal. [17] And they all seized Sos'thenes, the ruler of the synagogue, and beat him in front of the tribunal. But Gallio paid no attention to this . . .

[24]Now a Jew named Apol'los, a native of Alexandria, came to Ephesus. He was an eloquent man, well versed in the scriptures. [25]He had been instructed in the way of the Lord; and being fervent in spirit, he spoke and taught accurately the things concerning Jesus, though he knew only the baptism of John. [26]He began to speak boldly in the synagogue; but when Priscilla and Aq'uila heard him, they took him and expounded to him the way of God more accurately. [27]And when he wished to cross to Acha'ia, the brethren encouraged him, and wrote to the disciples to receive him. When he arrived, he greatly helped those who through grace had believed, [28]for he powerfully confuted the Jews in public, showing by the scriptures that the Christ was Jesus.

# READING 2

## Augustine's City of God

*Augustine of Hippo (354–430 A.D.), after converting to Christianity, became one of its foremost theologians. In this selection, Augustine is responding to those who attacked the Christians, blaming them for the sacking of Rome by the barbarians and other misfortunes in the Empire. Augustine argues that only one city is secure from destruction, the City of God. We here encounter the first shades of Christian withdrawal—a world view that would dominate the Middle Ages. The selection is taken from, Marcus Dads, trans.,* The Works of Aurelius Augustine, *Bishop of Hippo (Edinburgh: T.&T. Clark, 1897), Vol. II: Chap. 19 passim.*

---

### Discussion Questions

1. What is Augustine suggesting when he surmises that only the City of God is secure from destruction?
2. Look at the dates of Augustine's writings. How is the contemporaneous political situation afflicting the Roman Empire reflected in Augustine's writings?
3. How does this mentality impact the contemporaneous political situation?

### THE EARTHLY CITY VERSUS THE HEAVENLY CITY

17. The earthly city, which does not live by faith, seeks an earthly peace, and the end it proposes, in the well-ordered concord of civic obedience and rule, is the combination of men's wills to attain the things which are helpful to this life. The heavenly city, or rather the part of it which sojourns on earth and lives by faith, makes use of this peace only because it must, until this mortal condition which necessitates it shall pass away. Consequently, so long as it lives like a captive and a stranger in the earthly city, though it has already received the promise of redemption, and the gift of the Spirit as the earnest of it, it makes no scruple to obey the laws of the earthly city, whereby the things necessary for the maintenance of this mortal life are administered; and thus, as this life is common to both cities, so there is a harmony between them in regard to what belongs to it. . . .

This heavenly city, then, while it sojourns on earth, calls citizens out of all nations, and gathers together a society of pilgrims of all languages, not scrupling about diversities in the manners, laws, and institutions whereby earthly peace is secured and maintained, but recognizing that, however various these are, they all tend to one and the same end of earthly peace. It therefore is so far from rescinding and abolishing these diversities, that it even preserves and adopts them, so long only as no hindrance to the worship of the one supreme and true God is thus introduced. Even the heavenly city, therefore, while in its state of pilgrimage, avails itself to the peace of earth, and, so far as it can without injuring faith and godliness, desires and maintains a common agreement among men regarding the acquisition of the necessities of life, and makes this earthly peace bear upon the peace of heaven; for this alone can be truly called and esteemed the peace of the reasonable creatures, consisting as it does in the perfectly ordered and harmonious enjoyment of God and of one another in God . . .

20. Since, then, the supreme good of the city of God is perfect and eternal peace, not such as mortals pass into and out of by birth and death, but the peace of freedom from all evil, in which the immortals ever abide, who can deny that future life is most blessed, or that, in com-

parison with it, this life which we now live is most wretched, be it filled with all blessings of body and soul and external things? . . . But the actual possession of the happiness of this life, without the hope of what is beyond, is but a false happiness and profound misery. For the true blessings of the soul are not now enjoyed; for that is no true wisdom which does not direct all its prudent observations, manly actions, virtuous self-restraint, and just arrangements, to that end in which God shall be all and all in a secure eternity and perfect peace.

# READING 3

## A Scholar Says Goodbye to His Friends

*Decimus Magnus Ausonius (fl. 4th Cent. A.D.) was a native of Bordeaux in Gaul who became a famous grammarian and, eventually, a tutor to the Emperor Gratian (315–383 A.D.). Ostensibly a Christian, Ausonius, like many others at that time, struggled with his classical allegiances. In these brief commemorations dedicated to old friends and former teachers, Ausonius is bowing to an ancient tradition of teachers and pupils that stretched as far back as Homer—a legacy Ausonius knew was in its death throes. For this reading we are indebted to: "Poems Commemorating the Professors of Bordeaux" in Hugh G. Evelyn White, trans.,* Ausonius *(2 vols.; Cambridge, Mass.: Harvard University Press, 1919), Vol. 1: pp. 97–105.*

---

### Discussion Questions

1. Although Ausonius was a Christian, how does he portray the old values, myths and gods?
2. How does this passage depict the transition to a wholly Christian Empire?

### AUSONIUS TO HIS PROFESSORS

---

*I. Tiberius Victor Minervius, the Orator*

Minervius, chief ornament of Bordeaux . . . Your teaching in its day made glorious Constantinople, Rome, and lastly our native town . . . Your speech was like a torrent in full spate, yet one which whirled down pure gold without muddy sediment . . . Shall I speak also of your natural gifts and that divine blessing, your memory, which was so prodigious that you retained what you had heard or read over once as though it were engraven on your mind . . . No malice ever blackened your heart; your tongue, though free and full of wit, indulged only in kindly jests that held no sting . . . And when you died after six decades, although you left no heir, you were mourned by me as a father and a youth.

And now, if anything survives after Fate has struck her final blow you are living yet and not unmindful of your days gone by; or, if nothing at all remains, and death's long repose knows no feeling, you have lived your own life; we take pleasure in your fame.

*II. Latinus Alcimus Alethius, the Rhetorician*

[Alcimus,] In legal eloquence you were supreme, you were the Muses' pride, and our one model in those letters which learned Greece fostered at Athens, or which Rome fosters throughout the Latin world. Shall I speak of your character and of the rule of life maintained to your life's end? Or of the brilliance of your renown, and the devotion to learning which made you wholly shun ambition? No man was more dignified than you, yet none was more agreeable or more generous to the needy in undertaking the defense if legal aid was needed, or in zealously teaching some pupil in the schools . . .

If my pen, seeking to please, only offends, yet pardon me . . . I cannot voice aught worthy, I seek to pay my homage, harmfully zealous. Calm be your rest, and with renown outweigh the frail body's loss.

*IV. Attius Patera, the Elder, the Rhetorician*

Patera, renowned speaker . . . If report does not lie, you were sprung from the stock of the Druids of Bayeux, and traced your hallowed line from the temple of Belenus; and hence the names borne by your family: you are called Patera; so the mystic votaries call the servants of Apollo. Your father and your brother were named after Phoebus, and your own son after Delphi . . . Sound in memory as in learning, you had the gift of clear expression cast in sonorous and well-chosen phrase; your wit was chastened and without a spice of bitterness: sparing of food and wine, cheerful, modest, comely in person, even in age you were as an eagle or a steed grown old.

# LECTURE TOPIC 15

# The Early Middle Ages

I. Why Did the Barbarians Invade Europe?
  A. A *Voelkerwanderung*
  B. The Successors of Rome
  C. Germanic Tribes
    1. Visigoths and Ostrogoths
    2. Warrior Chieftians and the Comitatus
      a) Occasional Service in Roman Army
      b) Blurred Boundaries and Assimilation
      c) Alaric (370–410 A.D.)
    3. Wergeld
    4. Mythopoeic
    5. Ulfilas (311–381 A.D.)
      a) Christian Missionary
      b) Translated Bible into German
  D. Vandals
    1. Sacked Rome: 455 A.D.
    2. "Vandalism"
  E. Huns (Magyars)
    1. Attila (406–453 A.D.)
    2. Description by Ammianus Marcellinus (4th Cent. A.D.)
  F. What Is the Heritage of the Barbarians?
    1. Community Property
    2. Trousers
    3. "Daddy"

II. How Did The Franks Emerge in Western Europe?
  A. Merovingians: The "Do-Nothing" Kings?
    1. Clovis (466–511 A.D.)
    2. Converted to Christianity: 496 A.D.
    3. Lack of Primogeniture
  B. Why is Charles Martel Famous?
    1. Mayor of the Palace
    2. The Battle of Tours: 732 A.D.
  C. Carolingians
    1. Who Was Pepin the Short?
      a) The Donation of Pepin
      b) Partnership with the Pope
    2. What Made Charlemagne (742–814 A.D.) Great?
      a) Carolingian Renaissance
        (1) Palace School at Aachen or Aix La Chapelle
        (2) Einhard (770–840 A.D.)
        (3) The Caroline Miniscule

        b) Crowned Holy Roman Emperor: 800 A.D.
        c) Division of Frankish Empire after 814 A.D.

III. Three New Waves of Invasions
   A. Vikings: From the North
      1. King Knut or Cannute (c. 1026)
   B. Saracens (Muslims): From the South
   C. Magyars (Huns): From the East
      1. Battle of Leyfelt: 955 A.D.
   D. Importance of the Year 1000

IV. The Social Structure and Living Conditions of Medieval Europe
   A. Feudalism: Where Did It Come From and What Is It?
   B. Direct Transition of Institutions
      1. Roman *Latifundia, Coloni, Villa* become Fiefs, Serfs, and Villages
      2. Roman Officers become Counts and Dukes
   C. Hierarchical System of Loyalties Based on Land
      1. The Lord-Vassal Relationship
         a) Homage-Investiture Ceremony
         b) Immunity Provision
      2. The Role of the Church
      3. Were Serfs Happy or Miserable?

# READING 1

## Barbarians to the North

*Because he wrote about his campaigns in Gaul in the first century B.C., Caesar's Commentaries are perhaps our earliest description of these European peoples. To those living within the boundaries of Roman rule, everything outside was barbarous and uncivilized. Whether in the first century B.C. or the fourth century A.D., a sense of distance and savagery was always communicated by those who visited the barbarian tribes of the north. And none were more frightening than the Huns. The description provided by Ammianus Marcellinus conveys the terror in which this nomadic band was held. The first passage below is from Book VI of Caesar's Gallic Wars, translated into English by William Duncan and published under the title,* The Commentaries of Caesar *(2 vols.; London: J. Cuthell et al., 1819), Vol.I: pp. 412–420. For his portrait of the Huns, we are indebted to John C Rolfe, trans.,* Ammianus Marcellinus *(3 vols.; Cambridge, Mass.: Harvard University Press, 1958), Vol. III: pp. 381–387.*

---

### Discussion Questions

1. Caesar's description of the Gauls and the Germans is given as an outsider looking in. How might his background affect his viewpoint?
2. How is society in Gaul organized? Who holds authority and how do they achieve power?
3. How are the Germans different from the Gauls? What purpose does warfare serve?
4. Describe the reputation of Attila according to Marcellinus.

### GALUS JULIUS CAESAR (100–44 B.C.) AND HIS COMMENTARIES ON THE GALLIC WARS

---

XIII. Over all Gaul, there are only two orders of men, in any degree of honour and esteem; for the common people are little better than slaves. . . The two orders of men, with whom, as we have said, all authority and distinctions are lodged, are the Druids and nobles. The Druids preside in matters of religion, have the care of public and private sacrifices, and interpret the will of the gods. They have the direction and education of the youth, by whom they are held in great honour. In almost all controversies, whether public or private, the decision is left to them: and if any crime is committed, any murder perpetrated; if any dispute arises, touching an inheritance, or the limits of adjoining estates; in all such cases, they are the supreme judges. They decree rewards and punishments; and if anyone refuses to submit to their sentence, whether magistrate or private man, they interdict him the sacrifices. This is the greatest punishment that can be inflicted among the Gauls; because such as are under this prohibition, are considered as impious and wicked: all men shun them, and decline their conversation and fellowship, lest they should suffer from the contagion of their misfortunes. They can neither have recourse to the law for justice, nor are capable of any public office. The Druids are all under one chief, who possesses the supreme authority in that body. Upon his death, if anyone remarkably excels the rest, he succeeds; but if there are several candidates of equal merit, the affair is determined by plurality of suffrages. Sometimes they even have recourse to arms before the election can be brought to an issue. Once a year they assemble at a consecrated place in the territories of the Camutes, whose country is supposed to be in the middle of Gaul. Hither such as have any suits depending, flock from all parts, and submit implicitly to their decrees. . . . The Druids never go to war, are exempted from taxes and military service, and enjoy all manner of immunities. . . . They are taught to repeat a great number of verses, by heart, and often spend twenty years upon this institution; for it is deemed unlawful to commit their statutes to writing; though in other matters, whether public or private, they make use of Greek characters. . . .It is one of their principal maxims that the soul never dies, but after death passes from one body to another: which, they think, contributes greatly to exalt men's courage, by disarming death of his terrors. They teach likewise many things relating to the stars and their motions, the magnitude of the world and our earth, the nature of things, and the power and prerogatives of the immortal gods.

XIV. The other order of men is the nobles, whose whole study and occupation is war. Before Caesar's arrival in Gaul, they were almost every year at war, either offensive or defensive; and they judge of the power and quality of their nobles, by the vassals, and the number of men he keeps in his pay; for they are the only marks of grandeur they make any account of.

XV. The whole nation of the Gauls is extremely addicted to superstition: whence, in threatening distempers, and the imminent dangers of war, they make no scruple to sacrifice men, or engage themselves by vow to such sacrifices; in which they make use of the ministry of the Druids: for it is a prevalent opinion among them, that nothing but the life of a man can atone for the life of a man; insomuch, that they have established even public sacrifices of this kind. Some prepare huge Colossuses, of osier twigs, into which they put men alive, and setting fire to them, those within expire amidst the flames. They prefer for victims such as have been convicted, of theft, robbery, or other crimes; believing them the most acceptable to the gods: but when real criminals are wanting, the innocent are often made to suffer. Mercury is the chief deity with them: of him they have many images, account him the inventor of all arts, their guide and conductor in their journeys, and the patron of merchandize and gain. Next to him are Apollo, and Mars, and Jupiter, and Minerva. Their notions in regard to them are pretty much the same with those of other nations. Apollo is their god of physic; Minerva of works and manufactures; Jove holds the empire of heaven; and Mars presides in war. To this last, when they resolve upon a battle, they commonly devote the spoil. If they prove victorious, they offer up all the cattle taken, and set apart the rest of the plunder in a place appointed for that purpose: and it is common in many provinces, to see these monuments of offerings piled up in consecrated places. Nay, it rarely happens that anyone shows so great a disregard of religion, as either to conceal the plunder, or pillage the public oblations; and the severest punishments are inflicted upon such offenders.

XVI. The Gauls fancy themselves to be descended from the god Pluto; which, it seems, is an established tradition among the Druids. For this reason they compute the time by nights, not by days; and in the observance of birth-days, new moons, and the beginning of the year, always commence the celebration from the preceding night. In one custom they differ from almost all other nations; that they never suffer their children to come openly into their presence, until they are of age to bear arms, for the appearance of a son in public with his father, before he has reached the age of manhood, is accounted dishonourable.

XVII. Whatever fortune the woman brings, the husband is obliged to equal it out of his own estate. This whole sum, with its annual product, is left untouched, and falls always to the share of the survivor. The men have power of life and death over their wives and children: and when any father of a family of illustrious rank dies, his relations assemble, and, upon the least ground of suspicion, put even his wives to the torture like slaves. If they are found guilty, iron and fire are employed to torment and destroy them. Their funerals are magnificent and sumptuous, according to their quality. Every thing that was dear to the deceased, even animals, are thrown into the pile: and formerly such of their slaves and clients as they loved most, sacrificed themselves at the funeral of their lord.

. . . XIX. The Germans differ widely in their manners from the Gauls: for neither have they Druids to preside in religious affairs, nor do they trouble themselves about sacrifices. They acknowledge no gods but those that are objects of sight, and by whose power they are apparently benefited; the sun, the moon, fire. Of others they know nothing, not even by report. Their whole life is addicted to hunting and war; and from their infancy they are inured to fatigue and hardships. They esteem those most, who continue longest strangers to women; as imagining nothing contributes so much to stature, strength, and vigour of body: but to have any commerce of this kind before the age of twenty, is accounted in the highest degree ignominious. Nor is it possible to conceal an irregularity this way; because they bathe promiscuously in rivers, and are clothed in skins, or short mantles of fur, which leave the greatest part of their bodies naked.

XX. Agriculture is little regarded among them, as they live mostly on milk, cheese, and the flesh of animals. Nor has any man lands of his own, or distinguished by fixed boundaries. The magistrates, and those in authority, portion out yearly to every canton and family, such a quantity of land, and in what part of the country they think proper; and the year following remove them to some other spot. Many reasons are assigned for this practice; lest seduced by habit and continuance, they should learn to prefer tillage to war; lest a desire of enlarging their possessions should gain ground, and prompt the stronger to expel the weaker; lest they should become curious in their buildings, in order to guard against the extremes of heat and cold; lest avarice should get footing among them, whence spring factions and discords: in fine, to preserve contentment and equanimity among the people, when they find their possessions nothing inferior to those of the most powerful.

. . . XXII. Formerly the Gauls exceeded the Germans in bravery, often made war upon them, and as they abounded in people beyond what the country could maintain, sent several colonies over the Rhine. Accordingly the more fertile places of Germany, in the neighbourhood of the Hercynian forest, (which I find mentioned by Eratosthenes, and other Greek writers, under the name of Orcinia,) fell to the share of the Vokee, who settled in those parts, and have ever since kept possession. They are in the highest reputation for justice and bravery, and no less remarkable than the Germans for poverty, abstinence, and patience of fatigue, conforming exactly to their customs, both in habit and way of living. But the neighbourhood of the Roman province, and an acquaintance with traffic, has introduced luxury and abundance among the Gauls, whence becoming by little and little an unequal match for the Germans, and being worsted in many battles, they no longer pretend to compare with them in valour.

## Ammianus Marcelli Nus (Fl. 4th Cent. A.D.) on the Huns

1. However, the seed and origin of all the ruin and various disasters that the wrath of Mars aroused, putting in turmoil all places with unwonted fires, we have found to be this. The people of the Huns, but little known from ancient records, dwelling beyond the Maeotic Sea near the ice-bound ocean, exceed every degree of savagery. 2. Since there the cheeks of the children are deeply furrowed with the steel from their very birth, in order that the growth of hair, when it appears at the proper time, may be checked by the wrinkled scars, they grow old without beards and without any beauty, like eunuchs. They all have compact, strong limbs and thick necks, and are so monstrously ugly and misshapen, that one might take them for two-legged beasts or for the stumps, rough-hewn into images, that are used in putting sides to bridges. 3. But although they have the form of men, however ugly, they are so hardy in their mode of life that they have no need of fire nor of savory food, but eat the roots of wild plants and the half-raw flesh of any kind of animal whatever, which they put between their thighs and the backs of their horses, and thus warm it a little. 4. They are never protected by any buildings, but they avoid these like tombs, which are set apart from everyday use. For not even a hut thatched with reed can be found among them. But roaming at large amid the mountains and woods, they learn from the cradle to endure cold, hunger, and thirst. When away from their homes they never enter a house unless compelled by extreme necessity; for they think they are not

safe when staying under a roof. 5. They dress in linen cloth or in the skins of field-mice sewn together, and they wear the same clothing indoors and out. But when they have once put their necks into a faded tunic, it is not taken off or changed until by long wear and tear it has been reduced to rags and fallen from them bit by bit. 6. They cover their heads with round caps and protect their hairy legs with goatskins; their shoes are formed upon no lasts, and so prevent their walking with free step. For this reason they are not at all adapted to battles on foot, but they are almost glued to their horses, which are hardy, it is true, but ugly, and sometimes they sit them woman-fashion and thus perform their ordinary tasks. From their horses by night or day everyone of that nation buys and sells, eats and drinks, and bowed over the narrow neck of the animal relaxes into a sleep so deep as to be accompanied by many dreams. 7. And when deliberation is called for about weighty matters, they all consult as a common body in that fashion. They are subject to no royal restraint, but they are content with the disorderly government of their important men, and led by them they force their way through every obstacle. 8. They also sometimes fight when provoked, and then they enter the battle drawn up in wedge-shaped masses, while their medley of voices makes a savage noise. And as they are lightly equipped for swift motion, and unexpected in action, they purposely divide suddenly into scattered bands and attack, rushing about in disorder here and there, dealing terrific slaughter; and because of their extraordinary rapidity of movement they are never seen to attack a rampart or pillage an enemy's camp. 9. And on this account you would not hesitate to call them the most terrible of all warriors, because they fight from a distance with missiles having sharp bone, instead of their usual points, joined to the shafts with wonderful skill; then they gallop over the intervening spaces and fight hand to hand with swords, regardless of their own lives; and while the enemy are guarding against wounds from the sabre-thrusts, they throw strips of cloth plaited into nooses over their opponents and so entangle them that they fetter their limbs and take from them the power of riding or walking. 10. No one in their country ever plows a field or touches a plow-handle. They are all without fixed abode. without hearth, or law, or settled mode of life, and keep roaming from place to place, like fugitives, accompanied by the wagons in which they live; in wagons their wives weave for them their hideous garments, in wagons they cohabit with their husbands, bear children, and rear them to the age of puberty. None of their offspring, when asked, can tell you where he comes from, since he was conceived in one place, born far from there, and brought up still farther away. 11. In truces they are faithless and unreliable, strongly inclined to sway to the motion of every breeze of new hope that presents itself, and sacrificing every feeling to the mad impulse of the moment. Like unreasoning beasts, they are utterly ignorant of the difference between right and wrong; they are deceitful and ambiguous in speech, never bound by any reverence for religion or for superstition. They burn with an infinite thirst for gold, and they are so fickle and prone to anger, that they often quarrel with their allies without provocation, more than once on the same day, and make friends with them again without a mediator.

12. This race of untamed men, without encumbrances, aflame with an inhuman desire for plundering others' property, made their violent way amid the rapine and slaughter of the neighbouring peoples as far as the Halani, once known as the Massagetae.

# READING 2

## A Contemporary Description of Attila the Hun

*In 448 a Roman envoy named Priscus visited the home of Attila the Hun in a Scythian village near the Danube River. This encounter occurred only a few years before Attila's famous invasion of Italy. Priscus was aware of the reputation of Attila for savagery(see Reading 1, above), thus, the Roman was surprised to find him a simple and cultured man. The following account is taken from James Harvey Robinson, ed.,* Readings in European History, *Vol. 1 (Boston: Athenaeum, 1904), pp. 47–48.*

---

### Discussion Questions

1. How can we account for the discrepancy between this portrait of Attila and the previous description of the Huns by Ammianus Marcellinus?
2. Has history falsely portrayed the reputation of this fiercest of warriors?
3. What does it tell us about the Huns' system of justice that Attila dispensed judgments on the street as he walked?

Attila's residence. . . was made of polished boards, and surrounded with wooden enclosures, designed not so much for protection as for appearance's sake. . . . I entered the enclosure of Attila's palace, bearing gifts to his wife, whose name was Kreka. . . . Having been admitted by the barbarians at the door, I found her reclining on a soft couch. The floor of the room was covered with woolen mats for walking on. . . . Having approached, saluted her, and presented the gifts, I went out and walked to the other houses. . . . Attila came forth from [one of] the house[s] with a dignified strut, looking round on this side and on that. . . . Many persons who had lawsuits with one another came up and received his judgment. Then he returned into the house and received ambassadors of barbarous peoples. . . .

[We were invited to a banquet with Attila at three o'clock] The cupbearers gave us a cup, according to the national custom, that we might pray before we sat down. Having tasted the cup, we proceeded to take our seats, all the chairs being ranged along the walls of the room on either side. Attila sat in the middle on a couch; a second couch was set behind him, and from it steps led up to wrought coverlets for ornament, such as Greeks and Romans used to deck bridal beds. The places on the right of Attila were held chief in honor; those on the left, where we sat, were only second. . . .

The attendant of Attila first entered with a dish full of meat, and behind him came the other attendants with bread and viands [plates of food], which they laid on the tables. A luxurious meal, served on silver plate, had been made ready for us and the barbarian guests, but Attila ate nothing but meat on a wooden trencher [a wooden plate]. In everything else, too, he showed himself temperate; his cup was of wood, while to the guests were given goblets of gold and silver. His dress, too, was quite simple, affecting only to be clean. The sword he carried at his side, the latchets of his. . . shoes, the bridle of his horse were not adorned with gold or gems or anything costly. . . like those of the other Scythians.

[After two courses were eaten and] evening fell, torches were lit and two barbarians, coming forward in front of Attila, sang songs they had composed, celebrating his victories and deeds of valor in war.

# READING 3

## The Character of Charlemagne

*An exception to the negative appraisal of the Dark Ages is the reign of Charlemagne known as the Carolingian Renaissance. For this brief interlude, learning and culture flourished in the West, before again diminishing. Although only semiliterate, Charlemagne (c. 742–814) was a remarkable man. He patronized learning and the arts at his capital at Aachen (Aix-la-Chapelle) and established a palace school there to train clergy and sons of the court nobles. We are fortunate to have the complete history of Charlemagne written by Einhard (770–840 A.D.), a contemporary scholar, close friend and advisor of Charlemagne. His account, though not disinterested, still gives us an informative description not only of Charlemagne's military success and crowning as Holy Roman Emperor but a good picture of the king's private life. After reading this selection, one might have a clearer sense of how far culture and civilization had plunged after the demise of Roman authority. This is excerpted from the translation by A. J. Grant,* Early Lives of Charlemagne *by Einhard & The Monk of St. Gall (New York: Cooper Square Publishers, Inc., 1966), pp. 32–44.*

---

### Discussion Questions

1. What does Einhard tell us about the education and upbringing of royal children? How did the emperor treat his children, and was he a successful father?
2. Although Charlemagne was not literate, Einhard considered him a learned man. How did the Charlemagne deserve this distinction?
3. What message do you think the biographer is attempting to send with his work?

### EINHARD'S LIFE—THE EMPEROR CHARLES

19. In educating his children he determined to train them, both sons and daughters, in those liberal studies to which he himself paid great attention. Further, he made his sons, as soon as their age permitted it, learn to ride like true Franks, and practise the use of arms and hunting. He ordered his daughters to learn wool work and devote attention to the spindle and distaff, for the avoidance of idleness and lethargy, and to be trained to the adoption of high principles.

. . . He had such care of the upbringing of his sons and daughters that he never dined without them when he was at home, and never travelled without them. His sons rode along with him, and his daughters followed in the rear. Some of his guards, chosen for this very purpose, watched the end of the line of march where his daughters travelled. They were very beautiful, and much beloved by their father, and, therefore, it is strange that he would give them in marriage to no one, either among his own people or of a foreign state. But up to his death he kept them all at home, saying that he could not forego their society. . .

20. He had by a concubine a son called Pippin—whom I purposely did not mention along with the others—handsome, indeed, but deformed. When Charles, after the beginning of the war against the Huns, was wintering in Bavaria, this Pippin pretended illness, and formed a conspiracy against his father with some of the leaders of the Franks, who had seduced him by a vain promise of the kingdom. When the design had been detected and the conspirators punished Pippin was tonsured and sent to the monastery of Prumia, there to practise the religious life, to which in the end he was of his own will inclined.

Another dangerous conspiracy had been formed against him in Germany at an earlier date. The plotters were some of them blinded and some of them maimed, and all subsequently transported into exile. Not more than three lost their lives, and these resisted capture with drawn swords, and in defending themselves killed some of their opponents. Hence, as they could not be restrained in any other way, they were cut down.

The cruelty of Queen Fastrada is believed to be the cause and origin of these conspiracies. Both were caused by the belief that, upon the persuasion of his cruel wife, he had swerved widely from his natural kindness and customary leniency. Otherwise his whole life long he so won the love and favour of all men both at home and abroad that never was the slightest charge of unjust severity brought against him by anyone.

21. He had a great love for foreigners, and took such pains to entertain them that their numbers were justly reckoned to be a burden not only to the palace but to the kingdom at large. But, with his usual loftiness of spirit, he took little note of such charges, for he found in the reputation of generosity and in the good fame that followed such actions a compensation even for grave inconveniences.

22. His body was large and strong; his stature tall but not ungainly, for the measure of his height was seven times the length of his own feet. The top of his head was round; his eyes were very large and piercing. His nose was rather larger than is usual; he had beautiful white hair; and his expression was brisk and cheerful; so that, whether sitting or standing, his appearance was dignified and impressive. Although his neck was rather thick and short and he was somewhat corpulent this was not noticed owing to the good proportions of the rest of his body. His step was firm and the whole carriage of his body manly; his voice was clear, but hardly so strong as you would have expected. He had good health, but for four years before his death was frequently attacked by fevers, and at last was lame of one foot. Even then he followed his own opinion rather than the advice of his doctors, whom he almost hated, because they advised him to give up the roast meat to which he was accustomed, and eat boiled instead. He constantly took exercise both by riding and hunting. This was a national habit; for there is hardly any race on the earth that can be placed on equality with the Franks in this respect. He took delight in the vapour of naturally hot waters, and constantly practised swimming, in which he was so proficient that no one could be fairly regarded as his superior. Partly for this reason he built his palace at Aix, and lived there continuously during the last years of his life up to the time of his death. He used to invite not only his sons to the bath but also his nobles and friends, and at times even a great number of his followers and bodyguards.

23. He wore the national—that is to say, the Frankish dress. His shirts and drawers were of linen, then came a tunic with a silken fringe, and hose. His legs were cross-gartered and his feet enclosed in shoes. In winter-time he defended his shoulders and chest with a jerkin made of the skins of otters and ermine. He was clad in a blue cloak, and always wore a sword, with the hilt and belt of either gold or silver. Occasionally, too, he used a jewelled sword, but this was only on the great festivals or when he received ambassadors from foreign nations. He disliked foreign garments, however beautiful, and would never consent to wear them, except once at Rome on the request of Pope Hadrian, and once again upon the entreaty of his successor, Pope Leo, when he wore a long tunic and cloak, and put on shoes made after the Roman fashion. On festal days he walked in procession in a garment of gold cloth, with jewelled boots and a golden girdle to his cloak, and distinguished further by a diadem of gold and precious stones. But on other days his dress differed little from that of the common people.

24. He was temperate in eating and drinking, but especially so in drinking; for he had a fierce hatred of drunkenness in any man, and especially in himself or in his friends. He could not abstain so easily from food, and used often to complain that fasting was injurious to his health. He rarely gave large banquets, and only on the high festivals, but then he invited a large number of guests. His daily meal was served in four courses only, exclusive of the roast, which the hunters used to bring in on spits, and which he ate with more pleasure than any other food. During the meal there was either singing or a reader for him to listen to. Histories

and the great deeds of men of old were read to him. He took delight also in the books of Saint Augustine, and especially in those which are entitled the City of God. He was so temperate in the use of wine and drink of any kind that he rarely drank oftener than thrice during dinner.

In summer, after his midday meal, he took some fruit and a single draught, and then, taking off his clothes and boots, just as he was accustomed to do at night, he would rest for two or three hours. At night he slept so lightly that he would wake, and even rise, four or five times during the night.

When he was putting on his boots and clothes he not only admitted his friends, but if the Count of the Palace told him there was any dispute which could not be settled without his decision he would have the litigants at once brought in, and hear the case, and pronounce on it just as if he were sitting on the tribunal. He would, moreover, at the same time transact any business that had to be done that day or give any orders to his servants.

25. In speech he was fluent and ready, and could express with the greatest clearness whatever he wished. He was not merely content with his native tongue but took the trouble to learn foreign languages. He learnt Latin so well that he could speak it as well as his native tongue; but he could understand Greek better than he could speak it. His fluency of speech was so great that he even seemed sometimes a little garrulous.

He paid the greatest attention to the liberal arts, and showed the greatest respect and bestowed high honours upon those who taught them. For his lessons in grammar he listened to the instruction of Deacon Peter of Pisa, an old man; but for all other subjects Albinus, called Alcuin, also a deacon, was his teacher—a man from Britain, of the Saxon race, and the most learned man of his time. Charles spent much time and labour in learning rhetoric and dialectic, and especially astronomy, from Alcuin. He learnt, too, the art of reckoning, and with close application scrutinised most carefully the course of the stars. He tried also to learn to write, and for this purpose used to carry with him and keep under the pillow of his couch tablets and writing-sheets that he might in his spare moments accustom himself to the formation of letters. But he made little advance in this strange task, which was begun too late in life.

26. He paid the most devout and pious regard to the Christian religion, in which he had been brought up from infancy. And, therefore, he built the great and most beautiful church at Aix, and decorated it with gold and silver and candelabras and with wicket-gates and doors of solid brass. And, since he could not procure marble columns elsewhere for the building of it, he had them brought from Rome and Ravenna. As long as his health permitted it he used diligently to attend the church both in the morning and evening, and during the night, and at the time of the Sacrifice. He took the greatest care to have all the services of the church performed with the utmost dignity, and constantly warned the keepers of the building not to allow anything improper or dirty either to be brought into or to remain in the building. He provided so great a quantity of gold and silver vessels, and so large a supply of priestly vestments, that at the religious services not even the doorkeepers, who form the lowest ecclesiastical order, had to officiate in their ordinary dress. He carefully reformed the manner of reading and singing; for he was thoroughly instructed in both, though he never read publicly himself, nor sang except in a low voice, and with the rest of the congregation.

27. He was most devout in relieving the poor and in those free gifts which the Greeks call alms. For he gave it his attention not only in his own country and in his own kingdom, but he also used to send money across the sea to Syria, to Egypt, to Africa—to Jerusalem, Alexandria, and Carthage—in compassion for the poverty of any Christians whose miserable condition in those countries came to his ears. It was for this reason chiefly that he cultivated the friendship of kings beyond the sea, hoping thereby to win for the Christians living beneath their sway some succour and relief.

Beyond all other sacred and venerable places he loved the church of the holy Apostle Peter at Rome, and he poured into its treasury great wealth in silver and gold and precious stones. He sent innumerable gifts to the Pope; and during the whole course of his reign he strove with all his might (and, indeed, no object was nearer to his heart than this) to restore to the city of

Rome her ancient authority, and not merely to defend the church of Saint Peter but to decorate and enrich it out of his resources above all other churches. But although he valued Rome so much, still, during all the forty-seven years that he reigned, he only went there four times to pay his vows and offer up his prayers.

28. But such were not the only objects of his last visit; for the Romans had grievously outraged Pope Leo, had tom out his eyes and cut off his tongue, and thus forced him to throw himself upon the protection of the King. He, therefore came to Rome to restore the condition of the church, which was terribly disturbed, and spent the whole of the winter there. It was then that he received the title of Emperor and Augustus, which he so disliked at first that he affirmed that he would not have entered the church on that day—though it was the chief festival of the church—if he could have foreseen the design of the Pope. But when he had taken the title he bore very quickly the hostility that it caused and the indignation of the Roman emperors. He conquered their ill-feeling by his magnanimity, in which, doubtless, he far excelled them, and sent frequent embassies to them, and called them his brothers.

# READING 4

## The Services of a Serf

*By the fourteenth century, serfs were paid for their labor. This contract is from a manor in Sussex, England, and describes the services required of one particular serf named John of Cayworth. The contract stipulates the number of days the serf must devote to each task and the payment he is to receive from the lord in return for his work. Deductions for meals, which varied in price with the particular service performed, are factored into the serf's take-home pay. This excerpt is taken from James Harvey Robinson, ed.,* Readings in European History, *Vol. 2 (Boston: Athenaeum, 1906), pp. 400–402.*

---

### Discussion Questions

1. Does the work required of the serf appear excessive to you?
2. Does it seem worthwhile for the serf, given what he received in exchange?

John of Cayworth holds a house and 30 acres of land, and owes yearly 2 s[chillings] at Easter and Michaelmas [in rent to his lord]; and he owes a cock and two hens at Christmas [also in rent] of the value of 4 d[enarii] .

And he ought to harrow for 2 days at the Lenten sowing with one man and his own horse and his own harrow, the value of the work being 4d.; and he is to receive from the lord on each day 3 meals, of the value of 5d., and then the lord will be at a loss of 1 d. . . .

And he ought to carry the manure of the lord for 2 days with one cart, with his own 2 oxen, the value of the work being 8d.; and he is to receive from the lord each day 3 meals at the value as above. . . .

And he shall find one man for 2 days, for mowing the meadow of the lord, who can mow, by estimation, 1 acre and a half, the value of the mowing of an acre being 6d.; the sum is there 9d. And he is to receive each day 3 meals of the value given above. . . .

And he ought to carry the hay of the lord for 1 day with a cart and 3 animals of his own, the price of the work being 6d. And he shall have from the lord 3 meals of the value of 2 1/2d. . . .

And he ought to carry in autumn beans or oats for 2 days with a cart and 3 animals of his own, the value of the work being 12d. And he shall receive from the lord each day 3 meals of the value given above. . . .

And he ought to carry wood from the woods of the lord as far as the manor, for two days in summer, with a cart and 3 animals of his own, the value of the work being 9d. And he shall receive from the lord each day 3 meals of the price given above. . . .

The totals of the rents, with the value of the hens, is 2s. 4d.

# LECTURE TOPIC 16

# Fire from the Desert: The Rise of Islam

I. How did the Religion of Islam Originate?
  A. Muhammed the Prophet: Abdul-Kassim (570–632 AD.)
    1. Member of Aristocratic Clan, but Poor
    2. Married Rich Widow
    3. Visions Commenced at Age 40
II. How was the New Faith Initially Received?
  A. Hegira to Medina: 622 A.D.
  B. Return to and Forced Submission of Mecca: 630 AD.
  C. Death of Muhammed and Declaration to Proclaim Faith to All Nations: 632 A.D.
III. How did Islam Rapidly Transform into a World Religion?
  A. Incredible Expansion in all Directions
    1. Crossed Gibraltar: 711 A.D.
    2. Battle of Tours: 732 A.D.; Charles Martel
    3. Establishment of Islamic Civilization in Spain at Cordova
    4. Conquests by Islamic Seljuk Turks:11th Century A.D.
    5. The Mongol Assault: Jenghiz Khan (1162–1227 A.D.)
      a) First Mongol Ruler converts to Islam: 1295 A.D.
IV. How was the Islamic Empire Organized?
  A. The *Calif:* Elective at First; then Dynastic
    1. Disputes Over Succession
      a) Shi'a and Sunni
V. What are the Teachings of Islam?
  A. The "Five Pillars of Islam"
    1. Know the *Qur'an* and Declare in Arabic: "There is But One God, Allah, and Muhammad is his Prophet"
      a) Uncompromising Monotheism
    2. Pray to Allah, Facing Mecca Five Times Each Day
    3. Observe the Fast of Ramadan
    4. Go on a *Hadjj* and Visit Mecca at Least Once in One's Lifetime
    5. Give Alms to the Poor
  B. Other Tenets
    1. Centrality of the *Qur'an*
      a) Many of the Prophet's Teachings Gathered from Memory
        (1) The *Sunna*
    2. Prohibition of Intoxicating Drinks
    3. Ban on Usury
    4. Condemnation of Adultery
    5. Condemned Infanticide
    6. Condemned Oppression of the Poor
    7. Approved Polygyny and Divorce for Men
    8. Accepted Jewish and Christian Prophets

VI. What are Some Examples of the Scientific and Cultural Brilliance of Early Islam?
   A. al-Masudi (mid-tenth Cent. A.D.): 30 Vol. World History
   B. Hunayn ibn-Ishaq (d. 877 A.d.): Physician and Writer
   C. al-Kwarizmi (9TH Cent. A.D.): Father of Algebra; Popularized Zero (borrowed from India)
   D. Omar Khayam (d. 1123 A.D.): Poet and Mathematician
   E. Astrolabe
   F. al-Kimya
   G. Dyes and Fabrics: Cotton, Satin, Scarlet, Crimson, Saffron, Lilac
   H. Metalwork; Crystal and Ivory Carving; Leatherwork; Ceramic
   I. Paper Making and Block Printing
   J. Gunpowder (Borrowed from China)
   K. Triangular Sails and Magnetic Compass
   L. Windmill
   M. Almanacs
   N. Western Use Arabic Numerals

VII. Conclusion: What are the Contributions of Early Islam?
   A. One of World's Great Monotheistic Religions
   B. Astonishing Nature of Islamic Culture During Europe's Sleep
   C. Preservation of Classical Learning and Contribution to European Renaissance
   D. Islam's Joint Heritage with the West

# READING 1

## The Qur'an

*As with most world religions, Islam burst into existence as the product of a great prophet's visions. And as with most other founders, Muhammed (570–632 AD.) committed almost none of his revelations to writing, leaving that task to his disciples. The following are but a fraction of the one-hundred-fourteen Suras constituting the Moslem's holiest canon. Our source for these passages is: Rodwell, trans.,* The Qur'an *(London and Toronto., J. M. Dent & Sons, 1909), pp. 24–25, 31, 40–41, 88–91.*

---

### Discussion Questions

1. How does Muhammed view the Jewish Prophets?
2. According to the Qur'an, what sort of moral behavior is required of a Muslim?

## SELECTIONS FROM THE HOLY QUR'AN

*Sura LXXIII.—The Enfolded*

Commemorate the name of thy Lord, and devote thyself to Him with entire devotion.

Lord of the East and of the West! No God is there but He! Take Him for thy protector . . .

Lo! this is a warning. Let him then who will, take the way to his Lord.

Of a truth, thy Lord knoweth that thou prayest almost two-thirds, or half, or a third of the night, as do a part of thy followers. But God measureth the night and the day:—He knoweth that ye cannot count its hours aright, and therefore, turneth to you mercifully. Recite then so much of the Qur'an as may be easy to you. He knoweth that there will be some among you sick, while others travel through the earth in quest of the bounties of God; and others do battle in his cause. Recite therefore so much of it as may be easy. And observe the Prayers and pay the legal Alms and lend God a liberal loan: for whatever good works ye send on before for your own behalf, ye shall find with God. This will be best and richest in the recompense. And seek the forgiveness of God: verily, God is forgiving, Merciful.

*Sura CVII.—Religion*

In the name of God, the Compassionate, the Merciful

What thinkest thou of him who treateth our RELIGION as a lie? He it is who thrusteth away the orphan,

And stirreth not *others* up to feed the poor.

Woe to those who pray,

But in their prayer are careless;

Who make a shew of devotion,

But refuse help to the needy.

*Sura CII.—Desire*

In *the name of God, the Compassionate, the Merciful*

The DESIRE of increasing riches occupieth you,

Till ye come to the grave.

Nay! but in the end ye shall know

Nay! once more, in the end ye shall know *your folly.*

Nay! would that ye knew it with knowledge of certainty! Surely ye shall see hell-fire.

### *Sura LXXXVII.—The Most High*

In *the Name of God, the Compassionate, the Merciful*
Praise the name of thy Lord THE MOST HIGH,
Who hath created and balanced *all things*,
Who hath fixed their destinies and guideth them,
Who bringeth forth the pasture,
And reduceth it to dusky stubble.
We will teach thee to recite the Qur'an, nor aught shalt thou forget,
Save what God pleaseth; for he knoweth alike things manifest and hidden; And we will make easy to thee our easy ways.
Warn, therefore, for the warning is profitable:
He that feareth God will receive the warning,
And the most reprobate only will turn aside from it,
Who shall be exposed to the terrible fire,
In which he shall not die, and shall not live.
Happy he who is purified *by Islam*,
And who remembereth the name of his Lord and prayeth.
But ye prefer this present life,
Though the life to come is better and more enduring.
This truly is in the Books of old,
The Books of Abraham and Moses.

### *Sura XCV.—The Fig*

In *the Name of God, the Compassionate, the Merciful*
I swear by the FIG and by the olive,
By Mount Sinai,
And by this inviolate soil!
That of goodliest fabric we created man,
Then brought him down to be the lowest of the low;
Save who believe and do the things that are right, for theirs shall be a reward that faileth not.
Then, who after this shall make thee treat the Judgment as a lie?
What! is not God the most just of judges?
. . . We ourselves have sent down to thee the Qur'an as a missive from on high. Await then with patience the judgments of thy Lord, and obey not the wicked among them and the unbelieving:
And make mention of the name of thy Lord at morn, at even,
And at night. Adore him, and praise him the livelong night.

### *Sura XLIV.—Smoke*

In *the Name of God, the Compassionate, the Merciful*
By virtue of our behest. Lo! We have ever sent forth Apostles,
A mercy from thy Lord: he truly heareth and knoweth all things
Lord of the Heavens and of the Earth and of all that is between them,—if ye be firm in faith
There is no God but He!—He maketh alive and killeth!—Your Lord and the Lord of your sires of old!
Yet with doubts do they disport them.
But mark them on the day when the Heaven shall give out a palpable SMOKE,
Which shall enshroud mankind: this will be an afflictive torment.
*They will cry*, "Our Lord! relieve us from this torment: see! we are believers." But how did warning avail them, when an undoubted apostle had come to them;
And they turned their backs on him, and said, "Taught by others, possessed?"

Were we to relieve you from the plague even a little, ye would certainly relapse.

On the day when we shall fiercely put forth our great fierceness, we will surely take vengeance on them! . . .

Verily the day of severing shall be the appointed time of all:

A day when the master shall not at all be aided by the servant, neither shall they be helped;

Save those on whom God shall have mercy: for life is the mighty, the merciful . . . the pious shall be in a secure place,

Amid gardens and fountains,

Clothed in silk and richest robes, facing one another:

Thus shall it be: and we will wed them to the virgins with large dark eyes: Therein shall they call, secure, for every kind of fruit;

Therein, their first death passed, shall they taste death no more and He shall keep them from the pains of Hell:

'Tis the gracious bounty of thy Lord! This is the great felicity.

We have made this Qur'an easy for thee in thine own tongue, that they may take the warning.

# READING 2

## The Rubaiyat of Omar Khayyam

*Islamic creativity burned brightly during the centuries when European thought and culture were at their lowest ebb. Among the Moslems' many interests was a gift for poetry. And perhaps no Islamic poet achieved such popularity with later Europeans as Omar Khayyam (d. 1123 AD.). The skeptical, ironic edge he gave his verse reminds one of the ancient Jewish book of Ecclesiastes. These quatrains are taken from the most popular of Khayyam's English translators, Edward Fitzgerald. Edward Heron-Allen,* Edward Fitzgerald's Rubaiyat of Omar Khayyam with their Original Persian Sources. *(London: Bernard Quaritch, 1899), pp. 14, 22, 24, 34, 40.*

---

Discussion Questions

What do Kayyam's quatrains reveal about his attitude toward life and death?
How does this approach to life contradict or support the message in the Qur'an? What does this tell us about the "Golden Age of Islam."?

### THE RUBAIYAT

---

VII.
Come, fill the Cup, and in the fire of Spring
Your Winter-garment of Repentance fling: The Bird of
Time has but a little way
To flutter—and the Bird is on the Wing.

XII.
A Book of Verses underneath the Bough,
A Jug of Wine, a Loaf of Bread—and Thou
Beside me singing in the Wilderness
Oh, Wilderness were Paradise enow!

XIII.
Some for the Glories of This World; and some
Sigh for the Prophet's Paradise to come;
Ah, take the Cash, and let the Credit go
Nor heed the rumble of a distant Drum!

XVI
The Worldly Hope men set their Hearts upon
Turns Ashes—or it prospers; and anon,
Like Snow upon the Desert's dusty Face,
Lighting a little hour or two—is gone.

XXI.
Ah, my Beloved fill the Cup that clears
To-day of past Regrets and future Fears:

*To-morrow!*—Why, To-morrow I may be
Myself with Yesterday's Sev'n thousand Years.

XXIV.
Ah, make the most of what we yet may spend,
Before we too into the Dust descend;
Dust into Dust, and under Dust to lie,
Sans Wine, sans Song, sans Singer, and—sans End!

XXV.
Alike for those who for to-day prepare,
And those that after some to-morrow stare,
A Muezzin from the Tower of Darkness cries,
"Fools! your Reward is neither Here nor There."

XLVII
When You and I behind the Veil are past,
Oh, but the long, long while the World shall last,
Which of our Coming and Departure heeds
As the Sea's self should heed a pebble-cast.

LXIII
Oh threats of Hell and Hopes of Paradise!
One thing at least is *certain—This* Life flies;
One thing is certain and the rest is Lies;
The Flower that once has blown for ever dies.

LXIV
Strange, is it not? that of the myriads who
Before us pass'd the door of Darkness through
Not one returns to tell us of the Road,
Which to discover we must travel too.

LXXI
The Moving Finger writes; and, having writ,
Moves on: nor all your Piety nor Wit
Shall lure it back to cancel half a Line,
Nor all your Tears wash out a Word of it.

# READING 3

## Moslem Political and Philosophical Thought

*The amount of writing and scholarship produced by Islamic civilization is astonishing. And among those to be counted in this regard was ibn Khaldun (1332–1406 AD.). He wrote a comprehensive history of the Arabs and their neighbors and, in a masterly accompanying treatise on the philosophy of history, exhibited great insight. Two passages have been excerpted from his study and presented below. The other, as with Aristotle and others, underlines the importance of humankind's capacity for wonder and reflection. For the source of the selections that follow, see: ibn Khaldun, The Mugaddimah: An Introduction to* History, Franz Rosenthal translator *(3 vols.; New York: Pantheon Books, 1958), Vol. II: pp. 103–106, 414–426.*

---

### Discussion Questions

1. According to ibn Khaldun's, why should rulers respect property rights?
2. In the second reading, how is humankind's capacity for wonder and reflection viewed?
3. Would you consider these ideas to be "Western"? Give examples.

### IBN KHALDUN

---

*Injustice Brings About the Ruin of Civilization.*

It should be known that attacks on people's property remove the incentive to acquire and gain property. People, then, become of the opinion that the purpose and ultimate destiny of (acquiring property) is to have it taken away from them. When the incentive to acquire and obtain property is gone, people no longer make efforts to acquire any. The extent and degree to which property rights are infringed upon determines the extent and degree to which the efforts of the subject to acquire property slacken. When attacks (on property) are extensive and general, extending to all means of making a livelihood, business inactivity, too, becomes (general), because the general extent of (such attacks upon property) means a general destruction of the incentive (to do business). If the attacks upon property are but light, the stoppage of gainful activity is correspondingly slight. Civilization and its well-being as well as business prosperity depend on productivity and people's efforts in all directions in their own interest and profit. When people no longer do business in order to make a living, and when they cease all gainful activity, the business of civilization slumps, and everything decays. People scatter everywhere in search of sustenance, to places outside the jurisdiction of their present government. The population of the particular region becomes light. The settlements there become empty. The cities lie in ruins. The disintegration of (civilization) causes the disintegration of the status of dynasty and ruler, because (their peculiar status) constitutes the *form* of civilization and the form necessarily decays when its *matter* (in this case, civilization) decays.

When the King heard that, he proceeded to look into (the affairs of) his realm. The farms were taken away from the intimates of the ruler and restored to their owners. They were again treated, as they had formerly been treated. They began again to cultivate (their farms). Those who had been weak gained in strength. The land was cultivated, and the country became prosperous. There was much money for the collectors of the land tax. The army was strengthened. The enemies' sources of (strength) were cut off. The frontier garrisons were manned. The ruler proceeded to take personal charge of his affairs. His days were prosperous, and his realm was well organized.

*Man Is Essentially Ignorant, and Becomes Learned Through Acquiring (Knowledge).*

We have already explained at the beginning of these sections that man belongs to the genus of animals and that God distinguished him from them by the ability to think, which He gave man and through which man is able to arrange his actions in an orderly manner. This is the discerning intellect. Or, when it helps him to acquire from his fellow men a knowledge of ideas and of the things that are useful or detrimental to him, it is the experimental intellect. Or, when it helps him to obtain perception of the existent things as they are, whether they are absent or present, it is the speculative intellect.

Man's ability to think comes to him (only) after the animality in him has reached perfection . . . the noble verse of the Qur'an refers to it at the very beginning and opening of the revelation, and establishes through it the fact that (man) has received (from God) as a favor the first of the stages of his existence, which is humanity and its two conditions, the innate one and the acquired one.

"God has been knowing and wise."

← In order for a civilization to prosper, it needs security from injustices, so that they'll feel safe enough to settle & work on the prosperity of their society & in turn highlight the leadership of the upper class.

# READING 4

## Travels of Rabbi Benjamin of Tudela, 1164 A.D.

*Benjamin of Tudela, a native of Spain and a Jew, set out to explore the world between the years 1160–1173 A.D. and came back to report on the lives of Jews in various lands. His experiences throughout the Middle East give much insight into the Islamic world and their society, customs and governance and expose the advanced state of affairs in the Muslim world. His records also act as a great contrast to the governments in Medieval Europe during the same period. The excerpt below is from Thomas Wright, ed.,* Early Travels in Palestine... *(London: Henry G. Bohn, 1848)), pp. 95–97.*

---

### Discussion Questions

1. How do the Muslims treat the Jewish population in Baghdad? What does this tell us about this society and government? Compare this with the treatment of the Jews in Christian Europe.
2. How are the Caliph (Khalif) and the structure of his state viewed by Benjamin of Tudela? Do you note very modern concepts of governance? Compare this with Europe in the 12th century.

## His Travel to Baghdad

. . . Baghdad, the large metropolis of the khalif Emir-al-Mumenin al Abassi, of the family of their prophet, who is chief of the Mohammedan (Muslim) religion. All Mohammedan kings acknowledge him, and he holds the same dignity over them which the pope enjoys over the Christians . . . The great Abbasid is extremely friendly towards the Jews, many of his officers being of that nation; he understands all languages, is well versed in Mosaic law, and reads and writes the Hebrew tongue. He enjoys nothing except what he earns by labour of his own hands . . . The khalif is and excellent man, trustworthy and kind-hearted towards every one, but generally invisible to the Mohammedans . . .

The Khalif leaves his palace but once every year, at the time of the feast of Ramadan; on which occasion many visitors assemble from distant parts, in order to have an opportunity of beholding his countenance . . . The streets and squares are enlivened with singing and rejoicing, and by parties who dance before the great king, called khalif. He is saluted loudly by the assembled crowd, who cry: "Blessed art thou, our lord and king." He thereupon kisses his garment, and by holding it in his hand, acknowledges and returns the compliment . . . The Khalif never leaves his palace again for a whole year. He is a pious and benevolent man, and has erected buildings on the other side of the river . . . the buildings include large houses, streets, and hostelries for the sick and poor, who resort thither in order to be cured. There are about sixty medical warehouses here, all well provided for the king's stores with spices and other necessaries; and every patient who claims assistance is fed at the king's expense, until his cure is completed.

There is further a large building, called the Dar-al-Maraphtan, in which are confined all the insane persons who are met with, particularly during the hot season, every one of whom is secured by iron chains until his reason returns, when he is allowed to return home. For this purpose, they are regularly examined once a month by officers appointed by the king for this purpose; and when they are found to be possessed of reason they are immediately liberated.

All this is done by the king in pure charity towards all who come to Baghdad, either ill or insane; for the king is a pious man, and his intention is excellent in this respect.

Baghdad contains about one thousand Jews, who enjoy peace, comfort, and much honour under the government of the great king. Among them are very wise men and presidents of colleges, whose occupation is the study of Mosaic law. The city contains ten [Jewish]colleges . . .

Many of the Jews of Baghdad are good scholars and very rich. The city contains twenty-eight Jewish synagogues, situated partly in Baghdad and partly in Al-Khorkh, on the other side of the Tigris, which runs through and divides the city.

# LECTURE TOPIC 17

# *India and China*

I. India
   A. Gupta Empire: 320–480 A.D.
      1. A Dynasty of Kings Ruling from Bihar in Ganges Valley
      2. Brought Peace and Prosperity to Northern India
         a) Samudragupta (ca. 335–375 A.D.)
         b) Chandragupta II (375–415 A.D.)
      3. Scholarship, Poetry, and Mathematics (Invention of Zero)
   B. Invasion by Huns: ca. 450 A.D.
      1. Defeated by Guptas
   C. Decline of Gupta Dynasty
      1. Political and Military Fragmentation
      2. Hardening and Proliferation of Caste System: Subdivided along Trade and Tribal Lines
   D. How Did the Indian Culture View Women and Family Life?
      1. Sternly Patriarchal: Extended-Family Homes
      2. Status of Women
         a) Arranged Child Marriages
         b) Strict Subordination of Women to Fathers, Husbands, and Sons
      3. *Sati:* Especially Among Kshatriyas
      4. Children Prized: Especially Sons
   E. What Impact Resulted from India's Successive Invasions: 650–1400 A.D.?
      1. Muslim-Arabs Pushed Conquests Eastward: Afghanistan, Punjab and Ganges Beginning in 636 A.D.
      2. Muslim Turks: ca. 900–1200 A.D.
         a) Vast Destruction of Hindu and Buddhist Shrines
         b) Many Buddhists Escape to Himalayas
         c) Turks Establish Islamic Sultinate of Delhi: 1206–1526 A.D.
            (1) Islam Firmly Rooted in Northwest India (Pakistan)
            (2) Elsewhere Absorbed by Hindus
            (3) New Turkish Invasion by Timur: 1398 A.D.
               (a) Older Islamic and Hindu Jurisdictions Shattered

II. China: 580–1400 A.D.
   A. How Did Buddhism Come to China and Why Did it Spread?
      1. Arrived in China Between 300–500 A.D.
      2. Appeal of Egalitarian and Merciful Concepts
      3. Growing Wealth and Power of Buddhist Monasteries
   B. What Were the Achievements of the Tang Dynasty: 618–907 A.D.?
      1. Successors of the Sui (581–618 A.D.): A Short Lived Dynasty
      2. Widespread Prosperity
      3. Successful Bureaucratic Control
      4. Emphasis on Education: Advancement by Examination

    5. Gunpowder and Other Technological Innovations such as Abacus
    6. Withstood Islamic Advances in the West
C. Military Collapse and Confusion: 907–960 A.D.
D. Sung Dynasty: 960–1279 A.D.
    1. Return of Prosperity
        a) Trade Carried Via Arabs to Mediterranean
        b) Use of Paper Money
    2. Block Printing; Also Moveable Type
    3. Sensitive Painting and Beautiful Ceramics
    4. Widespread Scholarship; Encyclopedias
    5. Urban Growth
    6. Decline in Status of Women: Footbinding
        a) Ornamental Purpose as Product of Urban Prosperity
E. How Did the Mongol Invasions of 1215–1368 A.D. Impact China?
    1. Sung Dynasty Overrun by Jenghiz Khan and Grandson, Kublai Khan (1216–1294 A.D.)
    2. Establish Yuan Dynasty: 1271–1368 A.D.)
        a) Mandarins Displaced
        b) Native Chinese Humbled; New Classes Created
        c) Visit of Marco Polo (1254–1324 A.D.)
F. Ming Dynasty: 1368–1644 A.D.
    1. Chinese Revolt
    2. Hung Wu (1328–1398 A.D.): First Emperor of Ming Dynasty
    3. Return of Prosperity

# READING 1

## Religion in India Between the Fourth and Sixteenth Centuries

*The more liberal Mahayana sect of Buddhist belief took articulate form during the Gupta period of Indian history. Buddhism's most basic assumptions did not change, however. One such doctrine, that of "emptiness," is addressed in the first selection below. The second is a Buddhist appeal for harmony on the part of kings and leaders. It stands in contrast to traditional Hindu approval for conquest and territorial acquisition.*

*The third extract constitutes an Islamic description of the attributes of God. The fourth selection was written by Abd ul-Haqq al Dihlawi al-Bukhari and dates from the sixteenth century A.D. It is part of an exposition on Sunni doctrine and is a good example of Islamic thought in India. These three excerpts are taken from William Theodore de Bary et al., comps.,* Sources of Indian Tradition *(New York: Columbia University Press, 1958), pp. 176–177, 184–185, 259–261, 396–397.*

*The three documents that follow the above are excerpted from Vatsyayana's* Kama Sutra, *written between the first and the fourth centuries. They provide examples of Hindu thought during the Gupta period and offer alternative views of pleasure and culture, which balance the pessimistic, ascetic themes encountered in so many Hindu texts. Although once dismissed as little more than a sex manual, the* Kama Sutra *exhibits beautiful language, which gives it a continuing appeal. The centrality of sexuality to life and the importance of foreplay and equal pleasure to both partners is its principle theme. The excerpts come from* The Kama Sutra of Vatsyayana, *translated by Sir Richard Burton (New York; The Modern Library, a division of Random House, Inc., 2002), pp. 16–18, 58–59, 62–65.*

---

### Discussion Questions

1. According to the Kama Sutra excerpts, how is pleasure and culture viewed? What does this tell us about Hindu thought during the Gupta period? Do you think the majority of people in India were able to live their lives accordingly?
2. Consider the last excerpt on Islamic thought in India. Do you detect any hint of ancient Hindu or Buddhist beliefs? Why or why not?

### THE BUDDHIST DOCTRINE OF EMPTINESS

All things conditioned are instable, impermanent,
Fragile in essence, as an unbaked pot,
Like something borrowed, or a city founded on sand,
They last a short while only.

They are inevitably destroyed,
Like plaster washed off in the rains,

Like the sandy bank of a river
They are conditioned, and their true nature is frail.

They are like the flame of a lamp,
Which rises suddenly and as soon goes out.
They have no power of endurance, like the wind
Or like foam, unsubstantial, essentially feeble . . .

The mystic knows the beginning and end
Of consciousness, its production and passing away
He knows that it came from nowhere and returns to nowhere,
And is empty [of reality], like a conjuring trick...

Thus all things in this world of contingence
Are dependent on causes and conditions.
The mystic knows what is true reality,
And sees all conditioned things as empty and powerless.

## Buddhist Urgings of Peacefulness

Protect all those royal families, cities, lands, and provinces, save them, cherish them, guard them, ward off invasion from them, give them peace and prosperity. Keep them free from all fear, calamity, and evil portent. Turn back the troops of their enemies and create in all the earthly kings of India a desire to avoid fighting, attacking, quarreling, or disputing with their neighbors . . . When the eighty-four thousand kings of the eighty-four thousand cities of India are contented with their own territories and with their own kingly state and their own hoards of treasure they will not attack one another or raise mutual strife. They will gain their thrones by the due accumulation of the merit of former deeds; they will be satisfied with their own kingly state, and will not destroy one another, nor show their mettle by laying waste whole provinces. When all the eighty-four thousand kings of the eighty-four thousand capital cities of India think of their mutual welfare and feel mutual affection and joy, . . . contented in their own domains, . . . India will be prosperous, well-fed, pleasant, and populous. The earth will be fertile, and the months and seasons and years will all occur at the proper time. Planets and stars, moon and sun, will duly bring on the days and nights. Rain will fall upon earth at the proper time. And all living beings in India will be rich with all manner of riches and corn, very prosperous but not greedy.

## Islamic Thought In India

### *The Attributes of God*

In truth, the creation and the proper ordering of the world will not come right except with one creator and one governor . . . The Nourisher of the World is alive, is wise and powerful, and a free agent. Whatever He does is by His own intent and choice and not under compulsion and necessity. . . He is a speaker of speech, a hearer of hearing, and a seer of seeing, because to be dumb, deaf, and blind is to be deficient and deficiencies are not proper to God. The Holy Qur'an is eloquent as to that. It is impossible to comprehend the reality of these attributes, indeed of the totality of divine attributes by analogy and reason. But God has created a likeness of those in the essence of humankind, which he has interpenetrated in some way or other with His own attributes. But in truth, the attributes of man do not survive as God's attributes survive. "God's eternal attributes remain."

. . . He is not formed so that He has bodily shape and He is not compounded so that He is joined together repeatedly. He is not numbered so that it is possible to count Him. He is not limited so that He has a limit and He is not in a direction, that is to say, He is not above or below, before or after, left or right. He is not in a place and not in a moment, because all these are attributes of the world and the Nourisher of the World is not subject to worldly attributes and His purposes are not subject to time. . . .

*The Transcendence of God*

Whatever exists, except God's essence and attributes, is created, that is to say, it comes into existence from nonexistence and is not eternal. As proof, the tradition of the Prophet, "There was God and there was nothing besides Him." As proof too, the world changes and is a place of many vicissitudes. Whatever is of this description is not eternal, and whatever is eternal does not change . . . And Almighty God is capable of extinguishing the world. After existence it passes away. As the Word of God says: "Everything perishes except the mode [Him]." Thus the angels, paradise, hell, and such like things to whose lastingness a tradition has testified, also are perishable . . . Although God can annihilate in the twinkling of an eye, those who do not die will know that God is the creator of the world who has brought it into existence from nonexistence.

## Hindu Approval for Domestic and Civilized Pleasures

Having thus acquired learning, a man, with the wealth that he may have gained by gift, conquest, purchase, deposit,[1] or inheritance from his ancestors, should become a householder, and pass the life of a citizen. He should take a house in a city, or large village, or in the vicinity of good men, or in a place which is the resort of many persons. The abode should be situated near some water, and divided into different compartments for different purposes. It should be surrounded by a garden, and also contain two rooms, an outer and an inner one. The inner room should be occupied by the females, while the outer room, balmy with rich perfumes, should contain a bed, soft, agreeable to the sight, covered with a clean white cloth, low in the middle part, having garlands and bunches of flowers upon it, and a canopy above it, and two pillows, one at the top, another at the bottom. . .

Now the householder, having got up in the morning and performed his necessary duties, [2] should wash his teeth, apply a limited quantity of ointments and perfumes to his body, put some ornaments on his person and collyrium on his eyelids and below his eyes, colour his lips with alacktaka, [3] and look at himself in the glass. Having then eaten betel leaves, with other things that give fragrance to the mouth, he should perform his usual business. He should bathe daily, anoint his body with oil every other day, apply a lathering[4] substance to his body every three days, get his head (including face) shaved every four days, and the other parts of his body every five or ten days. All these things should be done without fail, and the sweat of the armpits should also be removed. Meals should be taken in the forenoon, in the afternoon, and again at night, according to Charayana. After breadfast, parrots and other birds should be taught to speak, and the fighting of cocks, quails, and rams should follow. A limited time should be devoted to diversions with Pithamardas, Vitas, and Vidushakas,[5] and then should be taken the midday sleep.[6] After this the householder, having put on his clother and ornaments, should, during the afternoon, converse with his friends. In the evening there should be singing, and after that the householder, along with his friend, should await in his room, previously decorated and perfumed, the arrival of the woman that may be attached to him, or he may send a female messenger for her, or go to her himself. After her arrival at his house, he

---

1 Gift is peculiar to a Brahman, conquest to a Kshutrya, while purchase, deposit, and other means of acquiring wealth belong to the Vaishya.

2 The calls of nature always performed by the Hindoos the first thing in the morning.

3 A colour made from lac.

4 This would act instead of soap, which was not introduced until the rule of the Mahomedans.

5 These are characters introduced in the Hindoo drama.

6 Noonday sleep is only allowed in summer, when the nights are short.

and his friend should welcome her, and entertain her with a loving and agreeable conversation. Thus end the duties of the day.

The following are the things to be done occasionally as diversions or amusements.

1. Holding festivals in honour of different duties.
2. Social gatherings of both sexes.
3. Drinking parties.
4. Picnics.
5. Other social diversions.

## "Of the Various Modes of Striking, and of the Sounds Appropriate to Them"

Sexual intercourse can be compared to a quarrel, on account of the contrarieties of love and its tendency to dispute. The place of striking with passion is the body, and on the body special places are:

The shoulders.
The head.
The space between the breasts.
The back.
The jaghana, or middle part of the body.
The sides.

Striking is of four kinds, viz.:

Striking with the back of the hand.
Striking with the fingers a little contracted.
Striking with the fist.
Striking with the open palm of the hand.

On account of its causing pain, striking gives rise to a hissing sound, which is of various kinds, and to the eight kinds of crying, viz.:

The sound of Hin.
The thundering sound.
The cooing sound.
The weeping sound.
The sound Phut.
The sound Phât.
The sound Sût.
The sound Plât.

Besides these, there are also words having a meaning, such as "mother," and those that are expressive of prohibition, sufficiency, desire of liberation, pain or praise, and to which may be added sounds like those of the dove, the cuckoo, the green pigeon, the parrot, the bee, the sparrow, the flamingo, the duck, and the quail, which are all occasionally made use of.

Blows with the fist should be given on the back of the woman, while she is sitting on the lap of the man, and she should give blows in return, abusing the man as if she were angry, and making the cooing and the weeping sounds. While the woman is engaged in congress the space between the breasts should be struck with the back of the hand, slowly at first, and then proportionately to the increasing excitement, until the end.

## About Women Acting the Part of a Man; and of the Work of a Man

When a woman sees that her lover is fatigued by constant congress, without having his desire satisfied, she should, with his permission, lay him down upon his back, and give him assistance by acting his part. She may also do this to satisfy the curiosity of her lover, or her own desire of novelty.

There are two ways of doing this, the first is when during congress she turns round, and gets on the top of her lover, in such a manner as to continue the congress, without obstructing the pleasure of it; and the other is when she acts the man's part from the beginning. At such a time, with flowers in her hair hanging loose, and her smiles broken by hard breathings, she should press upon her lover's bosom with her own breasts, and lowering her head frequently should do in return the same actions which he used to do before, returning his blows and chaffing him, should say, "I was laid down by you, and fatigued with hard congress, I shall now therefore lay you down in return." She should then again manifest her own bashfulness, her fatigue, and her desire of stopping the congress. In this way she should do the work of a man, which we shall presently relate.

Whatever is done by a man for giving pleasure to a woman is called the work of a man, and is as follows:—

While the woman is lying on his bed, and is as it were abstracted by his conversation, he should loosen the knot of her under garments, and when she begins to dispute with him, he should overwhelm her with kisses. Then when his lingam is erect he should touch her with his hands in various places, and gently manipulate various parts of the body. If the woman is bashful, and if it is the first time that they have come together, the man should place his hands between her thighs, which she would probably keep close together, and if she is a very young girl, he should first get his hands upon her breasts, which she would probably cover with her own hands, and under her armpits and on her neck. If however she is a seasoned woman, he should do whatever is agreeable either to him or to her, and whatever is fitting for the occasion. After this he should take hold of her hair, and hold her chin in his fingers for the purpose of kissing her. On this, if she is a young girl, she will become bashful and close her eyes. Any how he should gather from the action of the woman what things would be pleasing to her during congress.

Here Suvarnanabha says that while a man is doing to the woman what he likes best during congress, he should always make a point of pressing those parts of her body on which she turns her eyes.

The signs of the enjoyment and satisfaction of the woman are as follows: her body relaxes, she closes her eyes, she puts aside all bashfulness, and shows increased willingness to unite the two organs as closely together as possible. On the other hand, the signs of her want of enjoyment and of failing to be satisfied are as follows: she shakes her hands, she does not let the man get up, feels dejected, bites the man, kicks him, and continues to go on moving after the man has finished. In such cases the man should rub the yoni of the woman with his hand and fingers (as the elephant rubs anything with his trunk) before engaging in congress, until it is softened, and after that is done he should proceed to put his lingam into her. . .

When the woman is tired, she should place her forehead on that of her lover, and should thus take rest without disturbing the union of the organs, and when the woman has rested herself the man should turn round and begin the congress again.

There are also some verses on the subject as follows:

"Though a woman is reserved, and keeps her feelings concealed, yet when she gets on the top of a man, she then shows all her love and desire. A man should gather from the actions of the woman of what disposition she is, and in what way she likes to be enjoyed. A woman during her monthly courses, a woman who has been lately confined, and a fat woman should not be made to act the part of a man."

# READING 2

## Buddhism and Confucianism in China

*While Buddhism emigrated from India to China much earlier, with the Islamic onslaught after the seventh century A.D., Buddhist monks and devotees moved to China in large numbers. Slowly, the Chinese population converted to the new religion. This led, in turn, to attacks on Buddhism and questions as to its necessity. The first selection provides a Chinese Buddhist reply to this question.*

*The second reading is a petition written to a Sung emperor pleading greater regard for traditional Confucian values. The petitioner, one Ch'eng Yi (1033–1107 A.D.) acknowledged the prosperity of the Han and Tang dynasties but warns that it was inattention to Confucian precepts that brought on their decline.*

*Both these readings are found in Theodore de Bary et al., comps.,* Sources of Chinese Tradition *(New York: Columbia University Press, 1960), pp. 314, 315, 450–453.*

---

### Discussion Questions

1. In a society that greatly regards their ancestors, how does Mou Tzu validate the need for Buddhism despite the fact that ancient Chinese predecessors did not practice it?
2. In the second reading, what are Ch'eng Yi 's complaints about the government? Who is he trying to protect?

### WHY IS BUDDHISM NOT FOUND IN TRADITIONAL CHINESE TEXTS?

The questioner said: If the way of the Buddha is the greatest and most venerable of ways, why did Yao, Shun, the Duke of Chou, and Confucius not practice it? In the seven Classics one sees no mention of it . . . Mou Tzu said: All written works need not necessarily be the words of Confucius, and all medicine does not necessarily consist of the formula of [the famous physician] p'ien-chiieh. What accords with principle is to be followed, what heals the sick is good. The gentleman-scholar draws widely on all forms of good, and thereby benefits his character.

Tzu-kung [a disciple of Confucius] said, "Did the Master have a permanent teacher?" Yao served Yin Shou, Shun served Wu-ch'eng, the Duke of Chou learned from Lii Wang, and Confucius learned from Lao Tzu. And none of these teachers is mentioned in the seven Classics. Although these four teachers were sages, to compare them to the Buddha would be like comparing a white deer to a unicorn, or a swallow to a phoenix. Yao, Shun, the Duke of Chou, and Confucius learned even from such teachers as these. How much less, then, may one reject the Buddha, whose distinguishing marks are extraordinary and whose superhuman powers know no bounds! How may one reject him and refuse to learn from him? The records and teachings of the Five Classics do not contain everything. Even if the Buddha is not mentioned in them, what occasion is there for suspicion?

### MEMORIAL TO THE SUNG EMPEROR, JEN~TSUNG

In the Three Dynasties the Way was always followed; after the Ch'in it declined and did not flourish. Dynasties like the Wei and Chin indeed departed far from it. The Han and Tang achieved a limited prosperity, but in practicing the Way they adulterated it. . . .

In the *Book of History* it says: "The people are the foundation of the nation; when the foundation is solid the nation is at peace." Your servant thinks that the way to make the foundation firm is to pacify the people, and that the way to pacify the people is to see that they have enough food and clothing. Nowadays the people's strength is exhausted and there is not enough food and clothing in the land. When spring cultivation has begun and the seed has been sown, they hold their breath in anxious expectation. If some year their hopes are disappointed, they have to run away [and abandon the land]. In view of these facts, the foundation can hardly be called firm. Your servant considers that Your Majesty is kind and benevolent, loves the people as his children, and certainly cannot bear to see them suffer like this. Your servant suspects that the men around Your Majesty have shielded these things from Your Majesty's discerning sight, and prevented you from learning about them.

Now the government frequently has insufficient funds to meet its expenditures. Having an insufficiency, it turns to the Finance Commission, and the Finance Commission turns to the fiscal intendants of the various circuits. But where are the fiscal intendants to get the money? They simply have to wring it from the people . . . Surely Your Majesty, who is like a parent to the people, cannot help but take pity on them! The people have no savings and the government granaries are empty . . . If suddenly there is a famine for more than one year, such as the one which occurred in the Ming-tao period [1032–1033], I do not know how the government is going to deal with it. The soldiers who do no work and yet must be fed number more than one million. Since there is no means to support them, the people will be heavily taxed. And yet the people have already scattered. If strong enemies seize the opportunity to attack from without, or wicked men aspire to power from within, then we may well be fearful of a situation which is deteriorating and threatens to collapse.

Your servant considers that humanity is the foundation of the "Kingly Way." He observes that the humanity of Your Majesty is the humanity of Yao and Shun; and yet the empire has not had good government. This is because Your Majesty has a humane heart but not a humane government. Therefore Mencius [IV A:I] says: "There are now princes who have humane hearts and a reputation for humanity, while yet the people do not receive any benefit from them, nor will they leave any example to future ages—all because they do not put into practice the ways of the ancient kings". . . . Good government in the empire depends upon obtaining worthy men; misgovernment in the empire derives from a failure to obtain worthy men. The world does not lack worthy men; the problem is how to find them. The purpose of seeking out worthy men is good government, and the way to govern the empire is the way followed by the Five Emperors, the Three Kings, the Duke of Chou, and Confucius. Seeking out those who are familiar with the way of government employed by the Five Emperors, the Three Kings, the Duke of Chou, and Confucius, we should employ each of them according to the degree of his understanding of it . . .

In the selection of scholars for the civil service, though there are many categories under which men may qualify, yet there are only one or two persons who may be considered [under the category of] "wise, virtuous, square, and upright." Instead, what the government obtains are scholars who possess no more than wide learning and powerful memory. Those who qualify in [the examination on] Understanding of the Classics merely specialize in reciting from memory and do not understand their meaning. They are of little use in government . . . How can they know anything of the bases of education and cultivation found in the "Kingly Way"? They occupy the posts and are expected to fulfill their duties without ever having learned them. This is the same as having a nomad of the North steer a boat or having a riverman of the South be the driver of a horse. How can we possibly expect them to be any good? . . .

For two thousand years the Way has not been practiced. Foolish persons of recent times have all declared that times are different and things have changed, so that it can no longer be practiced. This only shows how deep their ignorance is, and yet time and again the rulers of men have been deceived by their talk. . . . But I see that Your Majesty's heart is filled with solicitude for the people, and if Your Majesty practices the Way of the sage-kings with such solicitude for the people, how can any difficulties stand in the way?

# READING 3

## Life at the Court of the Great Khan

*Marco Polo (1254–1324 AD.), a Venetian traveler and merchant, spent years in East Asia. He gained the confidence of the Emperor Kublai Khan (1216–1294 A.D.), performed diplomatic service for him and traveled throughout the Mongol empire. When he and his father, Nicolo, returned to Venice in 1295 after an absence of twenty-six years, they brought with them astonishing reports of a world both fabulous and foreign to nearly all Europeans. Below are excerpts describing life in China under the Mongol ruler. They are taken from* The Travels of Marco Polo, *revised from Marsden's translation and edited by Manuel Komroff (New York: Modern Library, 1953), pp. 118, 120, 122–124, 149, 150, 156–158, 160–164.*

---

### Discussion Questions

1. Why wouldn't the Great Khan convert to Christianity? Considering his expectations, do you think Christian missionaries could successfully convert him? Why or Why not?
2. What is Marco Polo's overall impression of the Great Khan and his empire? How does Marco Polo compare the customs of the East to those of Europeans?

## MARCO POLO

---

### *Chapter 6*

OF THE RETURN OF THE GREAT KHAN TO THE CITY OF KANBALU AFTER HIS VICTORY AND OF THE HONOUR HE CONFERS ON THE CHRISTIANS AND THE JEWS AND OTHER SUBJECTS

The Great Khan, having obtained this signal victory, returned with great pomp and triumph to the capital city of Kanbalu [Peking]. This took place in the month of November, and he continued to reside there during the months of February and March, in which latter was our festival of Easter. Being aware that this was one of our principal solemnities, he commanded all the Christians to attend him, and to bring with them their Book, which contains the four Gospels of the Evangelists.

After causing it to be repeatedly perfumed with incense, in a ceremonious manner, he devoutly kissed it, and directed that the same should be done by all his nobles who were present. This was his usual practice upon each of the principal Christian festivals, such as Easter and Christmas; and he observed the same at the festivals of the Saracens, Jews, and idolaters.

Upon being asked his motive for this conduct, he said: "There are four great Prophets who are reverenced and worshipped by the different classes of mankind. The Christians regard Jesus Christ as their divinity; the Saracens, Mahomet; the Jews, Moses; and the idolaters, Sogomombar-kan, the most eminent amongst their idols. I do honour and show respect to all the four, and invoke to my aid whichever amongst them is in truth Supreme in Heaven." But from the manner in which his majesty acted towards them, it is evident that he regarded the faith of the Christians as the truest and the best; nothing, as he observed, being enjoined to its professors that was not filled with virtue and holiness.

By no means, however, would he permit them to bear the cross before them in their processions, because upon it so exalted a personage as Christ had been scourged and put to death.

It may perhaps be asked by some, why, if he showed such a preference to the faith of Christ, he did not conform to it, and become a Christian?

His reason for not so doing, he assigned to Nicolo and Marco Polo, when, upon the occasion of his sending them as his ambassadors to the Pope, they ventured to address a few words to him on the subject of Christianity. "Wherefore," he said, "should I become a Christian? You yourselves must perceive that the Christians of these countries are ignorant, inefficient persons, who do not possess the faculty of performing anything miraculous; whereas you see that the idolaters can do whatever they will. When I sit at table the cups that were in the middle of the hall come to me filled with wine and other beverage, spontaneously and without being touched by human hand, and I drink from them. They have the power of controlling bad weather and obliging it to retire to any quarter of the heavens, with many other wonderful gifts of that nature. You are witnesses that their idols have the faculty of speech, and predict whatever is required.

"Should I become a convert to the faith of Christ, and profess myself a Christian, the nobles of my court and other persons who do not incline to that religion will ask me what sufficient motives have caused me to receive baptism, and to embrace Christianity. 'What extraordinary powers,' they will say, 'what miracles have been displayed by its ministers? Whereas the idolaters declare that what they exhibit is performed through their own sanctity, and the influence of their idols?'

"To this I shall not know what answer to make, and I shall be considered by them as labouring under a grievous error, whilst the idolaters, who by means of their profound art can effect such wonders, may without difficulty compass my death. But return you to your pontiff, and request of him, in my name, to send hither a hundred persons well skilled in your law, who being confronted with the idolaters shall have power to restrain them, and showing that they themselves are endowed with similar art, that which they refrain from exercising, because it is derived from the agency of evil spirits, shall compel them to desist from practices of such a nature in their presence. When I am witness of this, I shall place them and their religion under a ban, and shall allow myself to be baptized. Following my example, all my nobility will then in like manner receive baptism, and this will be imitated by my subjects in general. In the end the Christians of these parts will exceed in number those who inhabit your own country."

From this discourse it must be evident that if the Pope had sent out persons duly qualified to preach the gospel, the Great Khan would have embraced Christianity, for which, it is certainly known, he had a strong predilection.

## *Chapter 8*

### Of the Figure and Stature of the Great Khan of His Four Principal Wives and of the Annual Selection of Young Women For Him in the Province of Ungut

Kublai, who is styled the Great Khan, or Lord of Lords, is of middle stature, that is, neither tall nor short. His limbs are well formed, and in his whole figure there is a just proportion. His complexion is fair, and occasionally suffused with red, like the bright tint of the rose, which adds much grace to his countenance. His eyes are black and handsome, his nose is well shaped and prominent.

He has four wives of the first rank, who are esteemed legitimate, and the eldest born son of anyone of these succeeds to the empire, upon the decease of the Great Khan. They bear equally the title of empress, and have their separate courts. None of them have fewer than three hundred young female attendants of great beauty, together with a multitude of youths as pages, and other eunuchs, as well as ladies of the bedchamber; so that the number of persons belonging to each of their respective courts amounts to ten thousand.

When his majesty is desirous of the company of one of his empresses, he either sends for her, or goes himself to her palace. Besides these, he has many concubines provided for his use, from a province of Tartary named Ungut, the inhabitants of which are distinguished for beauty of features and fairness of complexion. Every second year, or oftener, as it may happen to be his pleasure, the Great Khan sends thither his officers, who collect for him, one hundred or more, of the handsomest of the young women, according to the estimation of beauty communicated to them in their instructions.

The mode of their appreciation is as follows. Upon the arrival of these commissioners, they give orders for assembling all the young women of the province, and appoint qualified persons to examine them, who, upon careful inspection of each of them separately, that is to say, of the hair, the countenance, the eyebrows, the mouth, the lips, and other features, as well as the symmetry of these with each other, estimate their value at sixteen, seventeen, eighteen, or twenty, or more carats, according to the greater or less degree of beauty. The number required by the Great Khan, at the rates, perhaps, of twenty or twenty-one carats, to which their commission was limited, is then selected from the rest, and they are conveyed to his court.

Upon their arrival in his presence, he causes a new examination to be made by a different set of inspectors, and from amongst them a further selection takes place, when thirty or forty are retained for his own chamber at a higher valuation. These are committed separately to the care of certain elderly ladies of the palace, whose duty it is to observe them attentively during the course of the night, in order to ascertain that they have not any concealed imperfections, that they sleep tranquilly, do not snore, have sweet breath, and are free from unpleasant scent in any part of the body. Having undergone this rigorous scrutiny, they are divided into parties of five, each taking turn for three days and three nights, in his majesty's interior apartment, where they are to perform every service that is required of them, and he does with them as he likes.

When this term is completed, they are relieved by another party, and in this manner successively, until the whole number have taken their turn; when the first five recommence their attendance. But while one party officiates in the inner chamber, another is stationed in the outer apartment adjoining. If his majesty should have occasion for anything, such as drink or victuals, the former may signify his commands to the latter, by whom the article required is immediately procured. In this way the duty of waiting upon his majesty's person is exclusively performed by these young females. The remainder of them, whose value had been estimated at an inferior rate, are assigned to the different lords of the household; under whom they are instructed in cookery, in dressmaking, and other suitable works; and upon any person belonging to the court expressing an inclination to take a wife, the Great Khan bestows upon him one of these damsels, with a handsome portion. In this manner he provides for them all amongst his nobility.

It may be asked whether the people of the province do not feel themselves aggrieved in having their daughters thus forcibly taken from them by the sovereign? Certainly not; but, on the contrary, they regard it as a favour and an honour done to them; and those who are the fathers of handsome children feel highly gratified by his condescending to make choice of their daughters. "If," say they, "my daughter is born under an auspicious planet and to good fortune, his majesty can best fulfill her destinies, by matching her nobly; which it would not be in my power to do." If, on the other hand, the daughter misconducts herself, or any mischance befalls her, by which she becomes disqualified, the father attributes the disappointment to the evil influence of her stars.

## *Chapter 22*

### Concerning the City of Kanbalu of the Multitude of Its Inhabitants and of the Commerce of the Place

The multitude of inhabitants, and the number of houses in the city of Kanbalu, as also in the suburbs without the city of which there are twelve, corresponding to the twelve gates, is greater than the mind can comprehend. The suburbs are even more populous than the city, and it is there that the merchants and others whose business leads them to the capital, take up their abode. Wherever, indeed, his Majesty holds his court, there these people flock from all quarters, in pursuit of their several objects.

In the suburbs there are also as handsome houses and stately buildings as in the city, with the exception only of the palace of the Great Khan. No corpse is suffered to be interred within the precincts of the city, and those of the Idolaters, with whom it is customary to burn their dead, are carried to the usual spot beyond the suburbs. There likewise all public executions take place. Women who live by prostituting themselves for money dare not, unless it be secretly, to exercise their profession in the city, but must confine themselves to the suburbs, where, as has already been stated, there reside above five-and-twenty thousand; nor is this number greater than is necessary for the vast concourse of merchants and other strangers, who, drawn there by the court, are continually arriving and departing.

To this city everything that is most rare and valuable in all parts of the world finds its way; and more especially does this apply to India, which furnishes precious stones, pearls, and various drugs and spices. From the provinces of Cathay itself, as well as from the other provinces of the Empire, whatever there is of value is brought here, to supply the demands of those multitudes who are induced to establish their residence in the vicinity of the court. The quantity of merchandise sold exceeds also the traffic of any other place; for no fewer than a thousand carriages and pack-horses, loaded with raw silk, make their daily entry; and gold tissues and silks of various kinds are manufactured to an immense extent.

In the vicinity of the capital are many walled and other towns, whose inhabitants live chiefly by the court, selling the articles which they produce in return for such as their own occasions require.

## Chapter 24

### Of the Kind of Paper Money Issued by the Great Khan and Made to Pass Current Throughout His Dominions

In this city of Kanbalu is the mint of the Great Khan, who may truly be said to possess the secret of the alchemists, as he has the art of producing money by the following process.

He causes the bark to be stripped from those mulberry-trees the leaves of which are used for feeding silk-worms, and takes from it that thin inner rind which lies between the coarser bark and the wood of the tree. This being steeped, and afterwards pounded in a mortar, until reduced to a pulp, is made into paper, resembling, in substance, that which is manufactured from cotton, but quite black. When ready for use, he has it cut into pieces of money of different sizes, nearly square, but somewhat longer than they are wide . . . The coinage of this paper money is authenticated with as much form and ceremony as if it were actually of pure gold or silver; for to each note a number of officers, specially appointed, not only subscribe their names, but affix their seals also. When this has been regularly done by the whole of them, the principal officer, appointed by his Majesty, having dipped into vermilion the royal seal committed to his custody, stamps with it the piece of paper, so that the form of the seal tinged with the vermilion remains impressed upon it. In this way it receives full authenticity as current money, and the act of counterfeiting it is punished as a capital offence.

When thus coined in large quantities, this paper currency is circulated in every part of the Great Khan's dominions; nor dares any person, at the peril of his life, refuse to accept it in payment. All his subjects receive it without hesitation, because, wherever their business may call them, they can dispose of it again in the purchase of merchandise they may require; such as pearls, jewels, gold, or silver. With it, in short, every article may be procured.

Several times in the course of the year, large caravans of merchants arrive with such articles as have just been mentioned, together with gold tissues, which they lay before the Great Khan. He thereupon calls together twelve experienced and skilful persons, selected for this purpose, whom he commands to examine the articles with great care, and to fix the value at which they should be purchased. Upon the sum at which they have been thus conscientiously appraised he allows a reasonable profit, and immediately pays for them with this paper. To this the owners can have no objection, because, as has been observed, it answers the purpose of their own disbursements; and even though they should be inhabitants of a country where this kind of money is not current, they invest the amount in other articles of merchandise suited to their own markets.

When any persons happen to be possessed of paper money which from long use his become damaged, they carry it to the mint, where, upon the payment of only three per cent, they receive fresh notes in exchange. Should any be desirous of procuring gold or silver for the purposes of manufacture, such as of drinking cups, girdles, or other articles wrought of these metals, they in like manner apply to the mint, and for their paper obtain the bullion they require.

All his Majesty's armies are paid with this currency, which is to them of the same value as if it were gold or silver. Upon these grounds, it may certainly be affirmed that the Great Khan has a more extensive command of treasure than any other sovereign in the universe.

## *Chapter 26*

### Of the Places Established on all the Great Roads for Supplying Post-Horses of the Couriers on Foot and of the Mode in Which the Expense is Defrayed

From the city of Kanbalu there are many roads leading to the different provinces, and upon each of these, that is to say, upon every great high road, at the distance of twenty-five or thirty miles, accordingly as the towns happen to be situated, there are stations, with houses of accommodation for travelers. These are called *yamb* or post-houses. They are large and handsome buildings, having several well-furnished apartments, hung with silk, and provided with everything suitable to persons of rank. Even kings may be lodged at these stations in a becoming manner, as every article required may be obtained from the towns and strong places in the vicinity; and for some of them the court makes regular provision.

At each station four hundred good horses are kept in constant readiness, in order that all messengers going and coming upon the business of the Great Khan, and all ambassadors, may have relays, and, leaving their jaded horses, be supplied with fresh ones. Even in mountainous districts, remote from the great roads, where there were no villages, and the towns are far distant from each other, his Majesty has equally caused buildings of the same kind to be erected, furnished with everything necessary, and provided with the usual supply of horses.

He sends people to dwell upon the spot, in order to cultivate the land, and attend to the service of the post; by which means large villages are formed. In consequence of these regulations, ambassadors to the court, and the royal messengers, go and return through every province and kingdom of the Empire with the greatest convenience and facility. In the management of all this the Great Khan exhibits a superiority over every other emperor, king, or human being.

In his dominions no fewer than two hundred thousand horses are thus employed in the department of the post, and ten thousand buildings, with suitable furniture, are kept up. It is indeed so wonderful a system, and so effective in its operation, as it is scarcely possible to describe. If it be questioned how the population of the country can supply sufficient numbers of these duties, and by what means they can be supported, we may answer, that all the Idolaters, and likewise the Saracens, keep six, eight, or ten women, according to their circumstances, by whom they have a prodigious number of children. Some of them have as many as thirty sons capable of following their fathers in arms; whereas with us a man has only one wife, and even although she should prove barren, he is obliged to pass his life with her, and is by that means deprived of the chance of raising a family. Hence it is that our population is so much inferior to theirs.

. . . In the space between the post-houses, there are small villages settled at the distance of every three miles, which may contain about forty cottages. In these are stationed the foot messengers, likewise employed in the service of his Majesty. They wear girdles round their waists, to which several small bells are attached, in order that their coming may be perceived at a distance; and as they run only three miles, that is, from one of these foot-stations to another next adjoining, the noise serves to give notice of their approach, and preparation is accordingly made by a fresh courier to proceed with the packet instantly upon the arrival of the former. Thus it is so expeditiously conveyed from station to station, that in the course of two days and two nights his Majesty receives distant intelligence that in the ordinary mode could not be obtained in less than ten days. It often happens that in the fruit season, what is gathered in the morning at Kanbalu is conveyed to the Great Khan, at Shangtu, by the evening of the following day; although the distance is generally considered as ten days' journey. . . . All these couriers are not only exempt from tax, but also receive from his Majesty good allowances.

. . . When it is necessary that the messengers should proceed with extraordinary dispatch, as in the case of giving information of disturbance in any part of the country, the rebellion of a chief, or other important matter, they ride two hundred, or sometimes two hundred and fifty miles in the course of a day. On such occasions they carry with them the tablet of the gerfalcon as a signal of the urgency of their business and the necessity for dispatch. And when there are two messengers, they take their departure together from the same place, mounted upon good fleet horses; and they gird their bodies tight, bind a cloth round their heads, and push their horses to the greatest speed. They continue thus till they come to the next post-house, at twenty-five miles distant, where they find two other horses, fresh and in a state for work; they spring upon them without taking any repose, and changing in the same manner at every stage, until the day closes, they perform a journey of two hundred and fifty miles.

In cases of great emergency they continue their course during the night, and if there should be no moon, they are accompanied to the next station by persons on foot, who run before them with lights; when of course they do not make the same speed as in the day-time, the light-bearers not being able to exceed a certain pace. Messengers qualified to undergo this extraordinary degree of fatigue are held in high estimation.

# LECTURE TOPIC 18

# *Ancient Peoples of the Western Hemisphere*

I. Who Were the Earliest Amerindians?
   A. Hunter Gatherers from Asia: 20,000–40,000 B.C.
   B. North American Societies
      1. Peoples of the Northwest
         a) The Chinook *et al.*
      2. Woodland Tribes
         a) The "Five Civilized Tribes" of the Southeast
         b) The Iroquois
      3. The Moundbuilders: 900 A.D.–1550 A.D.
      4. Peoples of the Southwest
         a) The Mogollon; Hohokam; Anasazi: 250 B.C.–1450 A.D.
         b) Their Pueblo Descendants

II. What Do We Know About Mesoamerican Societies?
   A. Olmecs: 1500–300 B.C.
      1. Remarkable Sculpture; Impressive Ceremonial Centers; Human Sacrifice; Ball Games
      2. Productive Agriculture
      3. Olmec Culture Assimilated by All Subsequent Mesoamerican Societies
   B. The Maya: 300–1500 A.D.
      1. Intensive Agriculture: Maize
      2. Large, Impressive Ceremonial Centers: Chichén Itzá; Uxmal; Copan; Palenque; et al.
      3. Widespread Trade
      4. Excellent Mathematics and Calendars
      5. Hieroglyphic Writing
      6. Reached Peak During "Classic Period" 600–900 A.D.
      7. Decline Owing to Soil Exhaustion and Spanish Conquest
      8. Tragic Destruction of Maya Records by Father de Landa
   C. Teotihuacán and Toltec Peoples: Contemporaries of the Maya, Located on Mexico's Mesa Central
      1. Both Urban and Agricultural
      2. Pyramids of the Sun and Moon
      3. Teotihuacán Overrun by Invaders, the Toltecs, from Southwest: 700 B.D.
      4. Toltecs Sought to Assimilate Culture of Teotihuacán
      5. Toltecs Overrun by Chichimeca (Aztec) Peoples in 13th Century
   D. The Aztecs: ca. 1250–1519 A.D.
      1. Settled in Valley of Mexico
      2. Rapidly Became Largest Imperial Power in Central Mexico

3. War Captives Sacrificed to God, Huitzliopochtli, God of the Sun

E. The Splendor of Tenochtitlán

F. The Prophecy of Quetzalcoatl and Arrival of the Spanish (1519)

1. Hernando Cortés vs. Montezuma II

G. Vast Destruction of Nahuatl Records by Catholic Conquerors

III. South American Societies

A. Moche Civilization and the Royal Tombs at Sipán: Peruvian Forerunners of Inca Rulers: 100 B.C.–500 A.D.

B. Inca Civilization: 200–1530 A.D.

1. Divine Kingship

a) "Cult of the Royal Mummies"

(1) Dead Kings Brought To Festivals To Advise Descendants

C. By 1438 A.D. Inca Imperial Rule Extended Over Most of Western Coast of South America: 16,000,000 Subjects

D. Master Stone Builders and Road Makers

1. The Runners: 175 Miles per Day; The Quipo

E. Arrival of the Spaniards under Francisco Pizarro (1470–1541) and his 168 Soldiers

F. Conquest and Destruction of Inca Civilization

IV. Conclusion

A. As With Ancient China, Western Hemispheric Civilizations Present us with the Spectacle of Human Achievement Separate from Mediterranean and European Peoples

B. The Debate over Advantages/Disadvantages of the Columbian Conquest

# READING 1

## A Mayan Creation Account

*The Popol Vuh of the Quiche Maya is a manuscript discovered in Spain in the nineteenth century. Written by a Quiché Indian shortly after the Spanish conquest, the document was transcribed by Father Francisco Ximénez in the early eighteenth century. It is one of the most complete cosmological accounts in all pre-Columbian literature. The passage here, dealing with the origin of humankind, is taken from Delia Goetz and Sylvanus G. Morley, eds.; Adrián Recinos, trans., Popol Vuh:* The Sacred Book of the Ancient Quiché Maya *(Norman: University of Oklahoma Press, 1950), Part 1, chs. 1–2, pp. 81–83, 86, 89.*

---

### Discussion Questions

1. What similarities do you see between the creation account in the *Popol Vuh* and the Judeo-Christian narrative of the Bible?

### THE POPOL VUH

---

This is the account of how all was in suspense, all calm, in silence; all motionless, still, and the expanse of the sky was empty.

This is the first account, the first narrative. There was neither man, nor animal, birds, fishes, crabs, trees, stones, caves, ravines, grasses, nor forests; there was only the sky.

There was nothing brought together, nothing which could make a noise, nor anything which might move, or tremble, or could make noise in the sky.

There was nothing standing; only the calm water, the placid sea, alone and tranquil. Nothing existed.

There was only immobility and silence in the darkness, in the night. Only the Creator, the Maker, Tepu, Gucumatz, the Forefathers, were in the water surrounded with light. They were hidden under green and blue feathers, and were therefore called Gucumatz. By nature they were great sages and great thinkers. In this manner the sky existed and also the Heart of heaven, which is the name of God and thus He is called.

Then came the word. Tepeu and Cucumatz came together in the darkness, in the night, and Tepeu and Gucumatz talked together. They talked then, discussing and deliberating; they agreed, they united their words and their thoughts.

Then while they meditated, it became clear to them that when dawn would break, man must appear. They then planned the creation, and the growth of the trees and the thickets and the birth of life and the creation of man. Thus it was arranged in the darkness and in the night by the Heart of Heaven who is called Huracán . . .

Then Tepeu and Gucmatz came together; then they conferred about life and light, what they would do so that there would be light and dawn, who it would be who would provide food and sustenance.

Thus let it be done! Let the emptiness be filled! Let the water recede and make a void, let the earth appear and become solid; let it be done. Thus they spoke. Let there be light, let there be dawn in the sky and on the earth! There shall be neither glory nor grandeur in our creation and formation until the human being is made, man is formed. So they spoke.

Then the earth was created by them. So it was, in truth, that they created the earth. Earth! They said, and instantly it was made . . .

[Unhappy with first efforts to create living creatures, the narrative continues.] For this reason another attempt had to be made to create and make men by the Creator, the maker, and the Forefathers.

"Let us try again! Already dawn draws near: Let us make him who shall nourish and sustain us! What shall we do to be invoked, in order to be remembered on earth? We have already tried with our first creations, our first creatures; but we could not make them praise and venerate us. So, then, let us try to make obedient, respectful beings who will nourish and sustain us." Thus they spoke.

Then was the creation and the formation. Of earth, of mud, they made [man's] flesh. But they saw that it was not good. It melted away, it was soft, did not move, had no strength, it fell down, it was limp, it could not move its head, its face fell to one side, its sight was blurred, it could not look behind. At first it spoke, but had no mind. Quickly it soaked in the water and could not stand.

And the Creator and the Maker said: "Let us try again because our creatures will not be able to walk nor multiply. Let us consider this," they said . . .

Then they talked and spoke the truth: "Your figures of wood shall come out well; they shall speak and talk on earth."

"So may it be," they answered when they spoke.

And instantly the figures were made of wood. They looked like men, talked like men, and populated the surface of the earth.

They existed and multiplied; they had daughters, they had sons, these wooden figures; but they did not have souls, nor minds, they did not remember their Creator, their Maker; they walked on all fours, aimlessly.

They no longer remembered the Heart of Heaven and therefore they fell out of favor. It was merely a trial, an attempt at man. At first they spoke, but their face was without expression; their feet and hands had no strength; they had no blood, nor substance, nor moisture, nor flesh; their cheeks were dry, their feet and hands were dry, and their flesh was yellow.l

Therefore, they no longer thought of their Creator nor their maker, nor of those who made them and cared for them.

These were the first men who existed in great numbers on the face of the earth.

# READING 2

## A Letter from Christopher Columbus

*Sailing for Spain, the Italian Christopher Columbus (1451–1506) was determined to attain the luxuries and profits possible by reaching the Far East by heading west across the Atlantic. After peddling his idea around the courts of Europe for nearly eight years, he finally persuaded the new young monarch of Spain, Queen Isabella of Castile, to finance his "Enterprise of the Indies." In an attempt to do an end run around the Ottoman Turks who had disrupted traditional Mediterranean trade routes, Columbus sailed west in 1492 from the Canary Islands and landed in the Caribbean, which he believed was the East Indies. One of the most alternately admired and vilified of the world's discoverers, Columbus gained little reward for his achievement, however finally assessed. The following excerpt is taken from* Christopher Columbus, Letters, *translated and edited by R. H. Major. (London: Hakluyt Society, 1847), pp. 1–17.*

---

### Discussion Questions

1. What seems to be Columbus's attitude toward the inhabitants of the islands?
2. How would you compare the attitudes of the Europeans and the Natives about trade?
3. What generalizations can you make about European views of Native culture at the time?

### A Description From His First Voyage

. . . The inhabitants of both sexes in this island, and in all the others which I have seen, or of which I have received information, go always naked as they were born, with the exception of some of the women, who use the covering of a leaf, or small bough, or an apron of cotton which they prepare for that purpose. None of them are possessed of any iron, neither have they weapons, being unacquainted with, and indeed incompetent to use them, not from any deformity of body (for they are well-formed), but because they are timid and full of fear.

They carry however in lieu of arms, canes dried in the sun on the ends of which they fix heads of dried wood sharpened to a point, and even these they dare not use habitually; for it has often occurred when I have sent two or three of my men to any of the villages to speak with the natives, that they have come out in a disorderly troop, and have fled in such haste at the approach of our men, that the fathers forsook their children and the children their fathers. This timidity did not arise from any loss or injury that they had received from us; for, on the contrary, I gave to all I approached whatever articles I had about me, such as cloth and many other things, taking nothing of theirs in return: but they are naturally timid and fearful. As soon however as they see that they are safe, and have laid aside all fear, they are very simple and honest, and exceedingly liberal with all they have; none of them refusing any thing he may possess when he is asked for it, but on the contrary inviting us to ask them. They exhibit great love towards all others in preference to themselves: they also give objects of great value for trifles, and content themselves with very little or nothing in return.

I however forbad that these trifles and articles of no value (such as pieces of dishes, plates, and glass, keys, and leather straps) should be given to them, although if they could obtain them, they imagined themselves to be possessed of the most beautiful trinkets in the world. It even happened that a sailor received for a leather strap as much gold as was worth three golden nobles, and for things of more trifling value offered by our men, especially newly coined blancas, or any gold coins, the Indians would give whatever the seller required: as, for instance, an ounce and a half or two ounces of gold, or thirty or forty pounds of cotton, with which commodity they were already acquainted. Thus they bartered, like idiots, cotton and gold for fragments of bows, glasses, bottles, and jars; which I forbade as being unjust, and myself gave them many beautiful and acceptable articles which I had brought with me, taking nothing from them in return; I did this in order that I might the more easily conciliate them, that they might be led to become Christians, and be inclined to entertain a regard for the King and Queen, our Princes and all Spaniards, and that I might induce them to take an interest in seeking out, and collecting, and delivering to us such things as they possessed in abundance, but which we greatly needed.

They practice no kind of idolatry, but have a firm belief that all strength and power, and indeed all good things, are in heaven, and that I had descended from thence with these ships and sailors, and under this impression was I received after they had thrown aside their fears. Nor are they slow or stupid, but of very clear understanding; and those men who have crossed to the neighbouring islands give an admirable description of everything they observed; but they never saw any people clothed, nor any ships like ours.

. . . As far as I have learned, every man throughout these islands is united to but one wife, with the exception of the kings and princes, who are allowed to have twenty: the women seem to work more than the men. I could not clearly understand whether the people possess any private property, for I observed that one man had the charge of distributing various things to the rest, but especially meat and provisions and the like. I did not find, as some of us had expected, any cannibals amongst them, but on the contrary men of great deference and kindness. Neither are they black, like the Ethiopians: their hair is smooth and straight: for they do not dwell where the rays of the sun strike most vividly, and the sun has intense power there, the distance from the equinoctial line being, it appears, but six-and-twenty degrees. On the tops of the mountains the cold is very great, but the effect of this upon the Indians is lessened by their being accustomed to the climate, and by their frequently indulging in the use of very hot meats and drinks.

Finally, to compress into few words the entire summary of my voyage and speedy return, and of the advantages derivable therefrom, I promise, that with a little assistance afforded me by our most invincible sovereigns, I will procure them as much gold as they need, as great a quantity of spices, of cotton, and of mastic (which is only found in Chios), and as many men for the service of the navy as their Majesties may require. I promise also rhubarb and other sorts of drugs, which I am persuaded the men whom I have left in the aforesaid fortress have found already and will continue to find; for I myself have tarried no where longer than I was compelled to do by the winds, except in the city of Navidad, which I provided for the building of the fortress, and took the necessary precautions for the perfect security of the men I left there. Although all I have related may appear to be wonderful and unheard of, yet the results of my voyage would have been more astonishing if I had had at my disposal such ships as I required.

But these great and marvelous results are not to be attributed to any merit of mine, but to the holy Christian faith, and to the piety and religion of our Sovereigns; for that which the unaided intellect of man could not compass, the spirit of God has granted to human exertions, for God is wont to hear the prayers of his servants who love his precepts even to the performance of apparent impossibilities. Thus it has happened to me in the present instance, who have accomplished a task to which the powers of mortal men had never hitherto attained; for if there have been those who have anywhere written or spoken of these islands, they have done so with doubts and conjectures, and no one has ever asserted that he has seen them, on which account their writings have been looked upon as little else than fables. Therefore let the king and queen, our princes and their most happy kingdoms, and all the other provinces of Christendom, render thanks to our Lord and Savior Jesus Christ, who has granted us so great a victory and such prosperity. Let processions be made, and sacred feats be held, and the temples be adorned with festive boughs. Let Christ rejoice on earth, as he rejoices in heaven in the prospect of the salvation of the souls of so many nations hitherto lost. Let us also rejoice, as well on account of the exaltation of our faith, as on account of the increase of our temporal prosperity, of which not only Spain, but all Christendom will be partakers.

Such are the events which I have briefly described. Farewell.

Lisbon, the 14th of March.

CHRISTOPHER COLUMBUS,

*Admiral of the Fleet of the Ocean.*

# READING 3

## The Conquest of Mexico

*Bernal Díaz del Castillo (1492–1581) was a Spanish soldier and historian who accompanied Cortez at the time of his conquest of the Aztecs and capture of Tenochtitlán in 1521. The following excerpt from his narrative tells how after many retreats and losses the Spaniards were near to losing the conflict. His description provides not only a picture of the fierce fighting that occurred but an account of how captives were sacrificed to the Aztec God, Huitzliopochtli (referred to below as Huichilobos). This excerpt is from Bernal Díaz del Castillo, A. P. Maudslay, translator,* The Discovery and Conquest of Mexico, *1517–1521 (New York: Farrar, Straus and Cudahy, 1956), pp.435–436.*

---

### Discussion Questions

1. In your opinion, were Aztec sacrifices as described be low more motivated by religious devotion or desire to frighten the Spaniards?

## The Spanish Siege of Tenochtitlán

At that time many companies of Mexicans came to the causeway and wounded the horsemen as well as all of us, and they gave Sandoval a good blow with a stone in the face. Then Pedro de Alvarado and other horsemen went to his assistance. As so many squadrons approached I and twenty other soldiers faced them, and Sandoval ordered us to retreat little by little so that they should not kill the horses, and because we did not retreat as quickly as he wished he said to us with fury: "Do you wish that through your selfishness they should kill me and all these horsemen? For the love of me, dear brothers, do fall back"—at that moment the enemy again wounded him and his horse. Just then we cleared our allies off the causeway, and we retreated little by little keeping our faces to the enemy and not turning our backs, as though to form a dam. Notwithstanding the number of Mexicans that the balls were sweeping away, we could not fend them off, on the contrary they kept on following us thinking that this very night they would carry us off to be sacrificed.

When we had retreated near to our quarters and had already crossed a great opening where there was much water the arrows, javelins and stones could no longer reach us. Sandoval, Francisco de Lugo and Andrés de Tápia were standing with Pedro de Alvarado each one relating what had happened to him and what Cortés had ordered, when again there was sounded the dismal drum of Huichilobos and many other shells and horns and things like trumpets and the sound of them all was terrifying, and we all looked towards the lofty Cue where they were being sounded, and saw that our comrades whom they had captured when they defeated Cortés were being carried by force up the steps, and they were taking them to be sacrificed. When they got them up to a small square in front of the oratory, where their accursed idols are kept, we saw them place plumes on the heads of many of them and with things like fans in their hands they forced them to dance before Huichilobos, and after they had danced they immediately placed them on their backs on some rather narrow stones which had been prepared as places for sacrifice, and with stone knives they sawed open their chests and drew out their palpitating hearts and offered them to the idols that were there, and they kicked the bodies down the steps, and Indian butchers who were waiting below cut off the arms and feet and flayed the skin off the faces, and prepared it afterwards like glove leather with the beards on, and kept those for the festivals when they celebrated drunken orgies, and the flesh they ate in *chimole [an Aztec gruel]*. In the same way they sacrificed all the others and ate the legs and arms and offered the hearts and blood to their idols, as I have said, and the bodies, that is their entrails and feet, they threw to the tigers and lions which they kept in the house of the carnivores which I have spoken about in an earlier chapter.

When we saw those cruelties all of us in our camp said the one to the other: "Thank God that they are not carrying me off to-day to be sacrificed."

# LECTURE TOPIC 19

# Late Medieval Europe

I. Economic Revival: How Does It Break the Fetters of Barbarism?
   A. Peace After 1000 A.D.
   B. Agricultural Innovations
   C. Increasing Trade
      1. Marco Polo (1254–1324 A.D.)
      2. Medieval Fairs
         a) Champagnes
         b) Venice and Genoa
         c) Money and Banks
II. Urban Revival: Why Now?
   A. The Decline of Feudalism
      1. Medieval Fairs Evolve into Cities
      2. Cities Emerge around Castles
   B. What Were Town Liberties?
III. Legal Developments: The Example of England
   A. What Was The Norman Conquest of 1066 A.D.?
      1. Common Law and the Jury System
      2. Magna Carta: 1215 A.D.
      3. Parliament
   B. Impact of the Norman Conquest
IV. How Did The Church and Religion Change?
   A. The Cluniac Reforms: 10th Cent. A.D.
   B. What Was the Investiture Controversy?
      1. College of Cardinals: 1059 A.D.
      2. Henry IV (1056–1106 A.D. vs. Pope Gregory VII (1073–1085 A.D.)
      3. Kidnapping the Pope: The Avignon Papacy: 1308–1378 A.D.
   C. New Methods of Discipline
      1. Excommunication
      2. Oral Confession
   D. The Crusades: 1096–1244 A.D.: What Did They Accomplish?
   E. Gothic Cathedrals
V. Rise of Universities
   A. Liberal Arts and Scholasticism
      1. Peter Abelard (1079–1142 A.D) and Heloise: *Sic et Non*
      2. Thomas Aquinas (1225–1274 A.D.)
   B. Irrepressible Secular Interest
      1. Frederick II (1194–1250 A.D.)
      2. Roger Bacon (1214–1294 A.D.)
   C. Revival of Aristotle and Greek Thought
VI. Decline of the Medieval World
   A. "The Waning of the Middle Ages"
   B. A Synthesis of Medieval and Classical Civilization

# READING 1

## Gregory VII Asserts the Authority of the Pope

*During the Middle Ages, the Catholic church and temporal rulers engaged in a long struggle for political power. Although at times the church seemed to gain the upper hand, in the long run, the secular powers won the final victory, taking control over secular matters while allowing the church to exercise authority over the spiritual domain. The aspirations of the medieval Catholic Church are revealed in the statements of Pope Gregory VII (c. 1020–1085), who is considered one of the most significant popes of the Middle Ages because he took a stand for the supremacy of the papacy over secular authorities. The pope asserts the political supremacy of the Catholic Church and describes the important role the church believed it should play in all aspects of life during the later Middle Ages. His challenge of secular authority led to a famous controversy with Emperor Henry IV. The following statements are taken from Ernest F. Henderson, trans, and ed.,* Select Historical Documents of the Middle Ages, *(London: George Bell & Sons, York St., Covent Garden, and New York, 1896), pp. 366, 367.*

### Discussion Questions

1. What image of the church empowered the challenge of Gregory to secular authority?
2. Which assertions might understandably cause contemporary rulers to think that the pope was claiming too much worldly as well as spiritual authority?
3. What position do you think the Catholic Church would take today on the question of temporal versus spiritual domination?

## THE DICTATE OF THE POPE

That the Roman Church was founded by God alone.

That the Roman Pontiff alone is rightly to be called universal.

That he alone can depose or reinstate bishops.

That, in a council, his legate, even if a lower grade, is above all bishops, and can pass sentence of deposition against them.

That the pope may depose the absent.

That, among other things, we ought not to remain in the same house with those excommunicated by him.

That for him alone it is lawful, according to the needs of the time, to make new laws, to assemble together new congregations, to make an abbey of a canonry; and, on the other hand, to divide a rich bishopric and unite the poor ones.

That he alone may use the imperial insignia.

That of the Pope alone all princes shall kiss the feet.

That his name alone shall be spoken in the churches.

That this is the only name in the world.

That it may be permitted to him to depose emperors.

That he may be permitted to transfer bishops if need be.

That he has power to ordain a clerk of any church he may wish.

That he who is ordained by him many preside over another church, but may not hold a subordinate position; and that such a one may not receive a higher grade from any bishop.

That no synod may be called a general one without his order.

That no chapter and no book shall be considered canonical without his authority.

That a sentence passed by him may be retracted by no one; and that he himself, alone of all, may retract it.

That he himself may be judged by no one.

That no one shall dare to condemn one who appeals to the apostolic chair.

That to the latter should be referred the more important cases of every church.

That the Roman Church has never erred, nor will it err to all eternity, the Scripture bearing witness.

That the Roman pontiff, if he have been canonically ordained, is undoubtedly made a saint by the merits of St. Peter; St. Ennodius, bishop of Pavia, bearing witness, and many holy fathers agreeing with him. As is contained in the decrees of St. Symmachus the pope.

That, by his command and consent, it may be lawful for subordinates to bring accusations.

That he may depose and reinstate bishops without assembling a synod.

That he who is not at peace with the Roman church shall not be considered catholic.

That he may absolve subjects from their fealty to wicked men.

# READING 2

## The Fourth Crusade

*One of the most dramatic developments in late medieval life was the repeated effort to expel the Muslim Turks from Jerusalem. Thousands of Europeans, soldiers and commoners alike, were swept up in these enterprises which involved at least eight successive efforts and stretched over a century and a half. In addition to Jerusalem, which was twice taken and twice lost, the fourth crusade made war on the Greek Orthodox capital of Constantinople. This sack of Constantinople in 1204 by western Crusaders ostensibly en route to the Holy Land cemented the split between these two main divisions of Christianity and signaled the rise of Western Europe as a world power.* It *also presented the world with the spectacle of Christians killing one another. The first excerpt by Robert de Clari, a poor knight, provides an account of the reasons for the diversion, which seem to be related to the need for money and supplies. Following are several excerpts from the account of a leader of the Crusaders, Geffroi de Villehardouin. They provide dramatic descriptions of storming and looting the city and division of the spoils. These passages are taken from Villehardouin and de Joinville: Memoirs of the Crusades, translated by Sir Frank Marzials, (London: J. M. Dent & Sons, Ltd.; New York: E. P. Dutton & Co., Inc., 1908), pp. 61–66. The last selection, by a Byzantine named Nicetas, clearly depicts the materialism and greed of the Crusaders who destroyed holy places and confiscated treasure. Both it and the first excerpt are taken from* Translations and Reprints from the Original Sources of European History, *Vol. 3 (Philadelphia: Department of History, University of Pennsylvania, 1909), pp. 7–18.*

### Discussion Questions

1. What is your opinion of the behavior of the Christian Crusaders? Were they expected to act differently?
2. What was the usual practice during a siege of a city? How did the siege of Constantinople compare?
3. What in the history of Rome and Constantinople might have influenced the Crusaders?
4. How is the Byzantine account different from the record of the western memoir?

### The Diversion to Constantinople

In the meantime the crusaders . . . considered how great the expense had been and said to one another that they could not go to Babylon [Cairo] or Alexandria or Syria ; for they had neither provisions nor money for the journey. They had already used up everything they had, either during the sojourn that they had made or in the great price that they had paid for the vessels. They said that they could not go and, even if they should go, they would accomplish nothing ; they had neither provisions nor money sufficient to support them.

The doge of Venice saw clearly that the pilgrims were ill at ease. He addressed them, saying : "Sirs, Greece is a very rich land and bountifully supplied with everything. If we can find a sufficient excuse for going there and taking food and other things, so as to recuperate ourselves, it would seem to me advisable, and then we could easily go across the sea." Then the marquis [Boniface, marquis of Montferrat, the leader of the crusaders] rose and said : "Sir, I was in Germany at the emperor's [Philip of Suabia] court last Christmas. There I saw a young man who was the emperor's brother in law [Alexis IV., brother of the queen Irene]. This young man was the son of the emperor *Kyrsac* [Isaac II] of Constantinople from whom his brother had taken the empire of Constantinople by treason. Whoever could get this young man," said the marquis, "could certainly go to the land of Constantinople and take provisions and other things ; for this young man is the rightful heir."

. . . [After the arrival of Alexis] Then all the barons of the army and the Venetians were summoned. When they had all assembled, the doge of Venice rose and said to them : "My lords, we have now a sufficient excuse for going to Constantinople, if you think it wise, for we have the lawful heir." Now some who did not want to go to Constantinople, spoke thus : "Bah! what are we going to do at Constantinople? We have our pilgrimage to make and intend to go to Babylon or Alexandria. Our ships are rented for only one year and the year is already half over."

The others said in reply : "What are we going to do at Babylon or Alexandria, since we have neither provisions nor money enough to go? It is better to go where we have a sufficient excuse for obtaining money and provisions by conquest, than to go where we shall die of hunger. Then we can do it, and he [Alexis] offers to go with us and to pay for our ships and our navy another year at his own expense." . . .

. . . When the pilgrims saw [that the first attack was repulsed], they were very angry and grieved much ; they went back from the other side of the harbor to their lodgings. When the barons had returned and had gotten ashore, they assembled and were much amazed, and said that it was on account of their sins that they did not succeed in anything and could not capture the city. Meanwhile the bishops and the clergy in the army debated and decided that the war was a righteous one, and that they certainly ought to attack the Greeks. For formerly the inhabitants of the city had been obedient to the law of Rome and now they were disobedient, since they said that the law of Rome was of no account, and called all who believed in it "dogs." And the bishops said that for this reason one ought certainly to attack them, and that it was not a sin, but an act of great charity.

Then it was announced to all the host that all the Venetians and every one else should go and hear the sermons on Sunday morning ; [April 11, 1204] and they did so. Then the bishops preached to the army, . . . and they showed to the pilgrims that the war was a righteous one ; for the Greeks were traitors and murderers, and also disloyal, since they had murdered their rightful lord, and were worse than Jews. Moreover, the bishops said that, by the authority of God and in the name of the pope, they would absolve all who attacked the Greeks. Then the bishops commanded the pilgrims to confess their sins and receive the communion devoutly ; and said that they ought not to hesitate to attack the Greeks, for the latter were enemies of God. They also commanded that all the evil women should be sought out and sent away from the army to a distant place. This was done ; the evil women were all put on a vessel and were sent very far away from the army.

## THE ASSAULT ON CONSTANTINOPLE

### *The Crusaders Take a Part of the City*

Before the assault the Emperor Mourzuphles had come to encamp, with all his power, in an open space, and had there pitched his scarlet tents. Thus matters remained till the Monday morning, when those on the ships, transports, and galleys were all armed. And those of the city stood in much less fear of them than they did at the beginning, and were in such good spirits that on the walls and towers you could see nothing but people. Then began an assault proud and marvellous, and every ship went straight before it to the attack. The noise of the battle was so great that it seemed to rend the earth.

Thus did the assault last for a long while, till our Lord raised a wind called Boreas which drove the ships and vessels further up on to the shore. And two ships that were bound together, of which the one was called the *Pilgrim* and the other the *Paradise,* approached so near to a tower, the one on the one side and the other on the other—so as God and the wind drove them—that the ladder of the *Pilgrim* joined on to the tower. Immediately a Venetian, and a knight of France, whose name was Andrew of Urboise, entered into the tower, and other people began to enter after them, and those in the tower were discomfited and fled.

When the knights see this, who are in the transports, they land, and raise their ladders against the wall, and scale the top of the wall by main force, and so take four of the towers. And all begin to leap out of the ships and transports and galleys, helter-skelter, each as best he can; and they break in some three of the gates and enter in; and they draw the horses out of the transports; and the knights mount and ride straight to the quarters of the Emperor Mourzuphles. He had his battalions arrayed before his tents, and when his men see the mounted knights coming, they lose heart and fly; and so goes the emperor flying through the streets to the castle of Bucoleon.

Then might you have seen the Greeks beaten down; and horses and palfreys captured, and mules, and other booty. Of killed and wounded there was neither end nor measure. A great part of the Greek lords had fled towards the gate of Blachernae. And vesper-time was already past, and those of the host were weary of the battle and of the slaying. And they began to assemble in a great open space that was in Constantinople, and decided that they would take up their quarters near the walls and towers they had captured. Never had they thought that in a whole month they should be able to take the city, with its great churches, and great palaces, and the people that were in it.

### Flight of Mourzuphles—Fire In Constantinople

As they had settled, so was it done, and they encamped before the walls and before the towers by their ships. Count Baldwin of Flanders and Hainault quartered himself in the scarlet tents that the Emperor Mourzuphles had left standing, and Henry his brother before the palace of Blachernae; and Boniface, Marquis of Montferrat, he and his men, towards the thickest part of the city. So were the host encamped as you have heard, and Constantinople taken on the Monday after Palm Sunday (12th April 1204).

Now Count Lewis of Blois and Chartres had languished all the winter with a quartan fever, and could not bear his armour. And you must know that this was a great misfortune to the host, seeing he was a good knight of his body; and he lay in one of the transports.

Thus did those of the host, who were very weary, rest that night. But the Emperor Mourzuphles rested not, for he assembled all his people, and said he would go and attack the Franks. Nevertheless he did not do as he had said, for he rode along other streets, as far as he could from those held by the host, and came to a gate which is called the Golden Gate, whereby he escaped, and avoided the city; and afterwards all who could fled also. And of all this those of the host knew nothing.

During that night, towards the quarters of Boniface, Marquis of Montferrat, certain people, whose names are unknown to me, being in fear lest the Greeks should attack them, set fire to the buildings between themselves and the Greeks. And the city began to take fire, and to bum very direfully; and it burned all that night and all the next day, till vesper-time. And this was the third fire there had been in Constantinople since the Franks arrived in the land; and more houses had been burned in the city than there are houses in any three of the greatest cities in the kingdom of France.

That night passed and the next day came, which was a Tuesday morning *(13th* April 1204); and all armed themselves throughout the host, both knights and sergeants, and each repaired to his post. Then they issued from their quarters, and thought to find a sorer battle than the day before, for no word had come to them that the emperor had fled during the night. But they found none to oppose them.

### The Crusaders Occupy the City

The Marquis Boniface of Montferrat rode all along the shore to the palace of Bucoleon, and when he arrived there it surrendered, on condition that the lives of all therein should be spared. At Bucoleon were found the larger number of the great ladies who had fled to the castle, for there were found the sister of the King of France, who had been empress, and the sister of the King of Hungary, who had also been empress, and other ladies very many. Of the treasure that was found in that palace I cannot well speak, for there was so much that it was beyond end or counting.

At the same time that this palace was surrendered to the Marquis Boniface of Montferrat, did the palace of Blachernae surrender to Henry, the brother of Count Baldwin of Flanders, on condition that no hurt should be done to the bodies of those who were therein. There too was found much treasure, not less than in the palace of Bucoleon. Each garrisoned with his own people the castle that had been surrendered to him, and set a guard over the treasure. And the other people, spread abroad throughout the city, also gained much booty. The booty gained was so great that none could tell you the end of it: gold and silver, and vessels and precious stones, and samite, and cloth of silk, and robes vair and grey, and ermine, and every choicest thing found upon the earth. And well does Geoffry of Villehardouin, the Marshal of Champagne, bear witness, that never, since the world was created, had so much booty been won in any city.

Everyone took quarters where he pleased, and of lodgings there was no stint. So the host of the pilgrims and of the Venetians found quarters, and greatly did they rejoice and give thanks because of the victory God had vouchsafed to them—for those who before had been poor were now in wealth and luxury. Thus they celebrated Palm Sunday and the Easter Day following (25th April 1204) in the joy and honour that God had bestowed upon them. And well might they praise our Lord, since in all the host there were no more than twenty thousand armed men, one with another, and with the help of God they had conquered four hundred thousand men, or more, and in the strongest city in all the world—yea, a great city—and very well fortified.

### *Division of the Spoil*

Then was it proclaimed throughout the host by the Marquis Boniface of Montferrat, who was lord of the host, and by the barons, and by the Doge of Venice, that all the booty should be collected and brought together, as had been covenanted under oath and pain of excommunication. Three churches were appointed for the receiving of the spoils, and guards were set to have them in charge, both Franks and Venetians, the most upright that could be found. . .

The spoils and booty were collected together, and you must know that all was not brought into the common stock, for not a few kept things back, maugre the excommunication of the Pope. That which was brought to the churches was collected together and divided, in equal parts, between the Franks and the Venetians, according to the sworn covenant. And you must know further that the pilgrims, after the division had been made, paid out of their share fifty thousand marks of silver to the Venetians, and then divided at least one hundred thousand marks between themselves, among their own people. And shall I tell you in what wise? Two sergeants on foot counted as one mounted, and two sergeants mounted as one knight. And you must know that no man received more, either on account of his rank or because of his deeds, than that which had been so settled and ordered—save in so far as he may have stolen it.

And as to theft, and those who were convicted thereof, you must know that stern justice was meted out to such as were found guilty, and not a few were hung. The Count of St. Paul hung one of his knights, who had kept back certain spoils, with his shield to his neck; but many there were, both great and small, who kept back part of the spoils, and it was never known. Well may you be assured that the spoil was very great, for if it had not been for what was stolen and for the part given to the Venetians, there would have been at least four hundred thousand marks of silver, and at least ten thousand horses—one with another. Thus were divided the spoils of Constantinople, as you have heard.

## THE CRUSADERS SACK CONSTANTINOPLE

How shall I begin to tell of the deeds wrought by these nefarious men! Alas, the images, which ought to have been adored, were trodden under foot! Alas, the relics of the holy martyrs were thrown into unclean places! . . . They snatched the precious reliquaries, thrust into their bosoms the ornaments which these contained, and used the broken remnants for pans and drinking cups—precursors of Anti-christ, authors and heralds of his nefarious deeds which we momentarily expect. Manifestly, indeed, by that race then, just as formerly, Christ was robbed and insulted and His garments were divided by lot only one thing was lacking, that His side, pierced by a spear, should pour rivers of divine blood on the ground.

Nor can the violation of the Great Church [of St. Sophia] be listened to with equanimity. For the sacred altar, formed of all kinds of precious materials and admired by the whole world, was broken into bits and distributed among the soldiers, as was all the other sacred wealth of so great and infinite splendor.

When the sacred vases and utensils of unsurpassable art and grace and rare material, and the fine silver, wrought with gold, which encircled the screen of the tribunal and the ambo, of admirable workmanship, and the door and many other ornaments, were to be borne away as booty, mules and saddled horses were led to the very sanctuary of the temple. Some of these which were unable to keep their footing on the splendid and slippery pavement, were stabbed when they fell, so that the sacred pavement was polluted with blood and filth. . . .

No one was without a share in the grief. In the alleys, in the streets, in the temples, complaints, weeping, lamentations, grief, the groaning of men, the shrieks of women, wounds, rape, captivity, the separation of those most closely united. Nobles wandered about ignominiously, those of venerable age in tears, the rich in poverty. Thus it was in the streets, on the corners, in the temple, in the dens, for no place remained unassailed or defended the suppliants. All places everywhere were filled full of all kinds of crime. Oh, immortal God, how great the afflictions of the men, how great the distress!

## READING 3

# The English Nobles Restrain King John

*In 1215 the vassals of King John of England, led by Stephen Langton, archbishop of Canterbury, forced their king to place his seal on a feudal document known as the Magna Carta. Meaning the Great Charter, the Magna Carta is a list of concessions to the king's barons reflecting royal encroachments on feudal law and past violations of traditional rights and liberties. The document illustrates the contractual element in feudalism—I'll keep my part of our agreement if you'll keep yours—and reveals the tensions that existed when feudal law was not observed. Although King John died nine weeks after signing it, the Magna Carta would become significant in English law and constitutional history as the foundation for the protection of rights against arbitrary power. The selections that follow are excerpted from Ernest F. Henderson, trans. and ed.,* Select Historical Documents of the Middle Ages, *(London: George Bell & Sons, 1896), pp. 135–148.*

---

### Discussion Questions

1. Who benefited most from the charter? What do you think was its original purpose?
2. What privileges seem to concern the barons most? How had the king infringed upon their rights?
3. What remedies were proposed and how were they to be enforced?
4. Many historians argue that the charter's significance lies in its making the king subject to the law. How does it do this, and why is this important?

## THE MAGNA CARTA

John, by the grace of God king of England, lord of Ireland, duke of Normandy and Aquitaine, count of Anjou: to the archbishops, bishops, abbots, earls, barons, justices, foresters, sheriffs, provosts, serving men, and to all his bailiffs and faithful subjects, greeting. . . .

1. First of all have granted to God, and, for us and for our heirs forever, have confirmed, by this our present charter, that the English church shall be free and shall have its rights intact and its liberties uninfringed upon. . . .

2. If any one of our earls or barons, or of others holding from us in chief through military service, shall die; and it, at the time of his death, his heir be of full age and owe a relief : he shall have his inheritance by paying the old relief;—the heir, namely, or the heirs of an earl, by paying one hundred pounds for the whole barony of an earl ; the heir or heirs of a baron, by paying one hundred pounds for the whole barony ; the heir or heirs of a knight, by paying one hundred shillings at most for a whole knight's fee ; and he who shall owe less shall give less, according to the ancient custom of fees.

3. But if the heir of any of the above persons shall be under age and in wardship,—when he comes of age he shall have his inheritance without relief and without fine.

4. The administrator of the land of such heir who shall be under age shall take none but reasonable issues from the land of the heir, and reasonable customs and services ; and this without destruction and waste of men or goods. . . .

5. The administrator, moreover, so long as he may have the custody of the land, shall keep in order, from the issues of that land, the houses, parks, warrens, lakes, mills, and other things pertaining to it. And he shall restore to the heir when he comes to full age, his whole land. . .

6. Heirs may marry without disparagement ; so, nevertheless, that, before the marriage is contracted, it shall be announced to the relations by blood of the heir himself.

7. A widow, after the death of her husband, shall straightway, and without difficulty, have her marriage portion and her inheritance, nor shall she give any thing in return for her dowry, her marriage portion, or the inheritance which belonged to her, and which she and her husband held on the day of the death of that husband. And she may remain in the house of her husband, after his death, for forty days; within which her dowry shall be paid over to her.

8. No widow shall be forced to marry when she prefers to live without a husband ; so, however, that she gives security not to marry without our consent, if she hold from us, or the consent of the lord from whom she holds, if she hold from another. . . .

10. If any one shall have taken any sum, great or small, as a loan from the Jews, and shall die before that debt is paid,—that debt shall not bear interest so long as the heir, from whomever he may hold, shall be under age. And if the debt fall into our hands, we shall take nothing save the chattel contained in the deed. . . .

12. No scutage (tax) or aid shall be imposed in our realm unless by the common counsel of our realm ; except for redeeming our body, and knighting our eldest son, and marrying once our eldest daughter. And for these purposes there shall only be given a reasonable aid. . . .

13. And the city of London shall have all its old liberties and free customs as well by land as by water. Moreover we will and grant that all other cities and burroughs, and towns and ports, shall have all their liberties and free customs. . . .

20. A freeman shall only be amerced (to punish by a fine) for a small offence according to the measure of that offence. And for a great offence he shall be amerced according to the magnitude of the offence, saving his contenement (property) ; and a merchant, in the same way, saving his merchandize. And a villain, (a free serf, bound only to his lord) . . .shall be amerced saving his wainnage (wagon). And none of the aforesaid fines shall be imposed save upon oath of upright men from the neighbourhood.

21. Earls and barons shall not be amerced [punished] save through their peers, and only according to the measure of the offence. . .

28. No constable (Governor of a Castle) or other bailiff of ours shall take the corn or other chattels of any one except he straightway give money for them, or can be allowed a respite in that regard by the will of the seller.

29. No constable shall force any knight to pay money for castle-ward (guard) if he be willing to perform that ward (guard) in person, or—he for a reasonable cause not being able to perform it himself—through another proper man. And if we shall have led or sent him on a military expedition, he shall be quit of ward according to the amount of time during which, through us, he shall have been in military service.

30. No sheriff nor bailiff of ours, (of the king) nor any one else, shall take the horses or carts of any freeman for transport, unless by the will of that freeman.

31. Neither we nor our bailiffs shall take another's wood for castles or for other private uses, unless by the will of him to whom the wood belongs. . . .

35. There shall be one measure of wine throughout our whole realm, and one measure of ale and one measure of corn—namely, the London quart ;—and one width of dyed and russet and hauberk cloths—namely, two ells below the selvage. And with weights, moreover, it shall be as with measures. . . .

38. No bailiff, on his own simple assertion, shall henceforth put any one to his law, without producing faithful witnesses in evidence.

39. No freeman shall be taken, or imprisoned, or disseized, or outlawed, or exiled, or in any way harmed—nor will we go upon or send upon him—save by the lawful judgment of his peers or by the law of the land.

40. To none will we sell, to none deny or delay, right or justice. . . .

60. Moreover all the subjects of our realm, clergy as well as laity, shall, as far as pertains to them, observe, with regard to their vassals, all these aforesaid customs and liberties which we have decreed shall, as far as pertains to us, be observed in our realm with regard to our own.

61. Inasmuch as, for the sake of God, and for the bettering of our realm, and for the more ready healing of the discord which has arisen between us and our barons, we have made all these aforesaid concessions,—wishing them to enjoy for ever entire and firm stability, we make and grant to them the following security : that the barons, namely, may elect at their pleasure twenty five barons from the realm, who ought, with all their strength, to observe, maintain and cause to be observed, the peace and privileges which we have granted to them and confirmed by this our present charter. . . .

Fairness!

What a piece of work is a man! How noble in reason! how infinite in faculty! in form, in moving, how express and admirable! in action how like an angel! in apprehension how like a god! the beauty of the world! the paragon of animals!

—William Shakespeare (1564–1616) Hamlet, Prince of Denmark Act II. Scene II

# LECTURE TOPIC 20

# Rebirth of the West: The Renaissance

I. How Significant Was Urban Revival?
  A. Agricultural Innovations
  B. Cities and Civilization
    1. Trade and Commerce
    2. The Italian City-State
    3. Universities
II. What Was The Islamic Contribution?
  A. Omayyad Spain
  B. Ottoman Conquest of Constantinople (1453)
III. Johann Gutenberg (1400–1468): Moveable Type
IV. The Renaissance Mentalite: What Was It?
  A. Contrast with the Medieval Worldview
  B. Fascination with Graeco-Roman Civilization
    1. Francesco Petrarch (1304–1374)
  C. How To Define Humanism
    1. A Liberal Arts Curriculum
    2. The Glorification and Admiration of Humankind
      a) Giovanni Pico della Mirandola (1463–1494)
      b) *Oration on the Dignity of Man*
V. Italy's Political Tragedy
  A. Rule by Despots and Invasion by Foreigners
  B. Secular Politics
    1. Nicolo Machiavelli (1469–1527)
      a) *The Prince*
      b) *Virtu and Homeric Arete*
VI. The Status of Women
VII. Art in the Italian Renaissance
  A. Its Characteristics
    1. Religious and Secular Subjects
    2. Bright Vibrant Colors
    3. Chiaroscuro and Linear Perspective
    4. Invention of Oil Paints
  B. Who Were the Major Renaissance Artists?
    1. Giotto (1266–1336)
    2. Masaccio (1401–1428)
      a) Adam and Eve Expelled from Garden of Eden
    3. Botticelli (1445–1510)
      a) "Primavera"
      b) "Birth of Venus"
      c) "The Adoration of the Magi"
      d) "The Wedding Feast"

4. Donatello (1386?–1466)
   a) "David"
   b) "Mary Magdalen"
5. Raphael (1483–1520)
6. Titian: Venus of Urbino (1538)
7. Leonardo da Vinci (1452–1519)
   a) "La Gioconda" or Mona Lisa
   b) "Last Supper"
8. Michelangelo Buonarroti (1475–1564)
   a) "Pieta"
   b) "David"
   c) Sistine Chapel

VIII. The Northern Renaissance
- A. Desiderius Erasmus (1466–1536): *In Praise of Folly*
- B. Michel de Montaigne (1533–1592)
- C. Thomas More (1478–1535): *Utopia*
- D. William Shakespeare (1564–1616): *Hamlet*

IX. Conclusion
- A. The Modern World View
- B. *"Crise de Conscience"*
  1. Ulrich von Hutten (1488–1523) and Centaurs
  2. The Story of Giralomo Savonarola (1452–1498)

# READING 1

## The High Nobility of Man

*Another important dimension of Renaissance humanism was its enthusiasm for man's extraordinary capacities. In the following passage, Giovanni Pico della Mirandola (1463–1494 AD.) lavishes such praise on humankind as is usually reserved for divinity. The encomium is taken from his "Oration on the Dignity of Man," found in Ernst Cassirer, Paul Oskar Kristeller, and John Herman Randall, Jr., eds.,* The Renaissance Philosophy of Man *(Chicago and London: University of Chicago Press, 1948), pp. 223–254.*

---

### Discussion Questions

1. What quality did Mirandola believe humans alone possessed?
2. What did the possession of this quality allow humans to do?

## "ORATION ON THE DIGNITY OF MAN"

---

*Giovanni Pico Della Mirandola*

At last it seems to me I have come to understand why man is the most fortunate of creatures and consequently worthy of all admiration and what precisely is that rank which is his lot in the universal chain of Being—a rank to be envied not only by brutes but even by the stars and by minds beyond this world. It is a matter past faith and a wondrous one. Why should it not be? For it is on this very account that man is rightly called and judged a great miracle and a wonderful creature indeed. . . .

But hear, Fathers, exactly what this rank is and, as friendly auditors conformably to your kindness, do me this favor. God the Father, the supreme Architect, had already built this cosmic home we behold, the most sacred temple of His godhead, by the laws of His mysterious wisdom. The region above the heavens He had adorned with Intelligences, the heavenly spheres He had quickened with eternal souls, and the excrementary and filthy parts of the lower world He had filled with a multitude of animals of every kind. But, when the work was finished, the Craftsman kept wishing that there were someone to ponder the plan of so great a work, to love its beauty, and to wonder at its vastness. Therefore, when everything was done (as Moses and Timaeus bear witness), He finally took thought concerning the creation of man. But there was not among His archetypes that from which He could fashion a new offspring, nor was there in his treasure-houses anything which He might bestow on His new son as an inheritance, nor was there in the seats of all the world a place where the latter might sit to contemplate the universe. All was now complete; all things had been assigned to the highest, the middle, and the lowest orders. But in its final creation it was not the part of the Father's power to fail as though exhausted. It was not the part of His wisdom to waver in a needful matter through poverty of counsel. It was not the part of His kindly love that he who was to praise God's divine generosity in regard to others should be compelled to condemn it in regard to himself.

At last the best of artisans [God] ordained that that creature [man] to whom He had been able to give nothing proper to himself should have joint possession of whatever had been peculiar to each of the different kinds of being. He therefore took man as a creature of indeterminate nature and, assigning him a place in the middle of the world, addressed him thus:

"Neither a fixed abode nor a form that is thine alone nor any function peculiar to thyself have we given thee, Adam, to the end that according to thy longing and according to thy judgment thou mayest have and possess what abode, what form, and what functions thou thyself shalt desire. The nature of all other beings is limited and constrained within the bounds of laws prescribed by Us. Thou, constrained by no limits, in accordance with thine own free will, in whose hand We have placed thee, shalt ordain for thyself the limits of thy nature. We have set thee at the world's center that thou mayest from thence more easily observe whatever is in the world. We have made thee neither of heaven nor of earth, neither mortal nor immortal, so that with freedom of choice and with honor, as though the maker and molder thyself, thou mayest fashion thyself in whatever shape thou shalt prefer. Thou shalt have the power to degenerate into the lower forms of life, which are brutish. Thou shalt have the power, out of thy soul's judgment, to be reborn into the higher forms, which are divine."

O supreme generosity of God the Father, O highest and most marvelous felicity of man! To him it is granted to have whatever he chooses, to be whatever he wills. Beasts as soon as they are born (so says Lucilius) bring with them from their mother's womb all they will ever possess. Spiritual beings, either from the beginning or soon thereafter, become what they are to be for ever and ever. On man when he came into life the Father conferred the seeds of all kinds and the germs of every way of life. Whatever seeds each man cultivates will grow to maturity and bear in him their own fruit. If they be vegetative, he will be like a plant. If sensitive, he will become brutish. If rational, he will grow into a heavenly being. If intellectual, he will be an angel and the son of God. And if, happy in the lot of no created thing, he withdraws into the center of his own unity, his spirit, made one with God, in the solitary darkness of God, Who is set above all things, shall surpass them all. Who would not admire this our chameleon?

. . . For, exalted to her lofty heights, we shall measure therefrom all things that are and shall be and have been in indivisible eternity; and, admiring their original beauty, like the seers of Phoebus, we shall become her own winged lovers. And at last, roused by ineffable love as by a sting, like burning Seraphim rapt from ourselves, full of divine power we shall no longer be ourselves but shall become He Himself Who made us.

## READING 2

# Machiavelli Gives Advice to Italy's Rulers

*No one understood the Italian despot better than Machiavelli and perhaps no other book illustrates so well the prevailing political spirit at the opening of the sixteenth century as does his little handbook for despots, The Prince. When he wrote it in 1513, Machiavelli had recently been arrested and tortured as a suspected enemy of the Medici government in Florence before being released from prison. Intended to be a guide to action, the book offered advice to rulers while its author probably hoped to acquire employment as an advisor. For Machiavelli, who had witnessed one foreign invasion of Italy after another, only the strongest state could hope to survive. Governments would always clash in wars, he believed; his goal was to be always on the side of the victor—and not be the victim. He admired success and survival and he advised rulers to use any means necessary in order to achieve and sustain political power. Although he was critical of his countrymen for lacking the "virtu" necessary to protect their homeland like the ancient Romans had done, in the last chapter of The Prince he called upon the Medici family to drive out the foreign "barbarians" who had invaded Italy, and by using the principles he had described to establish a strong government that could bring peace to his fragmented and chaotic country. The following selections are taken from James Harvey Robinson ed.,* Readings in European History, *Abridged Edition (Boston and New York:, 1906), pp. 219, 240–242.*

---

### Discussion Questions

1. How did Machiavelli's advice to princes differ from the teachings of Christian and medieval moralists?
2. How would you compare Machiavelli's view of human nature with that of Mirandola?
3. Do you think his advice would be useful to a politician in our society today?

## THE PRINCE

That prince who founds the duration of his government upon his mercenary forces will never be firm or secure; for they are divided, ambitious, undisciplined, unfaithful ; insolent to their friends, abject to their enemies, without fear of God or faith to men ; so the ruin of that person who trusts to them is no longer protracted than the attempt is deferred. In time of peace they plunder you, in time of war they desert you ; and the reason is because it is not love nor any principle of honor that keeps them in the field, but only their pay, and that is not a consideration strong enough to prevail with them to die for you. . . .

Every one understands how praiseworthy it is in a prince to keep faith, and to live uprightly and not craftily. Nevertheless we see, from what has taken place in our own days, that princes who have set little store by their word, but have known how to overreach men by their cunning, have accomplished great things, and in the end got the better of those who trusted to honest dealing.

Be it known, then, that there are two ways of contending,—one in accordance with the laws, the other by force ; the first of which is proper to men, the second to beasts. But since the first method is often ineffectual, it becomes necessary to resort to the second. A prince should, therefore, understand how to use well both the man and the beast. . . . But inasmuch as a prince would know how to use the beast's nature wisely, he ought of beasts to choose both the lion and the fox ; for the lion cannot guard himself from the toils, nor the fox from wolves. He must therefore be a fox to discern toils, and a lion to drive off wolves.

To rely wholly on the lion is unwise ; and for this reason a prudent prince neither can nor ought to keep his word when to keep it is hurtful to him and the causes which led him to pledge it are removed. If all men were good, this would not be good advice, but since they are dishonest and do not keep faith with you, you in return need not keep faith with them ; and no prince was ever at a loss for plausible reasons to cloak a breach of faith. Of this numberless recent instances could be given, and it might be shown how many solemn treaties and engagements have been rendered inoperative and idle through want of faith among princes, and that he who has best known how to play the fox has had the best success.

It is necessary, indeed, to put a good color on this nature, and to be skilled in simulating and dissembling. But men are so simple, and governed so absolutely by their present needs, that he who wishes to deceive will never fail in finding willing dupes.

One recent example I will not omit. Pope Alexander VI had no care or thought but how to deceive, and always found material to work on. No man ever had a more effective manner of asseverating, or made promises with more solemn protestations, or observed them less. And yet, because he understood this side of human nature, his frauds always succeeded. . . .

In his efforts to aggrandize his son, the duke [Caesar Borgia], Alexander VI had to face many difficulties, both immediate and remote. . . . It was consequently necessary that the existing order of things should be changed, and the states of Italy thrown into confusion, in order that he might safely make himself master of some part of them ; and this became easy for him when he found that the Venetians, moved by other causes, were plotting to bring the French once more into Italy. This design he accordingly did not oppose, but furthered by annulling the first marriage of King Louis of France. [So Louis XII could marry Anne of Brittany, who would bring the important fief of Brittany to the French crown].

King Louis therefore came into Italy at the instance of the Venetians, and with the consent of Pope Alexander ; and no sooner was he in Milan than the pope got troops from him to forward the papal schemes in Romagna, which province, moved by the reputation of the French arms, at once submitted. . . .

If, as I have said, it was necessary in order to display the valor of Moses that the children of Israel should be slaves in Egypt, and to show the greatness and courage or Cyrus that the Persians should be oppressed by the Medes, and to illustrate the excellence of Theseus that the Athenians should be scattered and divided, so at this hour, to prove the worth of some Italian hero, it was required that Italy should be brought to her present abject condition, be more a slave than the Hebrew, more oppressed than the Persian, more disunited than the Athenian, without a head, without order, beaten, spoiled, torn in pieces, overrun, and abandoned to destruction in every shape.

But though, heretofore, glimmerings may have been discerned in this man or that, whence it might be conjectured that he was ordained by God for Italy's redemption, nevertheless it has afterwards been seen in the further course of his actions that Fortune has disowned him ; so that our country, left almost without life, still waits to know who it is that is to heal her bruises, to put an end to the devastation and plunder of Lombardy and to the exactions and imposts of Naples and Tuscany, and to stanch those wounds of hers which long neglect has changed into running sores.

We see how she prays God to send some one to rescue her from these barbarous cruelties and oppressions. . . .

With what love he would be received in all those provinces which have suffered from the foreign inundation ; with what thirst for vengeance, with what firm fidelity, with what devotion and what tears, no words of mine can declare. What gates would be closed against him? What people would refuse him obedience? What jealousy would stand in his way? What Italian but would yield him homage? This barbarian tyranny stinks in all nostrils.

# READING 3

## A Contemporary Describes Leonardo

*Leonardo da Vinci, painter, architect, and engineer, is often considered the epitome of the "Renaissance Man." In this excerpt, Giorgio Vasari, friend and admirer of Leonardo, describes the remarkable versatility of the artist's work, actually claiming that it proved to be a handicap. The selection is taken from James Harvey Robinson, ed.,* Readings in European History, *Vol. 1 (Boston: Athenaeum, 1904), pp. 535–536.*

---

### Discussion Questions

1. Using Leonardo as the classic example, how would you define the "Renaissance Man"?
2. According to Vasari, what flaw does Leonardo have and how does it work against him?

### GIORGIO VASARI

The richest gifts are occasionally seen to be showered, as by celestial influence, upon certain human beings; nay, they sometimes supernaturally and marvelously congregate in a single person,—beauty, grace, and talent being united in such a manner that to whatever the man thus favored may turn himself, his every action is so divine as to leave all other men far behind him. This would seem manifestly to prove that he has been specially endowed by the hand of God himself, and has not obtained his preeminence through human teaching or the powers of man.

This was perceived and acknowledged by all men in the case of Leonardo da Vinci, in whom. . . there was a grace beyond expression, which was manifest without thought or effort in every act and deed, and who had besides so rare a gift of talent and ability that to whatever subject he turned his attention, no matter how difficult, he presently made himself absolute master of it.

In him extraordinary power was combined with remarkable facility, a mind of regal boldness and magnanimous daring. His gifts were such that the celebrity of his name was spread abroad, and he was held in the highest estimation not only in his own time but also, and even to a greater degree, after his death,—nay, he has continued, and will continue, to be held in the highest esteem by all succeeding generations.

Truly remarkable, indeed, and divinely endowed was Leonardo da Vinci. He was the son of Ser Piero da Vinci. He would without doubt have made great progress in learning and knowledge of the sciences had he not been so versatile and changeful. The instability of his character led him to undertake many things which having commenced he afterwards abandoned. In arithmetic, for example, he made such rapid progress in the short time that he gave his attention to it, that he often confounded the master who was teaching him by the perpetual doubts that he started and by the difficult questions that he proposed.

He also commenced the study of music, and resolved to acquire the art of playing the lute, when, being by nature of an exalted imagination and full of the most graceful vivacity, he sang to the instrument most divinely, improvising at once both the verse and the music.

[Verocchio, an esteemed artist of the period, upon seeing some of the drawings which Leonardo had made, gladly agreed to take him into his shop.] Thither the boy resorted with the utmost readiness, and not only gave his attention to one branch of art but to all those of which design makes a portion. Endowed with such admirable intelligence and being also an excellent geometrician, Leonardo not only worked in sculpture but in architecture; likewise he prepared various designs for ground plans and the construction of entire buildings. He too it was who, while only a youth, first suggested the formation of a canal from Pisa to Florence by means of certain changes to be effected in the river Arno. Leonardo likewise made designs for mills, fulling machines, and other engines which were run by water. But as he had resolved to make painting his profession, he gave the greater part of his time to drawing from nature.

READING 4

# A Renaissance Man's Advice on Wives

*Leon Battista Alberti constitutes a voice from Renaissance Florence. Though illegitimate, he was the son of one of the wealthiest merchants in Florence. He was a courtier, an athlete, an architect, and a musician as well as a writer. He both studied law and took orders in the church. His book on the family provides us with an interesting picture of Florentine merchant class perceptions about women and how to choose a wife. The following excerpt is taken from Leon Battista Alberti,* The Family in Renaissance Florence, *trans. by Renee New Watkins, (Columbia, S.C.: University of South Carolina Press, 1969), pp. 115–120.*

---

### Discussion Questions

1. How does Alberti's work reflect the trend of growing secularization during the Renaissance?
2. According to Alberti, what are the qualities of a good wife? Why do you think the author has nothing to say about the qualities of a good husband?

## LEON BATTISTA ALBERTI

They say that in choosing a wife one looks for beauty, parentage, and riches. . . . I think that beauty in a woman . . . must be judged not only by the charm and refinement of her face, but still more by the grace of her person and her aptitude for bearing and giving birth to many fine children.

Among the most essential criteria of beauty in a woman is an honorable manner. Even a wild, prodigal, greasy, drunken woman may be beautiful of feature, but no one would call her a beautiful wife. A woman worthy of praise must show first of all in her conduct, modesty, and purity. Marius, the illustrious Roman, said in that first speech of his to the Roman people: "Of women we require purity, of men labor." And I certainly agree. There is nothing more disgusting than a coarse and dirty woman. Who is stupid enough not to see clearly that a woman who does not care for neatness and cleanliness in her appearance, not only in her dress and body but in all her behavior and language, is by no means well mannered? How can it be anything but obvious that a bad mannered woman is also rarely virtuous? We shall consider elsewhere the harm that comes to a family from women who lack virtue, for I myself do not know which is the worse fate for a family, total celibacy or a single dishonored woman. In a bride, therefore, a man must first seek beauty of mind, that is, good conduct and virtue.

In her body he must seek not only loveliness, grace, and charm but must also choose a woman who is well made for bearing children, with the kind of constitution that promises to make them strong and big. There's an old proverb, "When you pick your wife, you choose your children." All her virtues will in fact shine brighter still in beautiful children. It is a well-known saying among poets: "Beautiful character dwells in a beautiful body." The natural philosophers require that a woman be neither thin nor very fat. Those laden with fat are subject to coldness and constipation and slow to conceive. They say that a woman should have a joyful nature, fresh and lively in her blood and her whole being. They have no objections to a dark girl. They do reject girls with a frowning black visage, however. They have no liking for either the undersized or the overlarge and lean. They find that a woman is most suited to bear children if she is fairly big and has limbs of ample length. They always have a preference for youth . . . particularly on the point that a young girl has a more adaptable mind. Young girls are pure by virtue of their age and have not developed any spitefulness. They are by nature modest and free of vice. They quickly learn to accept affectionately and unresistingly the habits and wishes of their husbands.

These things . . . are the things it makes sense to keep in mind in order to find and select a well-suited, prolific wife. To all this I might add one more point, that it is an excellent sign if a girl has a great number of brothers and no sisters. It is reasonable to hope that she will, when she is yours, fare like her mother.

Now we have spoken of beauty. Let us next consider parentage, and what are the qualities to look for there. I think the first problem in choosing a family is to investigate closely the customs and habits of one's new relatives. Many marriages have ruined the family . . . because they involved union with a litigious, quarrelsome, arrogant, and malevolent set of men. . . . I think that no one is so great a fool that he would not rather remain unmarried than burden himself with terrible relatives. Sometimes the links of family have proved a trouble and disaster to the man, who has had to support both his own family and that of the girl he married. Not infrequently it happens that the new family . . . all settle down in the house of their new kinsman. As the new husband you cannot keep them without harm to yourself, nor can you send them away without incurring censure.

To sum up . . . let a man get himself new kinsmen of better than plebeian blood, of a fortune more than diminutive, of a decent occupation, and of modest and respectable habits. Let them not be too far above himself, lest their greatness overshadow his own honor and position. Too high a family may disturb his own and his family's peace and tranquility . . . . I also do not want the new relatives to rank too low, for while the first error puts you in a position of servitude, the second causes expense. Let them be equals, then, and, to repeat, modest and respectable people.

The matter of dowry is next, which I would like to see middling in size, certain and prompt rather than large, vague, or promised for an indefinite future. I know not why everyone, as if corrupted by a common vice, takes advantage of delay to grow lazy in paying debts. Sometimes, in cases of marriage, people are further tempted because they hope to evade payment altogether. As your wife spends her first year in your house, it seems impossible not to reinforce the new bonds of kinship by frequent visiting and parties. But it will be thought rude if, in the middle of a gathering of kinsmen, you put yourself forward to insist and complain. If, as new husbands usually do, you don't want to lose their still precarious favor, you may ask your in-laws in restrained and casual words. Then you are forced to accept any little excuse they may offer. If you make a more forthright demand for what is your own, they will explain to you their many obligations, will complain of fortune, blame the conditions of the time, complain of other men, and say that they hope to be able to ask much of you in grater difficulties. As long as they can, in fact, they will promise you bounteous repayment at an ever-receding date. They will beg you, and overwhelm you, nor will it seem possible for you to spurn the prayers of people you have accepted as your own family. Finally, you will be put in a position where you must either suffer the loss in silence or enter upon expensive litigation and create enmity.

What is more, it will seem that you can never put an end to the pressure from your wife on this point. She will weep many tears, and the pleadings and insistent prayers of a new love that has just begun are apt to have a certain force. However hard and twisted your temperament you can hardly impose silence on someone who pleads with an outsider, thus softly and tearfully, for the sake of her own father and brothers. Then imagine how impossible for you to turn a deaf ear on your own wife doing so in your own house, in your own room. You are bound, in the end, to suffer either financial loss or loss of affection. This is why the dowry should be precisely set, promptly paid, and not too high. The larger the payments are to be and the longer they are to be carried, the more discussion you will be forced into, the more reluctantly you will be paid, and the more obliged you will feel to spend inordinate sums for all sorts of things. There will be indescribable bitterness and often totally ruinous results in setting dowries very high. We have said now how a wife is to be selected from outside and how she is to be received into the house. It remains to be seen how she is to be treated once she is within.

. . . One marries the girl who seems to have less faults than the others. One does not give up beauty for parentage or parentage in order to get a dowry. . . . One takes a wife, in fact, mainly to have children by her. . . . I say that when you have chosen your wife and decided on the girl you like best. . . pray to God that he graciously grant that your bride will be fertile, and that you may always have peace and honor in your house. . . . Not every man who seeks finds a good wife. Not every man who would like a faithful wife has one, though some perhaps think they have. . . .

. . . Now I think we should logically consider next in what manner it is best to conceive children. . . Husbands. . . should be careful not to give themselves to their wives while their mental state is troubled by anger, fear, or some other kind of disturbing emotion. The passions that oppress the spirit slow up and weaken our vital strength. . . . Hence it may often be found that a father who is ardent and strong and wise has begotten a son who is fearful, weak, and foolish. Sometimes from a moderate and reasonable man there springs a mad and bestial youth. Again, it is unwise to come together if body and limbs are not in good condition and health. The doctors say . . . that if a father and mother are low and troubled because of drink or bad blood or weaknesses and defects of energy and pulse, it is reasonable to expect the children to manifest these troubles. Sometimes, in fact, they will be leprous, epileptic, deformed, or incomplete in their limbs and defective.

. . . The doctors have ordained, therefore, that intercourse be undertaken only when one is sober, strong, and as happy as possible. They say that the hour of the night is best which comes after the first digestion is over, when you are neither empty nor full of heavy food, but flourishing and lightened by sleep. They say that in this act it is good to make oneself intensely desired by the woman. They also have many other counsels, and instruct one that when it is excessively hot or when every seed and root is petrified by frost in the earth it is better to wait for more temperate weather.

And now, if anyone who wants to know all of history accuses me of leaving out too much. . . I will defend myself by calling attention to . . . the infinite quantity of events. . . [for] it is impossible to satisfy our curiosity and know everything. . . But if, on the other hand, the labor of my studies has in some small measure given you what you expected, then I ask only that I be loved by you, though we are not personally acquainted, though I be shut up and dissolved in my grave. For in this same way I love those who helped me, though they have been but dust for a thousand years.

Francesco Petrach, from the preface to his *De viris illustribus* (1351–1353)